FOUNDATIONS

of Christian School Education

Colorado Springs, Colorado

Edited by James Braley • Jack Layman • Ray White

Books, Textbooks, and Educational Resources for Christian Educators and Schools Worldwide

Purposeful Design Publications is the publishing division of ACSI and is committed to the ministry of Christian school education, to enable Christian educators and schools worldwide to effectively prepare students for life. As the publisher of books, textbooks, and other educational resources within ACSI, Purposeful Design Publications strives to produce biblically sound materials that reflect Christian scholarship and stewardship and that address the identified needs of Christian schools around the world.

For additional information, write Purposeful Design Publications
PO Box 35097, Colorado Springs, CO 80935-3509.

Cover Design: Julia Evans

Printed in the United States of America

Foundations of Christian School Education
ISBN 1-58331-059-2 Catalog # 6502

Purposeful Design Publications
A Division of ACSI
PO Box 35097 • Colorado Springs, CO 80935-3509
Customer Service Department: 800/367-0798 • Website: www.acsi.org

Table of Contents

SECTION ONE

Biblical and Philosophical Foundations

It is by design that this book begins by describing our biblical and philosophical foundations. In the 1960s and 1970s, those early years of dramatic expansion, the Christian school movement was vision-driven. Its founders were men and women whose primary motive was to provide an education firmly based on biblical truth and the redemptive work of Jesus Christ crucified, risen, and living in His people through the Holy Spirit.

Christian schools have come a long way since those pioneer days in terms of adequate facilities, qualified teachers and administrators, improved curriculum, a broader ethnic and theological constituency, and a fuller understanding of learning and the learner. With Samuel Morse, whose words were the first ever sent by telegraph, we can exclaim, "What hath God wrought!"

Our schools' very success, however, makes them vulnerable to drifting away from the distinctives on which the movement was founded. That is why, before addressing educational psychology, pedagogy, and our cultural and social foundations, we must identify our core beliefs and values, and we must reiterate our philosophical and biblical foundations.

CHAPTER ONE

Introduction to Philosophy

Paul Spears

We as educators are inundated with competing philosophical paradigms, making it difficult to know which of many pedagogical approaches will best meet the needs of our students. As the intellectual gatekeepers, we must enable our students to interact with the world around them, and philosophy is a necessary part of the framework through which we approach that task. Though not replacing other disciplines, it is a tool by which one can examine academic and intellectual pursuits critically. While a degree in philosophy is not necessary, it is vital that educators clearly understand basic philosophical principles and terminology. This chapter will develop a framework to show that ideas about education are grounded in foundational beliefs that construct how humans interact with reality. Philosophy examines what underlying commitments we make regarding our beliefs and how our views come to be understood as knowledge, the concepts that form our worldview.

A Valuable Tool for Educators

Today's information age exposes us to an overwhelming amount of data, and it often seems impossible to sort out the true from the false. If it is hard for educated adults to determine what is true, how much harder it is for our students. We as teachers must be prepared to meet this challenge.

The Christian church has often seen philosophy as a roadblock to understanding our true purpose as humans and not a tool for learning what that purpose is. The apostle Paul said, "See to it that no one takes you captive through hollow and deceptive philosophy, which depends on human tradition and the basic principles of this world rather than on Christ" (Colossians 2:8, NIV). His admonition is often understood as an attack on all philosophy, but notice that the words *hollow* and *deceptive* modify *philosophy*. Philosophy can be hollow and deceptive, but like any tool it can be used for building up or tearing down. Proper philosophical understanding can allow an educator to distinguish ideas that could lead students to false conclusions from those that will give them access to a life of truth and fulfillment.

Philosophy enables us to justify our beliefs confidently and reasonably. It does not, of course, displace a thorough knowledge of Scripture as a necessary component of Christian education. Still, philosophy is an important part of an educator's toolbox. J. P. Moreland has an insightful and instructive discussion of this matter in his book *Love Your God with All Your Mind* (1997).

Our mind is an essential part of our whole person. C. S. Lewis writes, in regard to Christ's design for the mind, "He wants a child's heart, but a grown-up head.... He also wants every bit of intelligence we have to be alert at its job, and in first class fighting trim" (1952). Educators are on the front line in the battle for the mind, and we must understand the primary philosophical strategies for engaging in the conflict properly and effectively. These strategies are necessary if we are going to train students to think correctly and participate as active members of society.

The aim of education until the early nineteenth century was to cause humans to flourish, or to bring about their good. To flourish as a human is to understand what it means to act virtuously, or function properly as a human agent. Education enables us to understand what virtue is and how to know it, and virtue helps us know how we should act in order to flourish. For example, there are certain parameters that we use to judge whether a knife is good. A "virtuous" knife is durable and sharp; it cuts well. If we try to use a knife as a screwdriver, we find that it cannot fulfill its virtue—that is, cut our steak. Humans also have properties that make them virtuous. Humans need to understand who they are and how they can best act virtuously, doing what is right and proper. Happiness is not about getting what we think we want; it is about pursuing what will allow us to flourish. We act virtuously because it is the proper thing to do—not because of an expectation of punishment or reward. In the past, the pursuit of virtue was known to be holistic and attainable in the real world; that knowledge was never in question until recently. There was a normative standard of virtue—it was a given. Moral and ethical training was not based on socially constructed truth but on the truth of a transcendent reality.

Broadly speaking, modern education no longer has a unified vision, for education is pulled in many directions by competing allegiances. Training students how to get at truth through reason has been abandoned because the idea that one can actually have access to absolute truth is seen as foolish. As a result, the pursuit of knowledge is no longer understood as a coherent and unified quest, and the university, originally seen as a place where one discovers truths about the universe, has lost its real meaning. The purpose or mission of education has become unclear because truth is seen as relative, and the universities have often adopted purpose language that they have no right to use because that language is not commensurate with their philosophical commitments. If truth is relative, it is difficult if not impossible to construct clear purpose statements. Most institutions, although committed to a relativistic worldview, still dip into the well of transcendental truth because the world does not run on relativism but on eternal, unchanging truths.

To develop philosophical constructs, one must understand some categories historically used in the study of philosophy: metaphysics, logic, aesthetics, ethics, and epistemology. Each category answers basic questions about the universe and provides a framework for clarifying concepts about values and reality.

Metaphysics

The term *metaphysics,* which was coined by Aristotle, refers to the basic questions of reality, such as the nature and essence of things, cause and effect, and the nature of man. It is often called "first philosophy" because it deals with fundamental principles. Metaphysics examines the existence of things that cannot be known or understood through the senses, such as consciousness, the immortality of souls, freedom of the will, and of course God.

If education is to be successful, we must have a basic understanding of the nature and purpose of humankind. The study of metaphysics includes basic categories about humans so that teachers can make proper pedagogical and curricular decisions. Without an understanding of metaphysics, how can teachers prepare students for life? Through metaphysics, educators can understand their students and can craft pedagogical methods that will meet their needs.

Until the seventeenth century, most philosophical thinkers believed that an understanding of the world was not totally dependent on empirical, or sense-perceived, observation. Empirical data gave access to knowledge and understanding, but both metaphysical and empirical investigation were considered necessary if one was to have adequate information about existence. Driven by a belief in the power of human reason, philosophers and intellectuals, who were pragmatists at heart, believed human beings to be an end in themselves, a view that drove fallen man further toward his sinful tendencies of utilitarianism and hedonism. The Enlightenment, which can be seen as early modernism, fundamentally changed human attempts to understand the world, supplanting the epistemology of belief and replacing it with the epistemology of doubt. The question *How do you know?* drove the Enlightenment more than the questions *What is man?* and *What is man's purpose?*

Proponents of the Enlightenment agenda, who were bitter toward the church, wanted to remove God and metaphysical morality from the intellectual sphere and replace them with empiricism, in which sense experiences are the foundation of all knowledge. By replacing metaphysics with empiricism, they effectively removed God from the picture. The belief that the main source of knowledge is the investigation of the external world caused humankind to reject metaphysics as logically incoherent because it is not empirically verifiable. This commitment to knowledge as emerging only from the external, sensible world makes an understanding of God impossible, or at best a vague hope.

To understand the world around us, we Christians need to have a robust metaphysics. Knowable information and truths do exist outside the limits of our senses. One of the most important categories in metaphysics is *ontology*, the philosophy of being, the study of what exists or what it means to have existence. It is an attempt to categorize what is real, an interpretation of the fundamental aspects of the world of experience. Essence, unity, and function are ascribed to all things—rocks and atoms, plants and planets, animals and humans, and of course God. Ontology analyzes, explains, and defines real things so that humans can deliberate on these categories of existence. It is the most basic of the philosophical pursuits, the foundation of all other philosophical and academic enterprises.

What is a human being? Why do humans exist? What is my purpose as a human being? These questions ask for a list of properties that make up the construct called "human." A definition of what it means to be a human ("human qua human") is our "ontological commitment": for example, *A human has a unique kind of soul and is a rational thinker*. A human, from the point of conception, is and cannot be anything else. (He cannot become a horse or an oak tree.) He has a physical body existing in space and time. He is not just a brain; he is a different substance, neither mechanistic nor dependent on the functioning of the brain to exist. A soul is not just coextensive with the body (occupying the same space and time) but is always in a soul-body composite. A human has a purpose for existence, proper ways of functioning, and freedom of choice, and a human is made in the image of God. These are just a few of the constructs that make up the ontology of humanity.

Only ontology can describe the fundamental qualities of humanity and call it knowledge. Empiricism cannot do so. All an empiricist can do is describe information received through the senses. Humans then become property, or things—nothing more than a group of parts that function together in a machinelike manner with no unifying essence. An empiricist must limit knowledge about humanity to the physical realm, a position that leaves out the most important characteristics of humans, to be discussed in greater detail later.

An important aspect of metaphysics, one that works hand in glove with ontology, is the concept of universals. If two chairs are the "same," what makes us think they are the same? By universals we understand sameness or difference, and thus we can say that two chairs are the same (but not identical) because they share the essential properties that form the foundational components of the object we call a chair. Universals can be either properties or relations. Properties are attached to an object without relation to any other object—for example, colors or geometrical shapes. Relations involve at least two objects. Ideas such as bigger, taller, or heavier (a volleyball's size compared to that of a baseball, a sumo wrestler's weight compared to that of a jockey) are relations. Universals allow us to have permanent, foundational sources of order that are changeless whatever we experience in the external world. Universals are and always will be true. The concept of "circle" will never change regardless of one's experience. A particular circle may change, but the universal "circle" will never change.

Universals do not exist by themselves; a "substance" owns a universal. A substance owns a group of universal properties, but a substance is more than the sum of its properties, or parts. For example, let's think about my friend Fred, who is six feet tall, has fair skin and brown hair, and weighs 185 pounds. Many properties—such as color, weight, and height—make up Fred. But these properties could change. Fred could dye his hair, lose ten pounds, or get a tan. He could lose his legs in an auto accident! What would happen to him? Would he become "New Fred"? No, "Fred qua Fred"—whatever makes Fred "Fred"—exists regardless of whether he has two legs or no legs. Fred's essence is what unifies his properties regardless of change. An essence, for a human being, consists of the substantial things that make one human, such as an immortal soul, free will, and the ability to reason. All humans have an essence that does not change with changes in their accidental properties, such as limbs, that are not essential to being human.

Since Fred has basic metaphysical properties that make up his essence, he is able to exist as a unified whole through time. If Fred were just a property—a thing made up different kinds of "stuff"—every time he gained or lost something, there would be a "New Fred." It seems obvious that we do not gain a new person with every change, but an empirical model of reality makes it difficult to explain why.

Now consider how metaphysics affects the way you teach! If human beings are just property, or things, you should adopt a behaviorist model (advocated by B. F. Skinner; see chapter 3) for your pedagogy, and you should no longer be concerned with feelings. Under an empiricist model teachers train students by reinforcing their behavior with a series of rewards and punishments so that eventually they respond properly to certain stimuli. As long as students give the right responses, teaching is successful. Educators are no longer concerned with affecting immortal souls or instructing them in morality and ethics unless ethics can ensure that they will function properly in society.

Logic

Another important category in philosophy is logic, the study of arguments. Logic constructs ideas so that we are able to communicate certain concepts to each other by deducing them from a set of premises. The better we identify logical flaws in an argument, the easier it is to identify faulty beliefs.

God is a god of truth, wisdom, and logic. Jesus' use of logic shows us its value as a tool for teaching and learning. His debates with the Pharisees are a perfect example of the importance of logic as a tool to help us convey our ideas clearly to others. It would be useful to study a standard introduction to logic text; however, in this chapter we will look at only one part of such a study, deductive and inductive reasoning.

A deductive argument presents a conclusion that necessarily follows from the premises, which include all the information necessary to reach that conclusion. Here is a typical deductive argument:

All men are mortal.
Socrates is a man.
Therefore, Socrates is mortal.

An inductive argument presents a conclusion that is a probable truth. That is, to know that the conclusion is true, we need to know whether it is based on true information. This is an inductive argument:

The sun, since the beginning of time, has always risen in the morning.

Therefore, the sun will rise tomorrow morning.

Inductive arguments rely on probability, not necessity. The probability that the sun will rise in the morning is very high, but its rising is still only probable and not certain. We cannot make universal statements from general observations.

We often hear, and perhaps are guilty ourselves, of fallacious reasoning. For example, in an informal fallacy called "begging the question," the truth of a conclusion is assumed by the premises. For example: *Abortion is wrong because murder is wrong, and killing an unborn child is murder.* This conclusion may be true, but the speaker is equating abortion and murder without explaining why killing an unborn child is murder. The speaker needs to think of a way to form the argument without that assumption.

Philosophy and Biblical Truth Summarized

Metaphysics

The study or science of ultimate reality, which precedes and transcends truth derived from the world of the senses alone.

Biblical Truth

God is the basis of all reality. Because He exists, we exist. God is the unperceivable foundation of the physical, ordered universe.

Logic

The science of constructing ideas so that we are able to communicate truths to one another by deducing the consequences of a set of premises.

Biblical Truth

God is a God of truth, wisdom, and logic. Jesus' use of logic as He debated with the Pharisees is a paradigmatic example of its value.

Aesthetics

It asks, What is the schema by which one can consider the beautiful in art and nature?

Biblical Truth

God has made all things beautiful; beauty is a reflection of harmony with and function of God's created universe.

Ethics

It asks, What are the basis, nature, and reasons for right and wrong behavior?

Biblical Truth

God, who does not change, provides unchangeable standards of good and evil. His holiness demands that our lives become conformed to His perfect will, and thus we are made not only good but ultimately happy.

Epistemology

It asks, What are the origin, composition, and limits of knowledge?

Biblical Truth

Truth is not dependent on humans, though humans have the capacity to recognize truth, which is rooted in our discovery of God's creation.

Another informal fallacy is *tu quoque*, Latin for "you also." The answer is "Oh, yeah, you should talk," or "The pot is calling the kettle black." The argument is empty because the one making it has failed to follow her own advice. "Frieda told me to stop eating fatty foods because they are bad for me, but she eats a pound of french fries every day."

In a logical fallacy called *equivocation,* a key term in the argument can have more than one meaning. *It's a miracle that I passed the test even though I didn't study.* The student's definition of "miracle" is rather different from a theologian's! When I ask my son whether he has picked up his toys and he says yes, he is equivocating. He picked them up, but he put them right back on the floor!

Educators and students must be able to spot errors in reasoning. For this reason, it would be profitable to look for good examples of fallacies (Engel 1994) and train students to recognize and correct them. Dallas Willard writes, "Paying careful attention to how Jesus made use of logical thinking can strengthen our confidence in Jesus as master of the centers of intellect and creativity, and can encourage us to accept him as master in all of the areas of intellectual life in which we may participate" (1999).

Aesthetics

What is beauty? How do we know whether something is beautiful or ugly? Isn't beauty in the eye of the beholder? These questions are in the field of aesthetics, which attempts to define the nature of art and beauty. Art includes but is not limited to the written word, material art (painting, sculpting), music, and drama. Aesthetics attempts to develop a schema by which one can consider the beautiful, whether natural or man-made, and understand what happens in an artist when he creates.

Art can be limited to social construction. Artists can be the final arbiters for what is called art, or what is art may be determined by what is in vogue at a given point in history. While artists arbitrate what is art (which is transient), beauty is transcendent and unchanging. A community of art experts may correctly identify something as art that is "not-beautiful," and the craft or skill of the artist must be differentiated from the thing created. An artist may create an object that is very ugly if it is his desire to make a statement about a social issue or the state of humanity. In his painting *The Slaughtered Ox,* Rembrandt depicts an image that is far from beautiful, but it is certainly art. This amazing still life is a technical masterpiece, and it demonstrates Rembrandt's versatility.

Aesthetics deals with how we as human beings, through the arts and our senses, gain new understandings of the nature of truth, beauty, and goodness. Humans have an amazing ability to gain insight about the world through the artistic media, and the media are important tools as we strive to enable our students to develop all aspects of their persons. As students participate in art, they interact with an important part of their soul.

Ethics

Teachers often hear these questions: *Is it all right to steal if you have no money and need to feed your family? Is it ever right to lie? What if you can save a life by lying?* The aspect of philosophy that answers such questions is called ethics. Christian ethics is not based on values and customs that are agreed on by a certain society at a certain time but on universal principles revealed by God. Ethics is normative, and draws from sets of guidelines that do not change. It cannot be said strongly enough—ethics is not equivalent to social convention, nor is it subject to relativistic or situational constructions of proper action. Why is this so? To replace revealed, objective morality with social conventions denies God's authority and causes progressively degraded human behaviors that lead to social chaos.

Ethics evaluates the correctness of human acts, drawing from both metaphysics and epistemology to construct a schema by which humans should comport themselves. For Christians, ethics also draws from special revelation.

Ethics should be distinguished from morality, for every society, no matter how base, has a set of governing laws that guide conduct. Ethics studies the free acts of humans and deliberates on whether those acts are right or wrong.

Epistemology

Fundamentally, an educator attempts to train students to consider the world around them in such a way that they understand it and function properly within it as human beings. To do so, educators must understand epistemology, or the acquisition of knowledge. Epistemology is concerned with such questions as *How does someone come to know something?* and *How and why do we know that we know?*

Through epistemology we craft how to train students to access truths. Understanding the most influential constructions of epistemology will reveal how various pedagogical methods have come about and will enable us to refine our own classroom pedagogy.

A realist believes that things in the world are "real," or have existence. Tables are just tables, and we construct an idea of "table" in our head.

The reality of a thing is not dependent on the way we come to understand it. Things actually exist and continue to exist regardless of how or whether we find out about them. A realist can be confident that the things experienced through the senses actually exist. When we see a table in the external, sensible world, we can be confident we are correct that it is there. The existence of planets is not predicated on our knowledge of planets or on how we gain that knowledge.

Antirealists hold that knowledge is not transcendent: Beauty *is* in the eye of the beholder. Universal concepts are not inside the mind, nor are universal objects out there in the physical world. We come to understand the world by having experiences of external things that build the knowledge by which we access the world. Some antirealists hold that moral values are not objective but exist only as the feelings or attitudes of an individual or as agreed-upon community standards.

For the sake of brevity, I will combine *empiricism* (all knowledge must come through the senses) and *materialism* (all reality is physical) as EM. Believers in EM hold that knowledge is based on experiences that are composed of, or can be reduced to, physical forces, matter, or processes in the physical world. In order to say that something is reality, or that we know something, we need to have had an encounter with the thing (object) through our senses. We know nothing *a priori*, but everything we know can be explained by physical bodies or forces. Examining matter, the physical world, is the only way we can know what is real. Whatever we perceive or think about derives from our previous encounters with the thing on a physical or sensory level.

This construction of knowledge inevitably leads to agnosticism at best or atheism at worst. EM does not allow for the existence of spiritual entities or forces. One could argue, as philosopher Immanuel Kant does, that God may exist but we are unable to know Him because we are trapped by our inability to get at anything transcendent.

Educators define what knowledge is and how one obtains knowledge. We do not create new knowledge, but we develop methods that enable us and our students to have access to the real world. This is, of course, an interesting task given the empiricist paradigm out of which most modern universities function. It is unclear how, if one is committed to scientific naturalism (as all secular institutions are), one arrives at knowledge that is "true" when knowledge is seen as an agreed-upon method within a discipline, or an agreed-upon convention within academics as a whole. Philosopher Dallas Willard (2000) calls such handmade knowledge the "best profes-

About the Author

Paul Spears is a faculty member in the Torrey Honors Institute at Biola University. His main scholarly interest is in how educational theories are influenced by philosophical paradigm shifts inside the academy. His children, Ian 5 and Alexis 3, have taught him much about what it means to be an educator.

sional practice, or belief in a certain social setting." Such a view of knowledge is entirely inadequate for a Christian educator, since it is antithetical to the transcendent nature of God's truth as given through special revelation.

We as educators endeavor to teach our students truth, and philosophy endeavors to equip us with the proper tools to do so. We must understand what constitutes good and bad ideas, and we must remember that we have access to real knowledge that changes lives. As we do, we can enable our students to become persons who have a positive impact on their community and nation. This is a call not to the fainthearted but to those who understand the opportunity, privilege, and responsibility that are ours. We must train ourselves to recognize the importance of philosophy and to understand its applications to our work as educators.

Strengthen Your Foundations

1. Within a Christian worldview, what is the place of philosophy? How does philosophy affect an educator who is Christian?

2. What place does our metaphysics play in our understanding of God?

3. What place does our epistemology play in our understanding of God?

4. Most educational philosophies today are empirically driven. What is the impact of this fact on how most educators view and teach their students?

5. What is the difference between empiricism and materialism? How do you think each concept poses unique difficulties to the Christian thinker?

6. Historically, theology has been called the "queen of the sciences," and philosophy has been called its "handmaiden." What do those terms suggest about the place of theology and philosophy within the philosophy of education?

7. What are the metaphysical commitments of someone who is a materialist?

8. What are the epistemic commitments of someone who is a materialist?

9. How does philosophy enable you to expose philosophical commitments that are antithetical to your Christian beliefs? Think of this specifically in terms of the categories of informal logic discussed in this chapter.

References

Engel, S. M. 1994. *With good reason: An introduction to informal fallacies.* 5th ed. New York: St. Martin's Press.

Hurley, P. J. 1977. *A concise introduction to logic.* 6th ed. Belmont, CA: Wadsworth Publishing Co.

Lewis, C. S. 1952. *Mere Christianity.* New York: Macmillan.

Moreland, J. P. 1997. *Love your God with all your mind: The role of reason in the life of the soul.* Colorado Springs, CO: NavPress.

Willard, Dallas. 1999. Jesus the logician. *Christian Scholar's Review* 28, no. 4: 605–14.

——. 2000. How reason can survive the modern university: The moral foundations of rationality. Paper presented at the American Maritain Association, Notre Dame University.

CHAPTER TWO

Early History of Educational Philosophy

Jack Layman

The Renaissance artist Raphael illustrated the history of educational philosophy in his classic mural *The School of Athens.* At the center of the painting stand Plato and Aristotle, dominating and defining a crowd of philosophers and intellectuals from Pythagoras and Socrates to Euclid, Zoroaster, and Epicurus. Plato has his right arm raised and his index finger pointing upward; Aristotle's arm is outstretched with his palm held parallel to the earth.

Raphael used the body language of Plato and Aristotle to depict the two divergent approaches to truth that have marked philosophy and education for the past 2,500 years: Plato emphasized that the search for ultimate truth must be conducted outside the natural world, while Aristotle viewed the study of nature as a source of ultimate reality. These two approaches, sometimes referred to as *idealism* and *realism,* provide a broad structure for developing the ideas of this chapter.

Before discussing the division introduced by Plato and Aristotle, we may legitimately ask, *Why should Christian educators pay attention to pagan thinkers?* Cicero's comment that "there is nothing so absurd but that it may be found in the books of the philosophers" (Durant 1926, 2) holds as true today as it did 1,900 years ago, and Scripture warns us against being taken captive by "hollow and deceptive" human philosophies (Colossians 2:8).

So Why Study Philosophy?

The answer is twofold. First, philosophy is a legitimate and necessary field of Christian inquiry. Dictionaries define philosophy in terms that are at the heart of biblical revelation: an investigation of the truths and principles of being *(What is ultimate reality?),* of knowledge *(What can be known and how?),* and of human conduct *(How ought we to live?).*

A simpler description is that philosophy is an unusually stubborn attempt to think clearly about the basic questions of life. Those basic questions—*Who am I? Where did I come from? Why am I here?*—are answered authoritatively only by the Bible, which on one hand warns us against the empty philosophy of human tradition and on the other provides a sure foundation for a philosophy that "thinks clearly" about those basic questions of life.

Second, it is unwise to ignore philosophers (the apostle Paul certainly did not in Acts 17 and Colossians 2), whether scholars like Karl Marx and Richard Dawkins or celebrities like Steven Spielberg, Oprah Winfrey, and Britney Spears, who affect the direction of society and influence us and our students. We need to know what their ideas are, and whether they conflict with Scripture or offer legitimate choices within the circle of biblical revelation. For example, Christian educators who agree on the authority of the Bible often disagree on the appropriate application of its teachings in the same way that secular philosophers disagree among themselves.

Philosophy of Education

For much of recorded history there has been no distinct academic discipline called "philosophy of education," but there has been constant interaction between education and philosophy. The ideas of the philosophers, usually teachers themselves, often had educational implications. In the nineteenth century, with the emergence of the social and behavioral sciences, educational philosophy became a separate field, eventually settling into the curricula of schools of education rather than the philosophy departments of colleges and universities.

If philosophy is an unusually stubborn attempt to think clearly about the basic questions of life, then *educational* philosophy is an unusually stubborn attempt to think clearly about those basic questions *as they apply to education.* And in this, as in almost any discussion of the history of philosophy, one inevitably refers to Plato and Aristotle, whose body language, as Raphael portrayed it, is relevant to our discussion.

Plato and Idealism

Plato had little interest in the Greek gods. He saw those mythological characters caught in the same dilemmas as humankind, unable to offer solutions to the problems of life. Nor did Plato believe that the study of the world around us could provide answers. He rejected nature and its "facts" as a source of universal truth and believed that truth is obscured by our human preoccupation with the mundane experiences of the material world, a conviction he illustrated in an allegory about a cave.

The Allegory of the Cave

In a cave deep within the earth, prisoners are bound in such a way that their only source of knowledge is shadows cast on the cave wall by a fire behind them. These shadows become the prisoners' reality; status and prestige come to those who can best analyze and explain their significance.

Prisoners who manage to escape from the cave are dazzled and overwhelmed by the outside world, and they realize that this is reality and the shadows in the cave are of no consequence. A few return to share this insight with their comrades, but they are rejected. For the prisoners, the shadows are the only reality they know and can accept.

Plato's cave represents the world in which we live; the shadows are the particulars, the things around us: trees, mountains, chairs, horses, apples, and human beings themselves. Plato considered nature and its particulars, which are of utmost importance to most people, as mere shadows, insignificant distractions in the search for truth.

If Not the Shadows ...?

Plato's search for universal truths (often referred to as ideals, forms, or universals), and the ultimate reality from which everything in this world derives, led him past the material world to its origins. This concept is a familiar one to Christians, who believe that "in the beginning God created the heavens and the earth" (Genesis 1:1, NIV) and that "without him nothing was made that has been made" (John 1:3, NIV). But Plato had neither the Bible nor confidence in the assumptions of Greek mythology. He relied instead on a process of meticulous deliberation, stimulated by dialectics (logical argumentation), to bring ideas to their reasonable conclusions. Reason, applied to the meaningful questions of life, would provide an understanding of the first principles, the basic issues of life. Truth and ultimate reality could be found only by turning from investigation of the material world to the world of universal truths (forms or ideals). That is why Raphael pictured Plato pointing upward.

Plato suggested that we can comprehend the universals through reason because we once knew them, but in the process of birth, of becoming particulars ourselves, the truths we once knew were lost in our subconscious. Plato believed (his *doctrine of reminiscence*) that rigorous thought (the *dialectic*) could retrieve those memories. Truth is both outside nature and, somehow, innately within us, and it may be explored by both mind and intuition. *Idealism* emphasizes a dialectical search for the universal ideals from which everything in our world derives. Plato's idealism dominated philosophy and influenced religion and education in the West for well over a thousand years.

Idealism Across the Centuries

Plato considered the natural world unimportant, deceptive, and even contaminating. The influence of Plato can be seen, for example, in the gnostic and mystery religions that competed with and sometimes influenced the early Christian church. These emphasized the great gulf between the material world and the spiritual world, and the necessity of finding secret paths to spiritual purification. The gospel proclaimed Jesus Christ as "the Way," but the gnostic and mystery religions either rejected Him because He "became flesh and dwelt among us"—nothing material could be worthy—or denied that Christ was in fact a flesh-and-blood person (John 1:14; 1 John 2:20–23, 4:1–4).

Augustine

The Christian church was influenced by idealism in its first thousand years, particularly through the theologian Augustine. He believed that Plato's universals, forms, and ideals were ideas in the mind of God, and that God revealed these ideas through creation, the Bible, and Jesus Christ. His autobiographical work *Confessions* traces his conversion from the sights, sounds, and tastes of this world to the images in the mind of God.

In *The City of God,* Augustine contrasts the illusory world of men and material things, a world of sin and darkness, with the reality of God's city. Although Augustine's biblical theology nourished the church for six hundred years, his philosophy is marred by an extrabiblical negativism toward nature (for example, his suspicion of sexuality even within marriage) and by emphasis on an inner light that seemed to sanction intuitive and allegorical interpretations of Scripture.

For Augustine, education was essentially religious. Since the Bible provided authoritative universals, a biblically based education was a means for students to know God and to prepare for His kingdom. The dialectical process was a means of clarifying biblical truth, and contemplation a means of assimilating it. Idealism continued to influence philosophy and religion during the medieval period (325–1300), or "age of faith," but declined after the Renaissance. People became disillusioned with the established church and less willing to accept the authority of Scripture. They became more confident in human abilities, in the power of the human mind, and in humanity's growing control of nature through science. With the rediscovery of Aristotle, there was a slow but continuous drift away from what was often perceived as Plato's impractical emphasis on vague and unverifiable universals.

Summary: Idealism as a Philosophy of Education

Purpose and emphasis
To develop a reasoning mind and a virtuous character; emphasis on wisdom of the past, critical thinking, intuition (an inner sense of things), and personal responsibility.

Teachers
Model an inquiring mind and an admirable character; promote development of student minds, character, values, and personal responsibility.

Methodology
Emphasizes classic ideas rather than recent facts; analyzes the whole rather than masters a part (specialization); promotes thoughtful dialogue, and reflective and interactive thinking and writing (essay exams).

Curriculum
Introduces classical literature (the "great books"); emphasizes a core curriculum of language arts, history, and mathematics.

Positive perceptions
Preserves wisdom of the ages; emphasizes moral character, intellectual growth, thinking and writing skills; provides a broad preparation; emphasizes human worth and personal values (the teacher is a respected discipler).

Negative perceptions
Is outdated and elitist; too "religious"; inappropriate and impractical for many students. Does not lend itself to job training and the marketplace; assumes authority without verification and promotes unsubstantiated values and truths; an antitechnological bias; obsolete methodology for the mass media generation.

A Continuing Influence

Despite the decline of idealism, Plato's finger pointing upward still has its impact. The "father of modern philosophy," René Descartes (1596–1650), who decided to begin anew the search for knowledge and truth, began by doubting his own existence. Descartes turned not to physical evidence—which he thought unreliable—but to the mind: *Cogito ergo sum* (I think, therefore I am). Starting with his own existence, he reasoned (in the tradition of Plato's dialectic) that his existence presupposed a perfect being. Descartes' two basic principles, *Thought* and *Perfect Being*, were clearly in the idealist tradition.

Other influential thinkers of the eighteenth and nineteenth centuries shared Descartes' emphasis. Bishop George Berkeley

(1685–1753), for example, reacted to the materialism of the eighteenth century by arguing that nothing exists unless it is perceived to exist in the mind *(esse est percipi)*—of man or of God. Georg Wilhelm Frederick Hegel (1770–1831), the most influential philosopher of the nineteenth century, built an elaborate theory of process and progress in history on the existence of a reasoned universal, an *Absolute Spirit* or *World Soul* that somehow guides history through its progressive struggle.

Idealism continues to influence education and educators, providing a framework for schooling that emphasizes the training of the individual intellect. It gives priority to metaphysics over physics and to ideas over science and technology, and it sees education as a means of training students for their role in life while identifying those capable of higher thinking.

Aristotle and Realism

Plato's greatest pupil, Aristotle, agreed with him that the particulars of nature are the offspring of universal forms and that the dialectic is a primary means to contemplate the ideals (forms, universals). However, Aristotle taught that our world—Plato's "shadows"—is real and is a significant source of both natural and ultimate truth. Standing next to Plato in *The School of Athens,* Aristotle has the palm of his hand stretched toward the earth, emphasizing the study of nature as another entrance into the world of forms and ideals.

Aristotle argued that since the natural world is derived from universal forms, there is something of the universal in every particular, both in the particular itself and through its stages—the growth of a stream into a river, an acorn into an oak, or a newborn baby into an adult. By rigorously applying reason to the study of nature (in a process we call "science"), inquiring minds will learn the facts of nature. This process will lead to consideration of questions regarding the meaning, purpose, and essence (the questions raised by Plato), the universal aspects, of the particulars.

While Plato's idealism dominated Europe until the Renaissance, Aristotle's realism was kept alive in the East, where his works were translated by Syrian Christians, and his ideas were widely accepted throughout the Arab world. With the spread of Islam, the Crusades, and the ensuing collapse of the Eastern Roman Empire, refugee scholars from the East arrived in the West with fresh approaches to learning based on Aristotle's philosophy. Aristotle's emphasis on nature contributed greatly to technological innovation and the revival of art, prominent elements of the Renaissance. He also appealed to the Renaissance spirit by providing an alternative to the authoritarian church hierarchy that had dominated metaphysics and stifled new ideas.

Thomas Aquinas

The church also embraced Aristotle's realism, most notably through the theologian Thomas Aquinas (1224– or 1225–1274). Aquinas built a synthesis between biblical revelation, Roman Catholic tradition, and science. He concluded that God is Pure Reason; therefore, the universe He created must reflect His mind. By investigating God's creation, we learn about God and His ways. Over two thousand years earlier, long before Plato and Aristotle, the psalmist noted that "the heavens declare the glory of God; and the firmament shows His handiwork" (Psalm 19:1). Nature, perceived truly, produces a *natural theology,* which, if properly understood, would be in harmony with the church's interpretation of the Bible.

All Truth Is God's Truth

For the Christian educator as for Thomas Aquinas, any truth discovered in God's world is God's truth, so it is proper to give a prominent place in a Christian curriculum to the study of the natural sciences. There are, however, cautions that must be attached to the idea that "all truth is God's truth."

The first is that human beings are finite and fallible. They understand the secrets of nature slowly and partially, so that what appears at one point to be true may later prove to be incomplete, misleading, or just wrong. Humility is essential in the study of nature, especially when one is drawing conclusions from scientific evidence. The Christian realist, who begins with biblical revelation, assumes that the truths in Scripture and in nature are complementary.

In the same way, humility is appropriate and necessary in the study of the Bible. One who "sees" what is not clear to most others should give the issue careful thought. One should be cautious about moving from the clear teaching of the Bible to logical inference. As church leaders extended the Bible's infallibility to church pronouncements, *natural theology* grew beyond what Scripture taught, as demonstrated by Galileo's clash with the Roman Catholic Church.

Roman Catholicism reasoned that since Jesus, the Son of God, came to the planet earth, the earth must be the center of the universe. Therefore, church authority supported Ptolemy's theory that the earth stood still while the sun and other heavenly bodies circled around it. Although the logic was good, the facts were wrong, and the Bible does not teach this view. When Copernicus, Galileo, and others proved the theory to be wrong, the church stubbornly held to its untenable position.

Second, human beings are sinners. Our minds are affected by the Fall, so we tend to serve our own interests, limiting and interpreting what is found in nature by what we want or expect, by what supports our thesis and furthers our case. This tendency is evident in Charles Darwin's work. Darwin had accepted Hegel's idea of progress through struggle in history, and he looked for the same elements in nature. He found some, of course, but overlooked both the lack of evidence for parts of his theory and the contradictory evidence, such as genetic deterioration.

Third, science is limited to examining what can be proved through observation and experiment. It cannot speak authoritatively about the meaning of the particulars or about the basic questions of life involving the nature, purpose, and destiny of God and man.

Realism Across the Centuries

In the seven hundred years after Thomas Aquinas, realism became dominant. Despite pockets of Augustinian idealism on one hand and a steady deterioration of confidence in the Roman Catholic Church and religious faith on the other, the educational norm was a synthesis of faith and reason, of revelation and scientific inquiry.

Francis Bacon (1561–1626), for example, was a Christian who appreciated both God's Word (the Bible) and God's world (creation) as sources of knowledge but lamented the reliance on questionable traditions in both areas. He advocated greater emphasis on inductive learning (examining the evidence and then drawing conclusions) rather than blind acceptance of traditional authority and is widely credited as an architect of modern science.

John Amos Comenius

Another educator in the tradition of Aristotle was John Amos Comenius (1592–1670), a Moravian pastor and teacher who suffered severe persecution during the Thirty Years' War. During his forced exile, Comenius continued his pastoral ministry to Moravian exiles and became an influential writer and educator. His particular interest was how students learn.

Comenius developed approaches to education that use the senses and build on principles observed in nature. Nature, according to Comenius, is one of God's textbooks, from which principles of teaching and learning can be derived. Nature, for example, follows a developmental pattern. Things grow systematically, from the simple to the complex, with each step built upon previous progress. Teaching, then, ought to start with the simple and become progressively more complex as the simple is perceived and the student becomes ready for the next step. He also observed that we learn by relating ideas to things we see around us, everyday objects and familiar experiences.

Comenius described these and other educational theories in his books, most notably the *Didactica Magna.* His textbooks were highly influential. His *Janua Linguarum Reserata* (*The Gates of Languages Unlocked*) taught Latin and other languages by associating thousands of words with everyday situations and activities. Even more daring, in an age when learning was a solemn activity, was his *Orbis Pictus* (*The World in Pictures*), the first successful textbook to use illustrations as an integral part of instruction.

Aquinas, Bacon, and Comenius are representative of the development of Aristotle's ideas through the years. Although realism, like idealism, has been succeeded by twentieth-century theories that grew out of it, it continues to influence education.

Summary: Realism as a Philosophy of Education

Basis

Realism focuses on the facts and principles of the natural world.

Categories

Secular realism The natural world is all there is; the only truth is what is derived from observation and experience; values arise from nature and the rational mind.

Metaphysical realism The natural world has metaphysical origins and significance.

Biblical realism Nature reflects the Creator God; "all truth is God's truth," so there is unity between physics (God's world) and revelation (God's Word).

Teachers

Experts on the subject matter who lecture on and demonstrate principles and techniques, and are comfortable with scientific methodology.

Curriculum

Characterized by emphasis on science, mathematics, phonics, "back to basics," "time on task," standardized testing, computers, technical competence, and practical knowledge.

Positive perceptions

An emphasis on a work ethic, competence in the basics, ability to cope with technology and science, and career preparation.

Negative perceptions

Tends to neglect "human values" (to regard people as machines) and be biased toward control; produces a scientific elite while leaving the less able behind; overemphasizes the material world, specialization, and testing; underemphasizes values and contemplative thinking and writing.

Two Divergent Ways

Plato's and Aristotle's positions (Plato's on ideas and the intellect and Aristotle's on nature) provide useful categories to define and describe philosophical differences and educational strategies, but the two positions are complementary. Through the centuries educators, both idealists and realists, have avoided extremes and occupied a position near the middle, between the ends of the continuum—perhaps because educators, unlike professional philosophers, have to moderate their views in order to be successful in the classroom!

Two Ways: Their Strengths and Weaknesses

Both idealism and realism have much to offer. Idealism challenges the mind to think lofty thoughts, to consider the nature of reality and questions of "ought" and "why," addressing directly questions of truth and meaning. There is, however, a fatal weakness in this process. When the mind reaches conclusions concerning ultimate truth and meaning, perhaps supported by an intuitive deposit of reminiscence, how can those conclusions be verified? There would be no problem if we all came to the same conclusions, but obviously we do not. One person reasons that truth is such and such, and immediately others attempt to refute that conclusion and propose an alternative. Where then is the authority for the ideals of the idealists?

Christian idealists resolve this dilemma by referring to the authoritative revelation of God in the Bible and in Jesus Christ. This process moves one into realist territory, since God reveals Himself through two particulars, a book written in human language and Jesus Christ, who became flesh, a revelation verified historically through fulfilled prophecy, miracles, and His resurrection from the dead.

Since the Renaissance, however, there has been a growing lack of confidence in the established church, the Bible, religion in general, and any metaphysical authority, as well as a widening disagreement among philosophers themselves. Because of this uncertainty, philosophy no longer concentrates on seeking truth but on language analysis and, in effect, on attempts to establish that no authoritative metaphysics is possible.

Realism, on the other hand, offers a wide array of sources of authoritative verification. Scientific study of the particulars has resulted in an astonishing amount of evidence regarding the natural world. We know, for example, a great deal about human beings—

their respiratory system, circulatory system, and mental processes. We know the laws of physics, and we implement them in stunning ways—sending images through the air and astronauts to the moon.

What realism cannot do is tell us the *meaning* of things—such as the significance of human beings *(Who are we? What is the origin of our individual consciousness? What is our purpose and destiny?).* The authority of science is limited to describing and manipulating nature and cannot address the question of the meaning of the particulars.

Idealism provides meaning without verification, and realism provides verification without meaning. In either case, human philosophy is frustrated because, in spite of its stubborn attempt to think clearly about the basic questions of life, it cannot provide adequate answers.

Two Extremes

Realism, at its extreme, is a secular or scientific naturalism that denies the existence of anything but the natural world. There is nothing out there, or up there, or inside us that is not material or natural in origin and essence! This view, currently associated with "modernity," denies God, spirit, soul, life before birth or after death, or any reality except nature. The only way to gain any knowledge or truth is to investigate the material world, a search that reveals only a cold, impersonal universe.

At the other extreme, an exaggerated idealism divides the approach to truth and knowledge into a naturalistic approach for everyday life and a "how I see it" approach to the world of metaphysics and meaning. This postmodern view accepts no absolutes. Truth is determined within the individual (existentially), and the only verification necessary is one's inner experience.

The naturalistic extreme (modernity) flourished in the 1800s, the age of Darwin and Marx, as a secular religion based on the glory and progress of the human race. In the last half of the twentieth century, naturalism has been challenged by an existential philosophy borrowing from Plato's *doctrine of reminiscence* and from Eastern mysticism. Based on inner experience, this approach is the foundation of postmodernism. These competing views will be evident in the contemporary philosophies described in the next chapter.

Conclusion

Idealism and realism had interacted and competed throughout the centuries until, by the middle of the 1800s, radical naturalism had triumphed. This "modern" view declares that the only reality is the material world and denies there is anything—God, soul, spirit, ideals, forms, or universals—out there. There is, in fact, no "out there," only vast and impersonal space.

This *secular humanism,* or *scientific humanism,* infiltrated education and impacted both science and economics, as evidenced by the rise of Darwinism and Marxism. It attacked Christianity from without as religious superstition and from within through a modernist theology. Liberalism took control of church colleges and seminaries, and liberal theologians rejected the supernatural (the incarnation, the virgin birth, miracles, the atoning death and resurrection of Christ, and an infallible and inspired Bible), attempting to make Christianity more acceptable to the modern mind.

This triumph of naturalism was affirmed in 1823 in a series of lectures in which Auguste Comte presented his philosophy of positivism. Comte traced ascending steps in the intellectual evolution of humankind: the theological stage, in which human beings postulate the existence of a personal god; the metaphysical stage, which maintains that there are preexistent ideas; and science, the highest stage, in which the natural world is seen as the only reality and all knowledge must be based on empirical observation.

This process, Comte noted, had been established for the natural sciences; now it was time to turn to the social domain. For far too long the study of human society had been influenced by religion and metaphysics, and now it must be reconstructed using scientific methodology. A new field of science, the *social sciences,* emerged!

Comte coined the term "sociology" for the broad field of social study and laid out its naturalistic foundation. Others followed. Karl Marx related economic laws to cultural matters, Herbert Spencer applied Darwin's biological evolution to philosophy and ethics, and Sigmund Freud revolutionized scientific psychology and founded psychoanalysis. And in the last decade of the nineteenth century, in the hands of the scientific humanist John Dewey, education arrived as a social "science." Thus the foundations were laid for the modern philosophies of education addressed in the next chapter.

About the Author

Jack Layman teaches at Columbia International University in Columbia, South Carolina. Dr. Layman has served Christian schools in a number of positions—among them, member of the executive board of ACSI and director of the International Institute for Christian School Educators.

Strengthen Your Foundations

1. Compare and contrast the educational approaches of idealism and realism.
2. How is nature limited in its ability to reveal God and metaphysical truth? That is, what can be known and what cannot be known from the study of nature?
3. How are the human mind, intuition, and reminiscence limited in their ability to know metaphysical truth?
4. Consider your own educational experience. In what ways has it reflected the emphases of idealism and those of realism?
5. Discuss the statement "All truth is God's truth." In what ways is this true or not true? Are there limitations that ought to be noted? How does the statement help to clarify the study of our world?

References

Comenius, John Amos. 1967. *John Amos Comenius on education.* New York: Teachers College Press.

Durant, Will. 1926. *The story of philosophy: The lives and opinions of the greater philosophers.* New York: Simon and Schuster.

Plato. n.d. *The republic.* Translated into English by Benjamin Jowett. New York: Modern Library.

CHAPTER THREE

Modern Educational Philosophies

Jack Layman

Dramatic change came to the academic world with the emergence of the social and behavioral sciences in the nineteenth century. Auguste Comte (1798–1857) argued that the study of human beings as social creatures must reject the influences of religion and metaphysics and become a division of science. Social behavior, he emphasized, is not determined by mystical forces or philosophical theories but by the laws of nature, and should be observed and brought under control through the scientific method.

Comte's naturalistic approach was well received. What had once been social studies, with little formal academic status, became the social sciences, with the task of improving the human species. As a result, between 1890 and 1940, many new disciplines were established in American colleges and universities—departments of sociology, anthropology, psychology, political science, and, of particular interest to us, education (Kaminsky 1993).

By the close of the nineteenth century, naturalism—the belief that the natural world is the only and ultimate reality—dominated the intellectual world and was moving from academia into everyday life. Christianity, for example, was infiltrated by modernism, a naturalistic theology that denied supernatural elements, such as the bodily resurrection of Jesus Christ, and took control of denominational colleges and seminaries.

During the same period, the common or public school movement came into existence. Ostensibly Christian and Protestant, public education was deliberately constructed with an antisupernatural bias. Horace Mann and its other architects, many with ties to Unitarian and Universalist traditions, excluded miraculous elements of the Bible from the schools and in the guise of unity substituted a homogeneous and secularized liberal Christianity. Selected Bible readings and the Lord's Prayer started the day, but the divinity of Christ, His incarnation, atoning work, and resurrection were excluded as "sectarian" (Glenn 1988). This process of secularization gradually replaced the deposit of Christian truth that had been a traditional part of the schools, so that when prayer and the Bible were banished in 1963, the last leaves fell from a barren tree.

John Dewey

Progressive reformers, concerned about the impact of industrialization, urbanization, and massive immigration, looked to the social sciences to solve societal problems. One of these reformers was John Dewey, a professor of philosophy at the University of Chicago. Born the year Charles Darwin published his *Origin of the Species* (1859), Dewey was a child of his times. He believed in reliance on the "experiential method in the sciences [and] evolutionary ideas in the biological sciences" (Dewey 1944) and was an advocate of pragmatism (although he preferred the more scholarly term *instrumentalism*), a naturalistic philosophy with a distinctly American flavor. Pragmatism accepted "what works" (*pragma* is a Greek word for "what is practical"), and nothing else, as the definition of truth.

Dewey, who became involved in education at the close of the nineteenth century when naturalism and social reform were at their height and public education was approaching maturity, brought the three ideas together. He was committed to naturalism, supported the progressive agenda, and believed that public education offered an open door to social progress and reform.

Dewey's obvious and immediate influence was on classroom methods, but his philosophical base was more significant. He rejected religion based on revelation, and he was strident in his denial of God, the Bible, or anything else that transcended the natural world. Religious values, he argued, are useful only if they arise from nature and are not attached to the existence of God or divine revelation; "supernaturalism ... stands in the way" of human progress (Dewey 1964, 80).

Pragmatism's Methodology

To determine "what works" in schools, Dewey established a Laboratory School at the University of Chicago, where his goal was to change students from theoretical spectators to participants in the learning process (Dewey 1944, 124–25).[1] Teaching at the Laboratory School began with the interests of students, providing projects that integrated academic skills and content into cooperative experiences. Students worked together to make decisions and solve problems in situations comparable to life outside the classroom.

Although Dewey was committed to the scientific method, in practice he was intuitive, basing his "educational programme upon personal inspiration and shrewd hunches rather than upon rigorous scientific analysis of the evidence" (McClellan 1983, 180). His ideas were not new. In essence, he rediscovered and revived methods used by Jesus Christ, the Old Testament prophets, Martin Luther, John Amos Comenius, and others—teachers who began with the familiar, captured interest, used verbal and visual images, and provided interactive experiences.

Dewey's Laboratory School was successful, but it had many advantages: a select student body, small classes, highly motivated teachers, a low teacher-student ratio, plentiful resources, and the excitement of being part of something special. It is not surprising that the success of the Laboratory School proved difficult to duplicate in the broader arena of public education. This difficulty was partly due to the conservative nature of educators, school boards, and publishers but also to crowded classrooms and heavy teaching loads. Most teachers lacked the time, energy, and ability to prepare and implement life experiences that integrated academic skills and subject matter in a satisfactory way.

Dewey and Progressive Education

John Dewey's ideas invigorated public education, but they evolved into and became associated with "progressive education." The term "progressive" captured the excitement and adventure of social reform and became linked to the romantic naturalism idealized by Jean Jacques Rousseau in his educational novel *Emile.*[2] Confidence in the natural goodness and wisdom of children led to a reduction of adult restraint and discipline in classrooms. Eventually, progressive education became a pejorative synonym for schooling that catered to the whims of students, majored on trivial life adjustment themes, and left students deprived of the basics.

After World War II, as education deteriorated, criticism of progressive education grew clamorous. The outcry was not primarily from professional educators but from outsiders: parents, school board members, business leaders, intellectuals, legislators, and last but not least, humorists and cartoonists. Arthur Bestor, a product and proponent of progressive education, later became disturbed by the substitution of "life needs" for the basic academic disciplines. In *Educational Wastelands* he noted, "I ... do not believe that the American people have lost all common sense and native wit so that now they have to be taught in school to blow their noses and button their pants" (Ravitch 1983, 76).

Titles of similar books and articles are a commentary on the failure of progressive education, from the question-and-answer title *Shall We Have More Progressive Education? No!* to titles such as *Education or Indoctrination, Let's Talk Sense About Our Schools, Quackery in the Public Schools,* and *Time* magazine's article "Flapdoodle," on gimmicks in education.

When Russia orbited the first space satellite in 1957, there was rancorous debate on and reassessment of American education, with growing criticism of the results of progressive education. The irony, Diane Ravitch noted, was that ultimately "neither the Russians nor the critics killed progressive education. It died because it ... did not meet the [pragmatic] test of 'working' in public schools" (Ravitch 1983, 79–80).

Dewey's Legacy

In one sense John Dewey was the most influential educator in American history, dominating the field through his writings and the thousands of educators trained at the University of Chicago and Columbia University who staffed education departments at other universities. The Progressive Education Association and the journal *Progressive Education* disseminated his ideas; his name was synonymous with educational reform. But in another sense Dewey's influence faded.

After developing his ideas in the sheltered atmosphere of the Laboratory School, Dewey adopted a posture of "benevolent neglect" regarding their implementation, shifting his interest to writing and lecturing on issues such as world peace, religion, and civil liberties. Whether or not his lack of involvement was a contributing factor, the movement failed, and he himself lamented about what had been done in his name. In the 1950s, long after John Dewey had disassociated himself from the movement, the Progressive Education Association closed its doors and *Progressive Education* ceased publication.

Reconstructionists

Long before the post–World War II outcry against progressive education, revolt simmered in the ranks of professional educators, not because the movement had gone too far but because it had not gone far enough. Critics had grown impatient with the tendency of progressive education to promote adjustment to society rather than reform. They were disappointed that public education supported and maintained the status quo, particularly in regard to social and economic injustice.

This disaffection turned to anger when, from 1929 to the late 1930s, America was struck by a severe economic depression. As hardship piled upon hardship, a few prominent educators, led by George Counts of Columbia University Teacher's College, decided that education must be used to pursue radical change. After a visit to Russia in 1932, Counts, who had been favorably impressed by social progress under Communism, gave a series of lectures published under the title *Dare the Schools Build a New Social Order?* His thesis was "that the school must shape attitudes, develop tastes, and even impose ideas.... Teachers should deliberately reach for power" (Ozmon and Craver 2003, 193–94). Counts challenged educators to win the hearts of students and enlist their active support in the battle for an equitable and prosperous society.

The movement was short-lived. Americans, despite their economic trials, were not ready to abandon their tradition of self-reliance for the socialism implicit in Counts' proposals. Nor were the schools an easy place to begin a social revolution. Education was firmly in the hands of the establishment, supported by local property taxes and controlled by local school boards and superintendents who represented the status quo and were not eager to self-destruct.

Pragmatism as a Philosophy of Education

History

Rooted in naturalism, initiated by John Dewey and nurtured at Teacher's College, Columbia University, pragmatism dominated American educational philosophy from 1910–1950. It emphasized social adjustment and learning by experience, and had as its value base democracy and faith in human goodness and progress. His movement evolved into what was termed "progressive" education and, in the process, lost the confidence of Dewey himself.

Purpose

Its goal was to solve the problems of society through democratic and pragmatic methodologies.

Teachers

Teachers are guides, discussion leaders, and, above all, organizers of interactive group experiences.

Methods

Beginning with the child's natural curiosity, teachers emphasize learning by doing, problem solving, and group processes, and they integrate content and skills development into activity experiences.

Positive Perceptions

Emphasizes the importance of the child, the student as an active learner, and cooperative group processes. Subject matter is related to life, there is a minimum of rote learning, and the facilities welcome children and support the teaching methods.

Negative Perceptions

Demonstrates hostility toward Judeo-Christian values, traditional morality, and transcendent truth; promotes and indoctrinates its own absolutes: the basic goodness of humans, the inevitability of progress, and pragmatism, the idea that truth is whatever works. The projects approach was often impractical. The rise of "progressive education" became linked to neglect of basic academics and a tendency toward destructive permissiveness.

A Revolutionary Legacy

The idea of using schools to revolutionize society is a recurring one. In the 1960s and 1970s, for example, teachers actively indoctrinated students on issues such as Vietnam, antinuclear activism, and social justice. More recently, the focus has shifted to the environment, sexual morality, and "politically correct" textbooks. Moreover, control of schools has shifted from local boards to state and federal government and to professional teacher organizations, shielding the schools from protest by parents and taxpayers and opening the door to bolder initiatives.

The issue is not whether education should be used to mold the minds of students; that is the nature of education. The question is, *To whom do the students belong? Who has the right to decide what values should permeate education?* Christian schools, for example, are radically reconstructionist in the sense that they are attempting to instill into students the mind of Christ so that they will "turn the world upside down" in His name. But parents send their children to Christian schools voluntarily because they want the values of their children to be directed by the Bible. The public arena requires a greater degree of neutrality, perhaps more than is possible in our pluralistic society. Should parents and taxpayers be expected to support schools that intentionally indoctrinate children with values antithetical to their own?

Reconstructionism as a Philosophy of Education

Purpose
It is imperative to radically change society, and schools cannot be neutral. Education can and should be the primary agency for social change.

Teachers
Teachers must be convinced and convincing activists.

Methods
Expose and eliminate curriculum that supports and promotes the status quo, persuade and indoctrinate students with regard to the just society, and recruit and develop student activists.

Positive Perceptions
It is education that motivates and involves teachers and students.

Negative Perceptions
May neglect basic skills and content while indoctrinating gullible youth. It is unethical for any one ideology to take over public education. It blatantly interferes with parental roles, and society cannot allow one of its own institutions to undermine its way of life. In any case, evolutionary change is more effective in changing society.

Existentialism and the Humanistic Curriculum

The countercultural revolution of the 1960s was marked by Vietnam war protest, hippies and beatniks, neo-Marxism, marijuana and LSD, and an epidemic of rebellion against authority. Christian apologist Francis Schaeffer believed the revolution was partly the reaction of a new generation to the two materialistic values of their parents, affluence and personal security, and the emptiness and despair those values inevitably produce. Schaeffer thought their analysis of the problem was accurate but not their solutions: individual autonomy, New Left politics, drugs, and truth determined existentially by "how I see it" (1976, 105–110).

Existentialism teaches that truth is subjective, originating ("existing") in the experience of the individual. There are seeds of this idea in Plato's doctrine of reminiscence (see chapter 2)—that the meaning of things is somehow within us and can be retrieved intuitively. Soren Kierkegaard (1813–1855), a Danish Christian and philosopher, had a similar emphasis on the inner person. He attacked "dead" Christianity for limiting faith to mental assent to beliefs and conformity to prescribed practices. He believed that the only way to know God was through an intense inner experience, a personal "leap of faith."

A secularized and pessimistic existentialism became popular after World War I. The mood in Europe had turned from confidence in humankind to a pessimism born in the senseless slaughter of the war (10 million dead) and nurtured by a growing sense of the hopelessness inherent in a naturalistic philosophy. Jean-Paul Sartre argued persuasively that if there is no God, human beings are insignificant. His only advice was to live *as if* life had meaning. Karl Barth, the Swiss theologian, was more optimistic. He believed that the Christian faith and the Bible, while not true in themselves, could become true through our receiving and perceiving them.

Existentialism in America in the 1960s was even more optimistic: purpose, meaning, and truth were to be found within oneself, and a "humanistic" curriculum was designed to nourish the individual and reverse the impersonal emphasis of the 1950s. As one proponent wrote, "The teacher in America is warned by the psychologist

Existentialism as a Philosophy of Education

History

An emphasis on students as autonomous individuals rather than on cognitive outcomes; it came to the fore in the United States in the 1960s.

Teachers

Teachers treat students as friends and equals.

Methods

Encourage individuality and creativity without regimentation or manipulation. The curriculum is student-oriented, providing a variety of choices and emphasizing individual interests, self-awareness, and self-expression ("do your own thing"), with a de-emphasis on labeling, standardized testing, and grades.

Positive Perceptions

Emphasis on individual worth and de-emphasis on materialistic values and bureaucratic and technological mindsets.

Negative Perceptions

Hurts rather than helps individuals because without order, discipline, and content standards, student are ill prepared to fulfill their potential in a demanding and competitive society.

that he must nurture the self-concept of youngsters and extricate them from the academic jungle. As he reaches out to perform his rescue mission, he is attacked by the subject-matter specialists ..." (Manning 1971, vi).

The humanistic curriculum was an extreme form of the child-centered emphasis of progressive education. The focus was on the individual child and how she or he saw things; on "getting in touch with your feelings," "finding yourself," and "doing your own thing." The humanistic curriculum did not last long, partly because of general alarm at falling test scores, but it left a generation of students with a poor foundation in reading, grammar, and mathematics. A less obvious but more lasting result is the reinforcement it gave to *subjectivism,* an existential methodology that bases truth and morality on personal preference.

Although the humanistic curriculum did a lot of damage, it reminded educators that students should be treated as persons and not as things. Christian educators, too, must remember to be like gentle mothers and encouraging fathers (1 Thessalonians 2:7–12).

Behaviorism

Behaviorism is the antithesis of existentialism. According to the behaviorists, there is no "inner person" to develop. There is, in fact, no such thing as spirit, soul, or mind. What we call being good or bad, envious or loving, desires, fears, hopes, and beliefs are merely conditioned behaviors. Men and women are neither innately good nor innately bad; they are complex animals, an integral part of nature—and nothing more.

Behaviorism was influenced by three twentieth-century psychologists: Ivan Pavlov, John B. Watson, and B. F. Skinner, all of whom began with naturalistic presuppositions. Through experiments with animals, Pavlov established the principles of stimulus-response conditioning. Watson suggested conditioning ("engineering") infants and children. Skinner developed and popularized behavioral engineering as an educational science.

Conditioning is a natural process that affects all life forms, but, according to Skinner, we now have the technology to control the process and the behavioral tools to solve the social problems that have plagued humanity. Men and women can be made to want to do, and to do, what the behavioral engineers want them to do! The weak link in the process is the interference of parents and teachers who are unable to scientifically apply positive and negative reinforcement to conditioning procedures. To overcome this, teachers are de-skilled as teachers and re-skilled as technicians able to implement a scientifically designed curriculum. Skinner pioneered mechanical baby-care units to care for infants and teaching machines to provide programmed learning for students.

Behaviorism first appeared in the 1920s and reached its peak in the 1970s, partly as a welcome corrective to the excesses of existential education. While many of its techniques have proven helpful and continue to be used, behaviorism as a philosophy has lost ground for four reasons:

1. It does not work as well as was claimed. While useful for relatively simple operations, it requires too many tedious steps to work with complex ideas.
2. It underestimates the obstinacy of the human will. There are limits to the degree to which human behavior can be conditioned.
3. The notion that human beings are simply complex animals, a logical deduction from naturalism, is repugnant and depressing.
4. The control inherent in the process is seen as harmful. Skinner himself noted that "When we ask what Man can make of Man, we do not mean the same thing by 'man' in both instances. We mean to ask what a few men can make of mankind.... What kind of world can we build—those of us who understand the science of behavior?" (1948, 282). Who, then, will control the controllers?

Behaviorism as a Philosophy of Education

Basis
The science of behavior modification is applied to education.

Teachers
Teachers are technicians who implement a scientifically designed curriculum.

Methods
The teaching machine is symbolic of behaviorism. Each part of the curriculum is supported by positive (and, perhaps, negative) reinforcement.

Positive Perceptions
This "scientific" approach to education avoids reliance on individual teachers. It works well for teaching operational steps and is particularly effective with emotionally and developmentally impaired students.

Negative Perceptions
It does not live up to its messianic expectations. It is repetitive, can be boring, and is often ineffective. Its emphasis on manipulation and loss of individuality denies human freedom and dignity.

Essentialism and Perennialism

As one innovative educational approach follows another, are there schools that stick to traditional education? Or, as a teacher once asked, "Didn't we 'use to know' how to do this?" The answers are yes and yes.

"Traditional" is used here to refer to practices that have

distinguished "good" education through the ages. These practices are characterized by a core curriculum of traditional knowledge and skills, promotion of self-discipline and respect for authority, and high expectations for student achievement. When the curriculum emphasizes natural sciences in the tradition of Aristotle, it is often referred to as *essentialism*. When the emphasis is on a "liberal education," metaphysics, and the mind in the tradition of Plato, it is sometimes called *perennialism*. The boundaries between the two are vague, with many programs balanced between them, but both essentialism and perennialism stress foundational knowledge, and both are open to reconciling nature and science with faith and revelation.

Essentialism and perennialism are criticized as elitist and impractical, and are often referred to condescendingly in philosophy of education textbooks. For example, they may be included under the heading "Authoritarian Educational Theories" and described as "contributing to the slowness of educational change ...," "obsolete ...," and not satisfying "the needs of twentieth-century U.S. youth" (Johnson 2003, 276). These criticisms are unjustified. Traditional schools do well in low socioeconomic settings, adapt to technology, employ a variety of teaching methods, and produce successful students.

Conservative Alternatives

Traditional schooling has been the norm in some parts of the world, and it is common in many independent schools in America, particularly Roman Catholic, Lutheran, and evangelical Christian. Traditional education is also alive in the public sector. It is reflected in the back-to-basics movement that followed the USSR's space launch in 1957 as well as in subsequent reform efforts such as Mortimer Adler's *The Paideia Proposal*. Traditional education is also evident in advanced placement courses, upper-level tracks, and a myriad of individual classrooms where teachers close the door and attempt to educate their students.

Approximately 150 independent evangelical Christian schools existed between 1920 and 1960, but between 8,000 and 12,000 schools were founded between the mid-1960s (when achievement scores in public schools began to plummet and Bible reading and prayer were banished by the courts) and the 1990s. Almost without exception, these schools were educationally traditional.

In 1978 the Western Association, the Ohio Association, and the

National Christian School Education Association merged to form the Association of Christian Schools International (ACSI), and there are now more than 5,300 schools and 1,162,000 students attending ACSI schools in around 100 countries. Add the burgeoning home-school movement as well as those schools with another affiliation or none, and it is clear that the impact of Christian schooling is considerable. While the rate of the increase in Christian schools has slowed, the schools have matured educationally and have been invigorated by the growth of "classic" schools and the emergence of black Christian schools.

Systems, Spectrum, and Blend

The usual approach to educational philosophy is to categorize ideas into systems, as in this chapter. While such classifications are helpful for recognizing, organizing, and analyzing trends and ideas, they can be misleading. Lines drawn between systems are arbitrary; the differences are not nearly as distinct as they appear to be when categorized in a book. In reality, the ideas are not isolated from one another but mark points on a spectrum of concepts, and even when philosophical differences are extreme, there may be similarities in methodology.

Behaviorists, for example, recognize the need to welcome students warmly and the wisdom of building on student interests as a part of the conditioning process. On the other hand, existentialists understand that some conditioning is necessary—to train children to avoid danger, for example, or to develop skills that contribute to self-expression in music.

Every system has been built, to some extent, on false premises and is missing the essential foundation of biblical truth. On the other hand, each has something to offer in its emphasis, strategies, or methods, as can be illustrated in the Christian school movement.

A Christian school, to be truly Christian, must be established on the foundation of God Himself, the Creator, who has made Himself known through an authoritative and trustworthy Bible, and of Jesus Christ, His Son, the Savior of the world. Within this framework, however, Christian schools differ from one another, and even from course to course or teacher to teacher within a school. There is room for differences, both in our understanding of biblical teachings, which often reflects denominational distinctives, and in educational methodology, where differences between the schools are similar to those in the systems we have discussed.

Think of a choir. Though choirs have much in common, they differ in their selection of material, their special sound, their use of instruments, their dress, their degree of formality, and the musical level of their performance. Christian choirs differ from one another in a similar way, but in Christ they have common purposes and values that unify them and distinguish them from all other choirs. This is true of schools as well.

Some schools emphasize classical academics, while others stress nurturing children or reaching a lost world for Christ. Some concentrate on science and mathematics, others on the development of the mind, the arts, or communal body life. In some the teacher has little input, relying primarily on the curriculum, while in others the teacher is central, both as a model and as an organizer and presenter of material. Within the schools there are also differences, depending on the subject and the personality and gifts of the teacher. Biology focuses on nature, literature on the mind and the imagination, and history on social and political issues; but biology, literature, and history will be taught differently depending on the teacher and the curriculum (Pazmino 1988, 111–13).

Education is a blending of ideas, a balanced tension between academic content, the student as a person, and social behavior; between stress on the mind and ideas, on nature, and on personal relationships. Each school and class has a slightly different blend. Everything we do in schools, and the way we do it, reflects an educational point of view, and Christians can disagree on these. What we have in common, however—the truth found in the Bible and in Jesus Christ—must permeate our schools (we call this "integration") and, in the process, unify us despite theological and educational differences.

About the Author

Jack Layman teaches at Columbia International University in Columbia, South Carolina. Dr. Layman has served Christian schools in a number of positions—among them, member of the executive board of ACSI and director of the International Institute for Christian School Educators.

The Decline of Philosophy

With a few exceptions, philosophy is not considered important today in the education of teachers and administrators. There is usually a chapter or two in an introductory text, and perhaps a graduate course in educational philosophy, but the treatment is perfunctory. There is a review of philosophical systems, perhaps slanted by the view of the professor or textbook, but little or no stimulation for students to think through the issues and develop a philosophy of their own based on truth.

The reason for this is that secular colleges and universities are uncomfortable with metaphysics. Other than a vague humanism that reinforces the importance of human beings and a better life for all, there is a tacit understanding that ultimate truth is out of reach. There are competing opinions, but the only acceptable final statement is that whatever one believes is true—for oneself. Everything is subject to flux and change, and old absolutes are deposed by new uncertainties.

Educational philosophy has degenerated into a smorgasbord of conflicting speculations and a shift of focus from metaphysics to methodology. Most public educators cannot articulate their philosophy clearly because they are not sure what it is. Christian educators, however, need to be able to understand, articulate, and apply a biblical philosophy of education. The Christian school movement will thrive or fail to the extent that they do.

Notes

1. Dewey demonstrated the value of participation by noting the difference in the motivation of prisoners viewing the weather through their cell windows and farmers whose plans for planting and harvesting depended on the weather.

2. It is ironic that Rousseau is accepted as an educational authority. He had no experience in educating children and, in fact, sent his five infant children to orphanages!

Strengthen Your Foundations

1. List the educational institutions you have attended and try to describe and categorize educational philosophies and methodologies that you have experienced.

2. List under the four philosophical approaches described in this chapter—Pragmatism, Reconstructionism, Existentialism, and Behaviorism—methodologies that would be appropriate for Christian educators. How can/should one distinguish between philosophical foundations and methodologies?

3. What elements in John Dewey's educational methods can be illustrated by methods used by Jesus Christ?

4. Read chapter 33 of B. F. Skinner's *Walden Two* (New York: Prentice Hall, 1976) and outline Skinner's comparison of Christianity and behaviorism. In what sense is Skinner's philosophy "religious."

5. Prepare a skit illustrating progressive, reconstructionist, existential, and behaviorist education.

6. Replace the "choir" illustration in this chapter with another illustration and restate the point that the illustration makes.

References

Carper, James C. 2001. The changing landscape of U.S. education. *Kappa Delta Pi Record* (spring): 106–10.

Carper, James C., and Jack Layman. 1995. Independent Christian day schools: Past, present, and prognosis. *Journal of Research on Christian Education* 4, no. 1: 7–19.

———. 2002. Independent Christian day schools: The maturing of a movement. *Catholic Education: A Journal of Inquiry and Practice* 5, no. 4: 502–14.

Dewey, John. 1944. *Democracy and education.* New York: Macmillan.

——. 1964. *A common faith.* New Haven, CN: Yale University Press.

Glenn, Charles Leslie Jr. 1988. Ch. 3, The common school as a religious institution, and Ch. 4, The opposition to common school religion, in *The myth of the common school.* Amherst, MA: University of Massachusetts Press.

Johnson, James A., Victor L. Dupuis, Diann Musial, Gene E. Hall, Donna M. Gollnick, and Janet W. Lerner, eds. 2003. *Essentials of American education.* Boston: Allyn & Bacon.

Kaminsky, James S. 1993. *A new history of educational philosophy.* Westport, CN: Greenwood Press.

Manning, Duane. 1971. *Toward a humanistic curriculum.* New York: Harper & Row.

McClellan, V. A. 1983. Dewey, John. In *Twentieth-century culture: A biographical companion.* Edited by Alan Bullock and R. B. Woodings. New York: Harper and Row.

Ozmon, Howard A., and Samuel M. Craver. 2003. *Philosophical foundations of education.* 7th ed. Columbus, OH: Merrill Prentice Hall.

Pazmino, Robert W. 1988. *Foundational issues in Christian education: An introduction in evangelical perspective.* Grand Rapids, MI: Baker Book House.

Ravitch, Diane. 1983. *The troubled crusade: American education 1945–1980.* New York: Basic Books.

Schaeffer, Francis A. 1976. *How should we then live? The rise and decline of Western thought and culture.* Wheaton, IL: Crossway Books, 1983.

Skinner, B. F. 1948. *Walden two.* London: The Macmillan Company.

CHAPTER FOUR

Biblical Foundations of Education

Kenneth O. Gangel

In his much discussed book *The Soul of the American University: From Protestant Establishment to Established Unbelief*, George Marsden attempts to explain the fundamental reversal in American education. In his concluding paragraph, after observing that nonsectarianism has come to mean the exclusion of religious concerns, Marsden notes,

> As in earlier establishments, groups who do not match the current national ideological norms are forced to fend for themselves outside of the major spheres of cultural influence. Today, almost all religious groups, no matter what their academic credentials, are on the outside of this educational establishment, or soon will be, if present trends continue. Americans who are concerned for justice ought to be open to considering alternatives. (p. 440)

What a novel idea! An alternative to secular American education. An alternative that places the Bible back at the heart of what education is all about. An alternative that focuses curriculum around a core of absolute truth. Such is the foundation of biblical education.

Why do some young people grow into admirable adults? Somewhere, somehow, they learn a worldview based on a solid ethical and moral foundation, and they integrate that worldview, consciously or not, into their decision-making processes. Christian educators share the awesome responsibility of helping young people develop the kind of worldview that leads to holy and responsible life choices. Such a duty demands that educators themselves learn to think Christianly and then to effectively communicate that ability to their students.

The questions are many: *Where must we start? What is biblical thinking? What kind of knowledge must a person gain to hold a distinctively biblical worldview? Does such a worldview imply uniformity in politics, school choice, vocational decisions? What sources best support biblical education?* This chapter explores the necessary foundation for an education that can be called "distinctively biblical."

Where Does a Christian Worldview Begin?

Those familiar with my writings of the past four decades will expect me to stand on the platform of authority. In the postmodern scene, all the usual players—reason, tradition, revelation—have left the stage. The rejection of universal truth and absolute moral principles has broken the ideals that formerly linked us together and has left us with tribal loyalties that serve only to divide us. Standing against a secular education with little remaining commitment to authoritative underpinnings, I call Christian educators to return to the theology of David:

> The law of the Lord is perfect, reviving the soul. The statutes of the Lord are trustworthy, making wise the simple. The precepts of the Lord are right, giving joy to the heart. The commands of the Lord are radiant, giving light to the eyes. The fear of the Lord is pure, enduring forever. The ordinances of the Lord are sure and altogether righteous. They are more precious than gold, than much pure gold; they are sweeter than honey, than honey from the comb. By them is your servant warned; in keeping them there is great reward. (Psalm 19:7–11, NIV)

Although the gospel has always been transcultural, Christians have frequently adapted so dramatically to their culture that they fade into the scenery and become scarcely distinguishable. To be sure, this behavior often arises from sincere motives, such as a desire to contextualize the message or appear relevant to the times, yet it reflects Renaissance and Enlightenment thinking and a Christianity addicted to futurism, movements, groups, and slogans.

Any foundation for a Christian worldview must begin with Scripture. It is from the Word of God that we receive special revelation concerning the nature of God, humankind, ultimate reality, goodness, and life expectations. While all people have access to general revelation (through the study of God's creation) and to the world's accumulated knowledge, only Christians accept the Bible as our source for the ultimate answers to life. While all systems of philosophy require a measure of faith, a belief in Scripture provides the most internally consistent system on which to build a moral and purposeful life. Christians believe that through the Bible, God has given us "everything we need for life and godliness through our knowledge of him who called us by his own glory and goodness" (2 Peter 1:3, NIV).

Who Is God?

So much of what passes for theology today takes its cue from sociological pragmatism, ignoring or perverting authoritative biblical sources. The very process of education lends itself to a superficial pragmatism in which many behave as though crucial questions about the nature of God, the nature of humankind, and the relationship between them can be handled with neutrality. When technique becomes the center of educational process, we find ourselves handling only the shadows of truth, and we are only occasionally in search of a theology. Modern secularism affords neither a lesser nor a greater threat to biblical truth than Roman paganism; indeed, the similarities are striking. One needs no obsession with evil spirits to see satanic footprints all over the paths of contemporary culture.

Without apology or defense, the Bible's opening statement is a declaration of God and His power: "In the beginning God created the heavens and the earth" (Genesis 1:1). This God is presented throughout Scripture as a singular spirit Being (in opposition to the many gods of polytheism) who is the ultimate existence: "I am who I am" (Exodus 3:14). He is all knowing, all powerful, all present, all true, and the ultimate source of love, goodness, and beauty. God seeks those who will worship Him in spirit and in truth (John 4:23–24).

Where Did Humankind Come From?

At the end of each day of Creation, God looked at His work and pronounced it "good." The statement changed at the end of the sixth day, when God pronounced the work not just good but "very good." On that day, "God created man in his own image, in the image of God he created him; male and female he created them" (Genesis 1:27). Everything was good, but that which was in the image of God was *very* good.

Thus humankind was created in the image of God. This truth accounts for our spiritual nature, the vacuum within us that only the Spirit of God can fill. It also accounts for our human creativity, thinking skills, language, internal sense of right and wrong, sense of beauty, emotions, and ability to make choices. Psalm 8:3–6 (NIV) asks the question:

> When I consider your heavens, the work of your fingers, the moon and the stars, which you have set in place, what is man that you are mindful of him, the son of man that you care for him? You made him a little lower than the heavenly beings and crowned him with glory and honor. You made him ruler over the works of your hands; you put everything under his feet.

What Accounts for the Evil in Human Nature?

In education, the significance of anthropology is exceeded only by that of epistemology, and both must be viewed through theological eyes. Whatever one's hermeneutic of the early chapters of Genesis, their significance for understanding human nature can hardly be discounted. In the final and greatest creative act, the one person becomes two. We see the birth of the first human community, characterized by harmony with nature and unity with each other as the two recognize their interdependence.

Sadly, rebellion alters their relationship with God and results in disharmony with nature and disunity with each other. God has provided for every human need. Though He has given only one negative command, the man and woman choose to rebel. Their relationship with God, with each other, and with nature changes to one of disharmony and disunity. Original sin passes to all of humankind, bringing sorrow and separation. Ever since, human beings have had deceitful, wicked hearts and have been helpless to save themselves from the penalty of sin and restore their fellowship with God. On their own, humans are condemned to a life alienated from God and an eternity separated from Him.

Do Fallen Humans Still Bear God's Image?

Though different faith communities approach their understanding of humanity's creation in God's image from widely varying directions, we can hardly move forward with a philosophy of Christian education until we have built a biblical worldview based on certain theological components. A biblical worldview is an understanding of God and humankind in relation to everything else. Many regard our creation in God's image as the source of our rational and moral capacity, our need for community, even our dominion over nature (Genesis 1:26, 28). Seasoned Christian educators refresh their thinking with the theology of the restored image, although as some have put it, the image of God has not been erased in humanity, but it certainly has been defaced.

Thus humanity demonstrates God's likeness in that people retain the capacity to sincerely seek and find truth and to make moral decisions. Image anthropology acknowledges not only the tarnishing caused by sin but a means of restoring dignity and sanctity to life. Since all humans have the potential to become fully conformed to God's likeness, all human life is valuable. Sin has prevented the world and its people from fulfilling God's creative ideals, but in redemption He offers dignity to the dishonored and deliverance to the oppressed.

How Can Humans Be Restored to Fellowship with God?

Because God is holy, His nature demands payment for sin and a means of reestablishing righteousness before Him. From Genesis 3:15 on, the Old Testament foreshadows the coming of God's Son and the provision of a means of redemption. Although the sin of one (Adam) brought condemnation to all, one act of righteousness, Jesus' death on the cross, made justification and life available (Romans 5:19). As believers accept Christ's death as payment for their sin, God, who is rich in mercy, forgives them and makes them alive in Christ (Ephesians 2:8–9).

As finite human beings we cannot ultimately understand God, who is all powerful, all knowing, and present in all places at all times. None of these attributes are reflected in us as His image bearers. However, many of His other attributes do find expression in humanity—sacrificial love, unconditional forgiveness, a justice that knows no favoritism, and a choice of moral and ethical values in line with our Christian belief system. From such a combination of biblical epistemology and anthropology, we find the way to a restoration to fellowship.

What Is the Purpose of Humanity?

At Creation, humankind received two commands: to establish dominion over all that was created and to occupy the earth. The re-creative commands found in the New Testament note that it is the will of God that all people come to a saving knowledge of Him (2 Peter 3:9) and that all who are saved come into conformity with the new nature created in Christ (2 Corinthians 5:17). Thus these four commands form the basis for the integration of all of life:

Salvation	➠	a right relationship with God
Sanctification	➠	a maturing relationship within oneself
Dominion	➠	a caretaking relationship with the physical world
Occupancy	➠	a social relationship with others

Christian teachers carry the awesome responsibility of helping students develop a worldview that leads to responsible life choices. Built on the theological foundations that must form the heart of all our schools, such a worldview is distinguished by the integration of natural and special revelation into human learning and experience. A biblical worldview influences decisions to choose kindness and patience instead of pushing to be first and best. Christian teachers want to produce adults who have woven their moral and spiritual lives out of a worldview based on biblically ethical and righteous values.

What Is Truth?

Christian teachers must have a highly developed biblical awareness, enabling them to integrate scriptural truth with the realities of contemporary life. For all of us, God's revelation—personal (Christ), written (the Bible), natural (creation)—stands as the foundation for a theology of learning and therefore a theology of truth. We carry a two-edged sword. With one edge we slice through specialized academic disciplines, and with the other we apply biblical answers to academic and cultural questions.

Such an integrative process leads to a clear understanding of the nature, source, discovery, and dissemination of truth. Christian educators affirm that all truth is God's truth, by which they simply mean that all genuine truth can ultimately be traced back to God as its source. And since the God of revelation is also the God of creation, the true relationship between natural and special revelation begins in the foundation of absolute truth.

How Is a Biblical Education Integrated into a Unified Whole?

Yet another important dimension of biblical education is its holism, the holy unity of biblical living. The Puritans completely rejected a division of life that called some parts of it sacred, therefore of greater importance, and some secular, of less importance. Our contemporary world needs to become reacquainted with the view that every dimension of life is sacred. God's people bring salt and light to the world. They affirm and encourage the dignity of all life, asserting that God is uninterested in ethnic or gender boundaries in His redemptive call.

Christians find wholeness in a worldview that encompasses both the material and the spiritual, the sacred and the secular. This view is in opposition to the pervasive secular/sacred dichotomy maintained throughout history by many thinkers. Educators with a biblical worldview properly find that *for a Christian, there is no secular domain.*

One needs no special imagination to see Christian teachers equipping their students for tasks far greater than final exams or graduation. Our ultimate purpose finds reality in kingdom living, not academic honors. Biblical education promotes a worldview emphasizing that the God of Creation and revelation, not simply of nature and humanity, is the ultimate object of our worship.

What Personal Values Are Associated with a Biblical Education?

Life. Judeo-Christian ethics places a high value on human life. The Mosaic laws were among the first in history to provide instruction on the benevolent treatment of women, children, slaves, the elderly, and the handicapped. A biblical worldview incorporates a belief in the sanctity of life from conception to death, leading believers to work for the common good. Most charitable organizations established to relieve human pain and suffering are outgrowths of Christian concern.

Possessions. Believers are warned that we cannot serve both God and money, and that life does not consist in the abundance of things. While money and possessions are not wrong in themselves, the love of money is the root of all kinds of evil (1 Timothy 6:10). Believers are therefore warned against covetousness and materialism.

Family. God established the family as the first human institution when He said, "Therefore a man shall leave his father and mother and be joined to his wife, and they shall become one flesh" (Genesis 2:24). Throughout Scripture God provides clear counsel on relationships between husband and wife, and between parent and child. These are to be marked by respect, submission, love, and honor. Judeo-Christian teachings are unique in their demand for preservation of the marriage bond and for nurturing relationships with children, a core value in Christian education.

Children. Jesus emphasized the value of children when He said, "Let the little children come to Me, and do not forbid them; for of such is the kingdom of God" (Luke 18:16). Realizing that children represent the next generation of history, Christians share a deep concern for their tender care and proper instruction.

Work. Christians respect all work, whether secular or sacred, that brings honor to God through the fulfillment of His commands. We sense a personal obligation to provide honest work for honest pay, and we take seriously the Scriptures that convey the responsibilities of both a worker and a master. Paul best summarizes these principles: "And whatever you do in word or deed, do all in the name of the Lord Jesus, giving thanks to God the Father through Him" (Colossians 3:17).

Stewardship. God holds all people accountable for the resources entrusted to them, which include money and material possessions as well as personal resources—time, energy, talents, labor, and intelligence. Recognizing that God is the Author of all good and perfect gifts, we endeavor as Christians to be responsible stewards of the resources entrusted to us.

Church. Christians are to gather in local, corporate bodies of believers for the study of God's Word, prayer, ministry, and mutual encouragement. Biblical education incorporates strong support for local churches as well as worldwide missions organizations. As believers, we differ in many specific points of doctrine, and we support pluralism in the larger society, including the right of all people to live by their conscience as long as they neither harm others nor force their beliefs on them. At the same time, we accept the clear teaching of John 14:6 that Christ is the way, the truth, and the life, and that no one can come to the Father except through Him. In a society that treasures freedom of speech, the sharing of this truth of God will draw believers together and produce life-changing results.

The World. Humans were given responsibility to be caretakers of God's world. This gardening concept leads a farmer to take pride in the appearance and productivity of his land. In the same way, Christians view the world as a place of responsible gardening, where they plant and harvest in ways that do not pillage and destroy the earth.

The World to Come. While Christians sense a responsibility for the earth, we also recognize that it is not our final destination. God has a new heaven in preparation, so our values reflect eternal outcomes rather than exclusively earthbound ones. As Jesus said, "For what will it profit a man if he gains the whole world, and loses his own soul?" (Mark 8:36). Christians realize that the "real world" is that which maintains God at its center.

Other Values. The Bible specifically addresses some questions of eternal significance, such as the source of life, the sanctity of marriage, and the value of children; but it is silent on others, leaving us to form our own judgment. What guidance does theology hold for the way Christians decide matters not expressly addressed in Scripture? There are many issues on which Scripture does not speak specifically. How much easier certain decisions would be if there were a verse that said, *This is the one to vote for,* or *Here is the charity you should support financially.* Instead, students of Scripture must learn to use biblical principles as a framework from which to address life's questions, both practical and eternal.

School systems offering a value-laden curriculum that ignores the existence of meanings that transcend this world find themselves at odds with Christian parents. In biblical education the faculty and administration establish the theological and academic framework for the communication of truth.

How Can We Teach Our Students to Live Out Biblical Principles?

The difference in knowing the Bible and living biblically is the eighteen inches between head and heart. A simple knowledge of the "oughts" in no way ensures their incorporation into a student's lifestyle. That is why personal acceptance of Christ as Savior and Lord is absolutely essential for every person. At the moment of this decision, God sends His Holy Spirit to take residence in a believer's life. The Spirit's work is to teach and illumine the Word of God so that a Christian begins to know God's will. The Spirit begins the process of producing love, joy, peace, long-suffering, gentleness, goodness, faith, meekness, and temperance as a believer gradually becomes conformed to the character of Jesus Christ. Also, the Spirit convicts the believer of sin and begins to root out the unrighteous works of the flesh.

Why do Christians often fail miserably to demonstrate the true grace of Christ? Paul said that "to will is present with me, but how to perform what is good I do not find" (Romans 7:18). Similarly, a Christian who depends on self and on personal righteousness has no hope of success. Only by walking in the Spirit can a person achieve a consistently moral life that is pleasing to the Lord. A biblical education includes a view of oneself as totally dependent on the work of Christ for both salvation and sanctification.

Summary

Of the many types of human relationships there are, few require the attention to biblical thinking demanded of the relationship between teachers and students. Educators look at their students, whether preschoolers or final-term high school seniors, and wonder, *Will any of this affect their lives?* Yes. The testimony of thousands of Christian school graduates affirms the positive value of a biblical education, which can be summarized as follows:

- People were created to live in harmonious relationship with God, each other, and the world of material things (Genesis 1, 2).
- The initial purpose of Creation was thwarted by sin (Genesis 3), affecting all humanity and the material world as well (Romans 3:23, 8:22).
- Justification and reconciliation with God through Jesus Christ have been made available to all who accept Him in faith (Romans 5).
- Salvation begins a process whereby the Holy Spirit prunes

away the works of the flesh and produces the fruit of righteousness.
- Generally speaking, Christians live out this redemptive activity in relationship with one another (Ephesians 4, Colossians 3:12–17, James 2).
- A Christian integrates faith and biblical values into a lifestyle that reflects a Christian worldview.

Now a crucial epistemological question arises: *Can God's redemptive activity in a Christian's life provide a valid means for understanding truth and acting on it?* Certainly Scripture affirms that those who believe in Jesus Christ stand before God fully justified. Realistically, as the Scriptures witness, not all those who claim the name of Christ live in total harmony with a Christian worldview.

From the first century on, believers have faced problems similar to those of today. They struggled with the balance between liberty in Christ and licentious living, and between loving obedience and legalistic behavior. Immorality affected the first church communities; false theologies deceived new believers. Along the way Christians often stumbled. Early heresies drove good people into monastic isolation. A burning desire to "protect God" led some to burn at the stake those they thought might diminish Him. Many Christians hang their heads at the persecution, war, and brutality that have been perpetrated in the name of Jesus.

While the cultural context is different, the problems haven't really changed. Along with all of creation, today's Christians groan inwardly as we wait for the fullness of our adoption and the redemption of our bodies (Romans 8:22–23). Yet in our struggles we believers open our hearts to the mind of God as we evaluate natural revelation through eyes informed by special revelation. As students of Scripture, Christians must develop a reliance on divine truth in their constant search for human truth.

So, at the end of this chapter, humanity still walks the path of incomplete redemption. Some have come far on the path, but others have not yet begun. Here a basic truth must be understood: *Cognitive assent alone will not bring about life change.* Why is this fact important? Because the fallenness of human nature leads people to worship anything but God. Too many times people bow before the altar of knowledge, thinking its gods can solve life's problems. When some stumble and fall, others moan and say, "If only I had known better." In truth, they probably did, but knowledge alone does not redeem an individual from sin, or ensure right actions.

About the Author

Kenneth O. Gangel, Ph.D., serves as Distinguished Professor Emeritus of Christian Education at Dallas Seminary and as a Scholar-in-Residence at Toccoa Falls College in Georgia.

Christian educators teaching from a biblical worldview desire to affect the whole student, not just the intellect. We need to see our students as more than empty minds waiting to be filled. Students are fallen but redeemable people needing to live out their redemption in relationship to one another. In short, we as educators must translate our theology and philosophy into "street sense," enabling our students to live a Christlike life in the real world. They must learn not only what the Scriptures teach but how to live daily in accordance with a biblical worldview.

Strengthen Your Foundations

1. Since this chapter is introductory and broad, you may want to write a specific worldview that reflects the position of your personal life, your classroom, or your school. Be sure to utilize appropriate Scripture references.
2. Read John Stott's book *The Contemporary Christian* and reflect on its implications for Christian school teaching.
3. Design a strategy to help students reflect those attributes of God that He has allowed us to demonstrate.
4. Contemplate the significance of relationships at your school and what Christian "worldview thinking" can do to improve them.

References

Gangel, Kenneth O., and Warren S. Benson. 1983. *Christian education: Its history and philosophy.* Chicago: Moody Press, Wipf & Stock, 2001.

Gangel, Kenneth O., and Howard G. Hendricks, eds. 1993. *The Christian educator's handbook on teaching.* Grand Rapids, MI: Baker Books.

Hoffecker, W. Andrew. 1986. *Building a Christian world view,* vol. 1. Phillipsburg, NJ: Presbyterian and Reformed Publishing Company.

Lewis, Gordon R. 1976. *Testing Christianity's truth claims.* Chicago: Moody Press.

Marsden, George. 1994. *The soul of the American university: From Protestant establishment to established unbelief.* New York: Oxford University Press.

Stott, John R. W. 1992. *The contemporary Christian: Applying God's Word to today's world.* Downers Grove, IL: InterVarsity Press.

CHAPTER FIVE

Core Beliefs and Values of a Christian Philosophy of Education

Richard J. Edlin

All schooling helps children to learn about the world and their place and tasks in it. Christian schooling does this job in a context that challenges students to celebrate the lordship of Jesus Christ over all of creation. This chapter focuses on six core values that give meaning to the definition of Christian schooling. These values should act as signposts along the way, giving direction and focus to those involved in Christian schooling. Table 1 identifies the six values, their biblical foundations, and some affirmations that grow out of them.

Table 1: Summary of Core Values

Core Values	Biblical Foundations	Affirmations
Centrality of the Bible	Proverbs 3:1 Psalm 119 John 17:6–19 Colossians 3:16	The Bible, God's written Word, is preeminent in the life of the Christian. Divinely inspired and inerrant, it is authoritative for all of life, including the life of the Christian school.
A Biblical Worldview	Acts 17:16–34 Colossians 2:8 Joshua 1:8–9 Hebrews 1:1–2	Education is never neutral. Christian education must ensure that students learn about the world and their place and tasks in it from the perspective of a biblical worldview.
The Importance of Parents	Deuteronomy 6:4–9 Psalm 78:1–7 Ephesians 6:1–4	God has given parents the primary responsibility for the nurture of their children. The Christian school partners with parents to assist them in carrying out this responsibility.
The Importance of Teachers	Luke 6:39–40 Colossians 2:6–8 1 Timothy 4:6–11	Christian schools will fail without teachers who clearly understand, teach, and live from the perspective of a radical biblical worldview. Schools need to offer their teachers sustained, biblically authentic professional development.
Nurture in the Christian School	Psalm 8 Ephesians 2:10 Ephesians 4:20–24 Philippians 1:3–11	Children are gifted image bearers, but they are impacted by the Fall and need redemption in Christ. The school should help them discover God's peace and purpose for themselves and their world as stewards responsible to Him.
Responsive Discipleship and the Christian School	Luke 14:25–33 Jeremiah 29:7 Ephesians 3:13–19	Christian education does not just promote personal growth. It equips young people to share God's dynamic message of hope and peace in Christ, in every vocation and activity, to a lost and forlorn generation.

Core Value 1— The Centrality of the Bible

Affirmation

The Bible, God's written Word, is preeminent in the life of the Christian. Divinely inspired and inerrant, it is authoritative for all of life, including the life of the Christian school.

How firm a foundation, you
saints of the Lord,
is laid for your faith in His
excellent Word.

These lines were first given to us by John Rippon in 1787 and were later sung at the funerals of American presidents Theodore Roosevelt and Woodrow Wilson. These immortal words remind us of the starting and finishing point for all Christians—the Word of God. Christians live in different cultures. The denominational commitments of believers reflect differing historical and theological perspectives. Yet all true Christians seek to bring every thought into subjection to Jesus Christ as He has revealed His will in the Old and New Testaments.

Although the Bible is not a textbook, it nevertheless informs all our Christian educational activities in a foundational way. Consider the following examples:

- The Bible may not tell us whether a school should have a strict dress code, but it does give guidance about how we should view and clothe ourselves, and about what our lives should be like as individuals and in community. This guidance should be explored and articulated as the basis for any dress code.
- The Bible may not tell teachers how to arrange the desks and chairs in their classrooms, but it does give us an understanding of children (made in God's image, affected by the Fall, responsible to and for one another in community) that should impact the layout of a teacher's classroom.
- The Bible may not prescribe how we should teach mathematics or science, but it does show us the place and order of mathematics and science in God's world. They are parts of His created reality and are as steeped in faith commitment as any other aspect of God's world. Indeed, an entire issue of ACSI's journal *Christian School Education* (vol. 5, no. 4) provides guidance for biblically faithful education in these important areas. So too does the book *Mathematics in a Postmodern Age: A Christian Perspective* by Russell Howell and James Bradley (2001).
- The Bible may not provide examples of how schools should complete student report cards. However, an evaluation and assessment system in a Christian school that is not based on a biblically authentic pattern of giftedness and accountability (as informed, for example, by the parable of the talents) will not be pleasing to the God we seek to serve.

The curriculum development process in Christian schools must begin with God's Word at its center (Edlin 1999). The resulting biblical perspective on knowledge will involve much more than an understanding of ideas. True knowledge, in biblical terms, is not attained until it is lived out in the lives of teachers and students.

Working out from God's Word will also ground Christian education in a proper understanding of truth. Truth is not an autonomous, self-existing reality that scientific enquiry objectively discovers, as modernists would have us believe. Neither is truth a relativistic social construction as the postmodern radical constructivists who dominate contemporary educational theory would have us believe. According to the Bible, truth is propositional and incarnational. That is, truth is a revealed part of God's creation and is authentic across time and cultural boundaries. However, the full glory of truth is that it is also relational—found most fully in the person and work of the living Word, Jesus Christ. Jesus did not come just to tell us about the truth or give us true words. He *is* the truth (John 14:6). A Christian school's curriculum must start with this declaration and should bring its students to a deeper knowledge of it.

A proper use of the Bible in education is quite different from mere proof-texting, in which we attempt to justify everything with a biblical quotation. While it is important to indicate passages of Scripture that provide a foundation for certain concepts, the teaching should always be carried out in a way that respects and reflects the integrity of the context of the chosen passage. Satan's use of proof-texting in tempting Jesus (Matthew 4:6) reminds us of the error of just quoting Scripture to justify an activity.

Besides using the Bible in devotional and foundational ways, the Christian school will subject all its relationships and activities to the critique of Scripture to ensure that everything done is in accord with a biblical understanding of the world and our place and task in it. The odious trap of cultural idolatry that makes Christian school activities an unthinking reflection of contemporary culture cannot be overcome without this rigorous, sustained, communal critique. The simple task of asking *why* or *why not* about all school activities is a good place to start.

In recognizing the authority of Scripture for all of life, the Christian school should also be able to differentiate between the norms of God's Word, which apply in all cultural contexts, and the rules or cultural applications of these norms. As Craig Keener (1993) reminds us, the injunction in Deuteronomy 22:8 to build walls around our roofs to stop guests from falling off is a cultural expression of the biblical norm that we are our neighbor's keeper. A modern application could be to ensure that passengers in our cars have their seat belts fastened.

Finally, a biblically authentic understanding of the Bible in the Christian school, as it shapes the school's mission statement and its practice, should allow for diversity in disputable matters. Although conformity can be expected in organizational issues for the sake of the smooth operation of the school community, many of the ways that Christian schools apply the Bible to instructional activities are constructions on the Bible rather than the Bible itself. In the history class for example, a study of the origins of World War II may lead to a discussion about whether Christians should go to war. In the civics class, democracy will be compared with other governmental structures. In the economics class, capitalism and economic rationalism will be critiqued in the light of biblical norms.

In all these areas, Christians have differing perspectives. Paul's attitude about food offered to idols (Romans 14) reminds us that in disputable matters such as these we must allow for diversity. It is not important that all students agree with the teacher. What is important is that the teachers and students together are compelled to critique their perspectives on these issues in the light of God's Word. As they prepare children to live in the world, Christian schools must help them use God's Word to develop perspectives on reality that are biblically authentic and personally owned, and that will help them to glorify God and live for Him in all they do.

Core Value 2—A Biblical Worldview

Affirmation

Education is never neutral. Christian education must ensure that students learn about the world and their place and tasks in it from the perspective of a biblical worldview.

In Acts 17, Paul delivered his famous sermon to the Athenians on Mars Hill. In that sermon, he declared that all of life is inescapably religious. The famous American educator George Counts put it this way:

> Education conveys to the young responses to the most profound questions of life—questions of truth and falsehood, of beauty and ugliness, of good and evil. These affirmations may be expressed in what an education fails to do as well as in what it does, in what it rejects as well as in what it adopts. Education may serve any cause.... it may serve tyranny as well as freedom, ignorance as well as enlightenment, falsehood as well as truth, war as well as peace, death as well as life. It may lead men and women to think they are free even as it rivets upon them the chains of bondage. (1952, 29)

All of life, including education, is based on beliefs about the world. There is no neutrality. To acknowledge that life is religious means that we must reject modernism and scientism. These "isms" assume that the truth of certain "scientifically validated ideas" is self-evident, and that we therefore can base our beliefs on these supposedly neutral truths. However, there is no such thing as neutral truth. All ideas are based on belief commitments. As Francis Schaeffer taught, there is nothing back of God. All things, including scientific laws, depend on the creator-sustainer God, and we cannot understand anything fully without a faith commitment to Him.

Tragically, the last people to cling to the myth of religious neutrality in education seem to be Christians. This myth, based on the nonbiblical, dualistic idea that Christianity impacts only what happens on Sunday and in personal and family devotions, has been dispelled in earlier chapters of this book. What is important to establish here is that the approach to the world and education that we develop as Christian educators must be grounded in a biblical worldview. We must ensure that the way we look at schooling and education derives from a set of beliefs about the world that is distinctively Christian.

Probably the most helpful biblical worldview that dynamic Christian thinkers have articulated is that of Creation-Fall-Redemption-Fulfillment. (See *How Now Shall We Live?* by Chuck Colson and Nancy Pearcey; *The Life of the Mind: A Christian Perspective* by Clifford Williams; and *Creation Regained* by Alfred M. Wolters.) A sound grasp of this worldview should be a basic tool in every Christian teacher's intellectual toolbox. It must be used to shape the Christian school's view of the child. It will give foundational insight into curriculum construction. It will guide school and classroom relationships.

Christian educators committed to a Creation-Fall-Redemption-Fulfillment worldview may want to stop using the phrase "an integration of faith and learning." That phrase implies that learning exists without a faith commitment. It cannot. Learning is always faith-based. All curricula are based on the beliefs of their designers. Therefore, what Christian educators should be passionately committed to is the articulation of a *biblical* integration of faith and learning.

The relationship between the Bible and one's worldview must be reiterated. It is important that our worldview grows out of an understanding of God's Word and does not stand independent of it. Worldviews are human constructions; they are not divine revelation. In fact, our worldview shapes how we read the Scriptures. Therefore, we must be rigorous in critiquing our worldview in the light of Scripture to ensure that God's revelation, not our cultural prejudices, is at the root of our worldview and educational foundation. Our teacher training and evaluation programs must go behind worldview and ensure that teachers have a solid grasp of the Bible itself. We cannot assume that teachers will receive this input in many contemporary churches. And yet, unless our educational worldview constructions are based on an articulated biblical foundation, they can become what Brian Walsh calls "repressive ideologies" (Walsh 2000, 101) and can lead to distortion and error.

Core Value 3—The Importance of Parents

Affirmation

God has given parents the primary responsibility for the nurture of their children. The Christian school partners with parents to assist them in carrying out this responsibility.

Most Christians can quote passages of Scripture that highlight the God-given responsibility of parents to nurture their children in the discipline and instruction of the Lord. Christian parents are required to ensure that their children learn about the world and their place and task in it in a way that celebrates the lordship of Christ over all creation.

This responsibility applies to each kind of nurturing that parents provide—physical, spiritual, and educational. Christian parents do not yield this authority at the door to the doctor's office or the clubhouse of the local sports team. In the same way, they do not yield it at the school gate. In all these arenas, parents enlist the expertise of other people to help them carry out their biblical mandate. At the same time, because many of these enlistments are in a community context, parents agree to accept the authority of the supporting institution over their children. Parents carry out their biblical mandate by ensuring that the policies and procedures of the institution conform to biblical patterns and by involving themselves in appropriate ways in the life of the institution.

Because parental nurture is a God-given responsibility, Christian schools should beware of language, structures, and school cultures that strip parents of their responsibility. The Christian school must facilitate parents' informed involvement in the life of the school. Christian schools should not fear parents but should encourage their appropriate involvement. Classrooms should be open environments where parents are encouraged to observe and participate in a nondisruptive manner. Regular contact between home and school should not just be limited to times when children get into trouble.

The school and home can be mutually supportive only when there is meaningful cooperation and interaction built on a biblical perception of the relationship between the two. All too often in contemporary Western culture, the Christian school is seen as a business that works for people on a fee-for-service basis—not an appropriate way for the body of Christ to function. Before enrolling their children in the Christian school, parents need adequate nurture in a biblical pattern of schooling. Without such pre-enrollment nurture, the Christian values and worldview of the school can be overtaken by middle-class mediocrity.

Too many "Christian" schools in North America, Australia, and New Zealand are becoming mere "cheap" versions of the elitist private school across town. Biblical faithfulness is giving way to a socially acceptable, materialistic success mentality. School authorities and parents must work hard to combat the idea that the school exists to help students attain economic self-fulfillment. For the sake of the integrity of the school as well as the assimilation of the child, it is suggested that Christian schools normally make new student enrollments provisional. Final enrollment should depend on each new parent's participation in a seminar that explains the radical, socially nonconformist purpose and character of the school. As Nicholas Wolterstorff reminds us, "The idea of the Christian school in our society is the idea of a school producing dissenters and agents of change in the name of Christ. The Christian school is a training ground for ... dissent and reform" (2002, 170).

Core Value 4—The Importance of Teachers

Affirmation

Christian schools will fail without teachers who clearly understand, teach, and live from the perspective of a radical biblical worldview. Schools need to offer their teachers sustained, biblically authentic professional development.

Teachers are not mere extensions of parents. Although the context is theological, Ephesians 4 reminds us that the office of teacher is biblically mandated. Teachers have gifts and abilities appropriate to their calling, and schools should be structured in a manner that allows them to exercise their talents in a God-honoring way. The metaphors used by Van Brummelen (1998)—artist, facilitator, storyteller, steward, priest, and guide—paint a useful picture of the multiple tasks of the Christian teacher. Three particularly important issues concerning teachers are training and professional development, relationships, and community.

Thinking and teaching Christianly does not come naturally. In fact, like Peter (Mark 8:33), many teachers whose instruction is modeled on the secular teaching they received may well be doing the devil's work for him, even inside the Christian school. Sustained, ongoing professional development from a biblically informed perspective must be non-negotiable, for it is more fundamental to a Christian school's ultimate survival than electricity. School boards should generously fund (in time and money) opportunities for their teachers to think deeply and critically from a biblical perspective about all aspects of the educational task. Teachers' contracts should require them to commit themselves to such training.

Recently, the president of Handong Christian University in Korea was talking with the president of Wheaton College in the United States. The Handong president asked his Wheaton counterpart why Wheaton had maintained its Christian distinctive whereas institutions like Yale and Harvard had lost theirs. The response was that the key to Wheaton's continued faithfulness has been its sustained, corporate commitment to rigorous, biblically authentic professional development of its teachers. Let us learn this lesson well!

Biblically authentic professional development leading to a dynamic curriculum is of strategic importance. However, in Luke 6:40 Jesus did not say that a student when he is fully trained will be like his curriculum. No, Jesus said that a student, when he is fully trained, will be like his teacher. Relationships are at the heart of the Christian gospel, and they are at the heart of Christian nurture within the Christian school. Paul blends these twin aspects of truth in instruction and godly interaction with students in his comments in 1 Thessalonians 2:8 (NIV): *We loved you so much that we were delighted to share with you not only the gospel of God but our lives as well.*

Finally, Christian teachers must work in community. Many Christian schools are structured in such a way that teachers become individualists working in their own disconnected classrooms. Others have disempowering, dictatorial leadership models. Once again, these patterns are contrary to the biblical model of the body of Christ. According to Van Dyk,

> The staff must constitute a team, consisting of differently gifted people all working together with a shared perspective.... When such a unity of perspective is absent, the school is no longer a genuine

organic community but merely an organization held together by externally imposed rules and regulations. (2000, 18)

Core Value 5—Nurture in the Christian School

Affirmation

Children are gifted image bearers, but they are impacted by the Fall and need redemption in Christ. The school should help them discover God's peace and purpose for themselves and their world as stewards responsible to Him.

A biblical worldview gives the educator a wonderful perspective on the children, whose ultimate worth is found not in their beauty or intelligence but in the fact that they are made in God's image. As God's image bearers, all children have a unique set of gifts and talents that the school should help them and their families identify and develop. Recent decades have seen new light shed on such issues as multiple intelligences and learning styles, and knowing about these enables Christian educators to respond appropriately to each child's uniqueness.

As God's image bearers, students also have the need to make moral choices and be held accountable for them. Therefore, pedagogy in the Christian school will go far beyond direct instruction to include discovery learning, in which teachers and students together learn about the world and their place and task in it. The Christian school will also celebrate community among the students and will recognize the place of collaborative instruction and appropriate classroom layout in enhancing community.

However, children are not just created in God's image. They, like their teachers, are deeply scarred by the Fall and impacted by sin, and true nurture in the Christian school will acknowledge this reality. Accountability and discipline will be evident. However, the discipline should not be separated from nurture but should focus on truth, confession, and restoration, using a discipling model. (Note that the root of the word *discipline* is *disciple.*) Discipline will go beyond mere behavior modification and will address the heart. Within its structures, the school will also acknowledge the right of adolescents to defect from the school's religious commitment while at the same time requiring the defector to conform to its prescribed standards as long as he or she is belongs to the school community.

A biblical view of the child and of giftedness should inform the Christian school's approach to evaluation and awards. Evaluation should be based on the uses of a student's giftedness more than the mere possession of it. Awards in Christian schools, which range from simple stickers to prizes presented in elaborate ceremonies, often seem to have more to do with behavior modification and the reinforcement of personal fulfillment than with celebrating the biblically faithful use of gifts and abilities.

Core Value 6—Responsive Discipleship and the Christian School

Affirmation

Christian education does not just promote personal growth. It equips young people to share God's dynamic message of hope and peace in Christ, in every vocation and activity, to a lost and forlorn generation.

The instruction and nurture provided by the Christian school are not offered only for the sake of the student. In challenging students with the celebration of the lordship of Christ over all creation, Christian education demands a response. The apostle Peter reminded his readers that they were the recipients of all sorts of good things, but for an explicit purpose—to declare to a needy world the wonderful light of the good news of true life in Jesus Christ (1 Peter 2:9–12). Christian schools should not exist to produce another generation of pew-sitters. They should be equipping young people, as they come to know the King of kings, to be His ambassadors in the world, seeking to bring His peace into all of life. This is responsive discipleship.

True worship and service to God for the Christian school graduate do not always mean becoming a pastor or missionary. The Christian school experience should equip young Christians in every vocation to critique the idolatrous culture they live in and bring God's message of hope, peace, and reconciliation into that culture. The task belongs to every Christian, in commerce, industry, service industries, homemaking, the arts, unemployment, the military, medicine, or any other area.

In every area of life, we find people chasing after false hopes—particularly in our contemporary societies where commercialism and economic rationalism shout their counterfeit claims. Carl Henry claimed that if ever this generation is to become one of virtue, it must be dramatically confronted by those who have smelled the acrid, enveloping smoke of our pagan age and will share with others the incomparable rewards of new life in Christ that alone can lift the pall of darkness. This confrontation will mean that Christian school programs must help students find out about the world as it really is, even to the extent of studying and genuinely comprehending false perspectives. Only then will our students be able to speak coherently with people who are wedded to those false views and lead them toward the light.

Graduates from Christian schools are their schools' living report cards. If Christian schools are to receive a passing grade, their graduates should be evident in the world, challenging the idolatrous status quo and offering an alternative view that is biblically authentic and that genuinely seeks the welfare of the city they live in. Never has this been more important than in contemporary society, in which individualism, economic rationalism, and despair have reached record levels. Zygmunt Bauman believes that modern society has fractured into a series of hopeless, monologic discourses, a mere "series of soliloquies with the speakers no more insisting on being heard, but refusing to listen into the bargain" (1997, 81). If Christian schools are doing their job properly, their teachers and students should be salt-and-light beacons of hope in this postmodern nightmare. By representing God and His way as they have taught and learned it in school, they have the opportunity to stand tall themselves and reach out with God's shalom into all areas of this desperate and needy world.

About the Author

Richard J. Edlin, Ed.D., is director of the National Institute for Christian Education, a graduate Christian teacher training school in Sydney, Australia. Originally from New Zealand, he has served on governing bodies of Christian schools on four continents. Edlin's publications include *The Cause of Christian Education.*

Strengthen Your Foundations

1. What is cultural idolatry? Give some examples from your experience of how cultural idolatry has shaped Christian schooling. Identify three strategies we can use to reduce the impact of cultural idolatry in the Christian school community.

2. Clarify your understanding of these terms: *relativistic social construction; propositional; incarnational; relational.* How might a certain view of truth shape the way a Christian teacher or parent understands education? How would you compare the views of a Christian teacher with those of a non-Christian teacher?

3. What is meant by the claim that there is no neutrality in education? Tell how that claim relates to: (1) the urgency for Christian educators to develop a Christian worldview, and (2) the importance of sustained, biblically-based professional development programs for Christian teachers.

4. What do you think Wolterstorff does (and does not) mean by claiming that Christian schools should be training grounds for dissent and reform? Do you agree with Wolterstorff? Why or why not? Note three ways in which Wolterstorff's perspective would shape the teaching and learning that occurs in a Christian school community.

5. Form six small groups, each responsible for one core value identified in this chapter. Each group will develop an information brochure about your school, focusing on that core value. Include pictures (digital cameras are great here). This activity can be rewarding and fun for parents, teachers, and even students. Not only will it help cement your vital core beliefs into the school culture, it may also produce an array of contextualized brochures to use in the school's vision-based growth programs.

References

Bauman, Zygmunt. 1997. *Postmodernity and its discontents.* New York: New York University Press.

Colson, Charles, and Nancy Pearcey. 1999. *How now shall we live?* Wheaton, IL: Tyndale House.

Counts, George. 1952. *Education and American civilization.* New York: Teachers College Press.

Edlin, Richard J. 1999. *The cause of Christian education.* Colorado Springs, CO: Association of Christian Schools International.

Howell, Russell W., and W. James Bradley, eds. 2001. *Mathematics in a postmodern age: A Christian perspective*. Grand Rapids, MI: Eerdmans.

Keener, Craig. 1993. *IVP Bible background commentary—New Testament.* Downers Grove, IL: InterVarsity Press.

Van Brummelen, Harro. 1998. *Walking with God in the classroom.* Seattle: Alta Vista College Press.

Van Dyk, John. 2000. *The craft of Christian teaching.* Sioux City, IA: Dordt Press.

Walsh, Brian. 2000. Transformation: Dynamic worldview or repressive ideology? *Journal of Education and Christian Belief* 4, no. 2: 101–14.

Williams, Clifford. 2002. *The life of the mind: A Christian perspective.* Grand Rapids, MI: Baker Academic.

Wolters, Alfred M. 1985. *Creation regained.* Grand Rapids, MI: Eerdmans.

Wolterstorff, Nicholas. 2002. *Educating for life.* Grand Rapids, MI: Baker Academic.

SECTION TWO

Psychological Foundations

From biblical and philosophical foundations, we turn to the psychological foundations of Christian school education. We will look at learners, their psychological makeup and learning styles, and at teachers and the qualities that best facilitate their students' learning.

An understanding of the psychological foundations of education, built firmly on a biblical philosophy, brings order and cohesiveness to a Christian school's curriculum. Teachers need to understand and provide for the varied learning styles found in every classroom. Christian school teachers are more than simply dispensers of knowledge. They become role models and mentors for all students.

Every Christian school educator must come to grips with the importance of the psychological foundations of the education process. A working knowledge of the psychology of the learner and its relationship to learning is critical to the success of the classroom teacher.

CHAPTER SIX

The Nature of the Learner

Gloria Goris Stronks

The intelligent and frightening Masai warriors of eastern Africa use the traditional greeting *Kasserian ingera* when they meet each other. I am told that greeting means "And how are the children?" The greeting acknowledges the great value the Masai people place on the safety and protection of their children. The expected response, "All the children are well," means that the young are safe and protected.

I do not know whether that greeting still retains its original meaning. But think how it would be if the president of the United States were required to begin each State of the Union address by answering truthfully the question, *And how are the children?* Knowing how our children fare, how they think, and how they learn is extremely important to us.

Christians know that the search for meaning is innate. God created us so that we long to find meaning when we learn new things, especially in matters concerning God's creation. This fact is important for Christian teachers to remember because creation tells us about God.

Learning and the Human Brain

We live in a time when researchers know more about the human brain and how people learn than ever before. The following insights concerning the brain can be found in *Education on the Edge of Possibility* by Renate Nummela Caine and Geoffrey Caine and *A Biological Brain in a Cultural Classroom* by Robert Sylwester:

1. The search for meaning occurs through creating patterns in the mind. Knowing this helps teachers understand the importance of using instructional strategies that enable students to create mental categories.
2. Learning always involves conscious and unconscious processes. Some learning occurs below the level of awareness, and a student

may not understand a concept until weeks or even months after it has been taught. Knowing this helps teachers understand that they must continually look for opportunities to creatively connect new learning with old.

3. The brain is modular, and various parts of it have to work together. Knowing this helps teachers understand that when a student's brain functions perfectly well except for one module, the result may be a very intelligent student who has a particular learning difficulty.
4. During the second ten years of a person's life, the frontal lobes of the brain mature, allowing it to make decisions more easily and to solve more complex problems. Knowing this encourages teachers in grades five and up to use problem-solving strategies in their teaching.
5. People learn best when they are challenged, but the challenge must happen in a safe, nonthreatening environment. A healthy emotional environment is critical to learning. Knowing this helps teachers understand the dangers inherent in the use of sarcastic or threatening comments to students or in allowing such comments within the school or on the playground.
6. Every brain is uniquely organized, and no teacher can understand the organization of anyone's brain. That is why we cannot know when we teach something whether the student has only memorized or has truly learned it.

While we value insights such as these, we are aware that often those who apply research findings to education in the form of special programs or materials have vested interests and blind spots. Thus we are cautious about becoming too accepting of their way of thinking about learners, particularly when we try to understand learners from a biblical perspective.

When bombarded with research findings as applied to education, some teachers are too quickly persuaded that these findings represent the best way to view students. Others say that research can prove anything you want it to, so they think they need not consider any research important to how they think about learners.

Developing a Framework for Thinking About Learners

Teachers must develop frameworks for thinking about learners. Having a framework helps them examine each theory to see whether any part of it fits into their framework or might shape it appropriately. Such a framework must be based on personal beliefs, which are shaped by biblical teachings, about what it is to be human. It must also be based on teachers' professional knowledge informed by a careful study of the research. A teacher's framework may change, but only when that teacher has carefully thought through the impetus for change to determine that the change will clarify and improve the framework.

What might this kind of framework look like? Fifth-grade teacher Lorraine J. describes it this way:

> After doing a good bit of reading and listening to speakers, I now think about learners, including myself, very much as people who live in relationships. First of all is our relationship with our triune God. Our response to God in this relationship is to live obediently and to work to mend whatever we can in this broken world. Our relationship with God also can make us aware of a deep loneliness within ourselves, loneliness that really is a result of our feeling separate from God while we are on this earth. That is what St. Augustine was talking about when he said, "Our hearts are restless until they find their rest in thee."
>
> The learner also stands in relationship to himself or herself. People cannot have identities, cannot even know themselves, apart from God's revelation. That, I think, is what C. S. Lewis referred to in his novel *Till We Have Faces*. Al Greene says, "We must, for God's sake, develop in all directions in order to be something and mean something in the world."
>
> The learner stands in relationship to others. Often, we come to know much more about ourselves when we see how we react to others who are here on earth with us. When we think of others in a competitive or jealous manner, we look inside ourselves and see the monster deep within us. Jesus tells us to "love one another as I have loved you." This kind of love is filled with caring. When we support those who need our care and work to serve others, we see God's grace working deep inside of us.
>
> The learner also stands in relationship to God's creation. Because of sin, this creation is no longer the way God intended it to be. But because of the sacrifice of Jesus Christ on the cross, we are now able to work to heal the brokenness of creation. That is our task while we are on this earth.

Lorraine went on to say that each of these relationships carries with it certain responsibilities, and an important part of teaching in Christian schools is to teach students how to fulfill these responsibilities:

> What is the responsibility that flows from our relationship with God? It is a willingness to act in obedience to God's word in response to our

salvation, a willingness to set aside our own longings and desires in order to live as God wants us to live. It includes a willingness to care for the earth and to care for others because of our relationship with God.

What is the responsibility that flows from our relationship with ourselves before God? I believe it is to be willing to be all God made it possible for me to be; to be willing to look at myself, my own gifts, and to say, "I must do all I can to develop my knowledge, my skills, and my ways of thinking to use them for God's glory."

When I think about my students and about their learning, all of the above shapes my thinking. So when I hear new information about learning, I examine it and ask two questions: (1) *What evidence is there that this information is based on careful research?* (2) *If the information appears to be valid, how can I think about it in light of all that I believe and know?*

Our students should learn that out of gratitude for being saved from our sinful selves we must become all that God has made it possible for us to be. In doing so, each student must come to know how to take responsibility for his or her own learning in ways that are appropriate for that student's developmental level.

Our relationship with others means that out of gratitude for our salvation we will learn to take responsibility for the safety and care of others. Christian schools must be places of *shalom*; places where the distress of others makes one feel compassion and long to take action so that justice will prevail. Caring for others is one of the most splendid ways in which human beings image God.

In school, taking responsibility for others means that it really matters how students speak to each other on the playground and in the hallways as well as in class. If one student is hurting because of inappropriate teasing, teachers and other students must take notice and do what they can to support that person and stop any behavior that is causing pain. Students must learn that God's people work for justice for others, even for those who have done wrong, and must do what they can to protect the rights of others.

There are teachers who will say, "But I can't be everywhere. I can't possibly know what students are saying and doing all the time." It is a tall order to suggest that teachers are responsible to be on constant guard to assure that students treat each other with respect and dignity. However, we are educating students for life. The tendencies developed during childhood and adolescence to act with care toward others will stay with them throughout their lives.

Using the Framework

Some time ago I was with a group of teachers listening to a speaker who said that we should be using tangible reward tokens in the classroom, in the form of candy and stars as well as grades. His argument was that teachers and parents get paychecks for their work. Why should we expect children and young people to work for less? He went on to say that expecting students to do schoolwork without rewards isn't even biblical. "After all," he continued, "Every command to follow Jesus Christ always carried with it the reward of being with Him in glory. Therefore, to expect students to work hard without tangible rewards implies that on their own they can have good intentions, a mark of secular humanism rather than of personal piety."

The discussion in the teachers' lounge the next day centered on arguments for and against tangible reward tokens. Finally one teacher said:

> I would agree that tangible rewards in the form of grades or other things likely have a place in schooling. My concern is that overuse of tangible rewards reduces the intrinsic motivation that most of our students have. Also, the research I have been reading says that when we give tangible rewards to some students, others who do not get the reward perceive it as punishment. When I teach my students to keep self-assessment charts, I find they learn better and also seem to feel good about their progress in learning.
>
> Let's go back to the original framework we agreed we would use. What does the use of tangible reward tokens do to the students' responsibility toward each other? What does it do to their responsibility toward themselves? And how does all of this fit with a Christian view of learners?

Focusing that discussion went a long way toward clarifying issues, and the vote came down on the side of finding better ways of promoting individual and communal learning in classes rather than the use of tangible reward tokens.

Many years later I asked teachers from that school whether they still spoke in terms of a framework of relationships and responsibilities that might help them understand how to think about their students as learners. I heard the following:

> *Angie:* That way of thinking continues to help us. For example, we have all read Howard Gardner's description of multiple intelligences. After considerable discussion we agreed it is more in keeping with our view of learners to think of the eight he describes, along with two others we

have identified, as gifts or talents rather than as intelligences. That does not mean that we don't value his insights. However, discussing them in terms of our framework of relationships and responsibilities helped us to understand that we do not want to create an entire curriculum around them. Instead, it is better for our students if we keep his insights in mind as we plan a variety of activities for our integrated units and also for ways of assessing learning.

George: Some of us visited a neighboring school that was teaching even very young students to use Bloom's taxonomy to understand categories of questions their teachers asked. After some discussion we concluded that the instruction is more developmentally appropriate for older students. The visit and discussion, however, encouraged all of us to ask higher-level questions and to help students understand the difference between higher- and lower-level questions. Bloom's taxonomy fits within our framework in that with it we are helping students take more responsibility for their own learning.

Jim: The framework also helps us when we fall into the trap of thinking too easily of our students as labels. You know, some are the "gifted," others are "ordinary," still others are "ADHDs" or "LDs" or "EDs." Certainly, understanding and knowing how to teach students with learning problems is important, as is meeting the needs of all learners. But the framework keeps us focused on our ultimate goals for each student, as well.

Angie: This way of thinking keeps us from swinging too far with the pendulum on any issue. For example, when split-brain theory was popular, we read articles and books on that topic. After considerable discussion we agreed that we did not think the research should be applied to our classrooms by assigning tasks we had identified as the "right brain" or "left brain" to specific children. Again, we agreed that we must teach in ways that are appropriate for people who are either visual or linguistic learners but that most of our students are likely some combination of the two. It seemed to us limiting, and thus inappropriate, to try to identify each learner as one or the other. Recent research has borne out the fact that doing so is unsuitable for learners.

The Moral Life of the Learner

We sometimes say to students, "Let your conscience be your guide," assuming that the students who come to us have already formed an inner voice that tells them when they are doing wrong. Certainly they will have formed some of the moral attitudes that we call the voice of conscience, but the task of the Christian teacher is to help them develop a mature conscience.

James Fowler named the kinds of conscience that learners need to form (Fowler 1992, 239), and I have described them as a student might:

1. *Conscience of craft.* "I make a habit of doing tasks thoroughly and well. I take pride in the fact that people can count on me to complete a task."
2. *Conscience of membership.* "I do not pretend to be something I am not. The person that others see when they look at me is the person I really am."
3. *Conscience of responsibility.* "If I give my word, I will keep my word. If you ask me not to tell what you have told me, I will keep your confidence unless doing so will cause painful or sinful actions to be repeated."
4. *Conscience of memory and conscience of imagination.* "Thinking of the strength, courage, weaknesses, and suffering of those who have gone before me helps me understand what it takes to live as God wants me to live. I hope to be a person of courage and justice, and I will commit myself to helping those who are poor, afflicted, or oppressed."

When students take pride in doing tasks thoroughly and well, they are respecting themselves and taking responsibility for themselves. When they present themselves honestly and without pretension, they are displaying regard for their own worth and that of others. Remembering heroes of the past helps them think about possibilities for their own lives.

Striving to have these consciences will encourage students to develop hope, which is a positive, realistic vision of the future that allows them to dream and to take positive steps toward their dream. They will be encouraged to develop love that draws their focus away from themselves and leads them into actions of care for others. And knowing that God holds the future, students will be encouraged to believe in a reliable future that allows constructive actions to go forward.

Our Students as Lifelong Learners

An important goal in Christian schooling is that our students will not only learn in ways that enrich their lives today but will also become lifelong learners, adults who find joy and delight in knowing more, and who know how to learn what they don't know. We should teach in ways that will give our students a continual longing to know more about this wonderful world God made for our home, and be able to do more in it.

There has been a great deal written about adults who continue to learn well into their later years. Some people believe that being interested in learning throughout life is a characteristic one is born with. Others say a zest for lifelong learning develops because of what happens in one's family, community, or school experience and therefore can, to some extent, be learned.

Is it possible to teach students in such a way that they will actually want to continue learning and will know how to learn effectively later in life? I believe it is possible, but in order to do so we must first identify the characteristics of lifelong learners. In a study of 1,500 learners for the purpose of discovering characteristics and dispositions of effective lifelong learners, Ruth Deakin-Crick identified the following dimensions of learning that lifelong learners develop. She expressed them as an effective individual learner might:

Learnability Versus Stuckness

- *Enthusiastic (vs. uninterested)* I am usually excited by the prospect of learning, and I have a good deal of energy for learning tasks and situations. In general, I'm attracted to learning and enjoy a challenge.
- *Growth-oriented (vs. static)* I see learning as something that is capable of being improved, and myself as an improving learner. This often reflects a more general interest in "self-improvement," along with faith in the possibility.
- *Responsible (vs. conscripted)* I tend to take ownership of my own learning, and I like to be responsible for what and how I'm learning. I'm usually quite ready to "sign up" for learning tasks that are presented to me.
- *Meaning making (vs. accumulating data)* I tend to look for patterns, connections, and coherence in what I'm learning, and to seek links between new situations and my current knowledge and interests. I'm on the lookout for "horizontal meaning."
- *Critically curious (vs. passive)* I like to get below the surface of things and see what is really going on. I like to work things out for myself and to ask my own questions. I tend to go looking for things to understand better rather than just responding to problems that come my way. I seek out "vertical meaning."

Resilience Versus Dependence

- *Persistent (vs. brittle)* I tend to stick at things for a while, even when they are difficult. I don't give up easily. I often enjoy grappling with difficult things.

- *Robust (vs. fragile)* I can handle the feelings that tend to crop up during learning: frustration, confusion, apprehension, and so on. I have quite a high degree of emotional tolerance when it comes to learning. I'm not easily upset or embarrassed when I can't immediately figure something out.
- *Self-reliant (vs. dependent)* I don't immediately look for someone to help me out when I am finding things difficult, or when I get stuck. I'm usually happy to keep trying on my own for a while. I don't mind if there's nobody around to "rescue" me.

Creativity and Challenge Versus Sameness

- *Risk-taking (vs. "playing it safe")* I enjoy being pushed to the edge of my ability, and I am often willing to take on challenges when I really don't know how to proceed. I like new situations and will sometimes create novelty and uncertainty just to see what will happen. I'll spice things up to keep them from being boring. I don't mind going "out on a limb" in terms of my thoughts and opinions.
- *Playful (vs. literal)* I like playing with possibilities and imagining how situations could be otherwise. I am able to look at problems from different perspectives. I sometimes increase the complexity of what I'm doing rather than try to reduce it. I like trying things out even if I don't know where they will lead or what the point is.
- *Intuitive (vs. rule-bound)* I sometimes get my best ideas when I let my thoughts float freely, and I don't mind giving up mental control for a while to see what bubbles up. I often use my imagination when I'm learning, and pay attention to images and physical promptings as well as rational thoughts.

Learning Relationships Versus Isolated and Dislocated Relationships

- *Collaborative (vs. being a loner)* I like working on problems with other people, especially my friends. I have no difficulty sharing thoughts and ideas with others, and I find it useful. Still, I am quite capable of working away at problems on my own, and I often prefer it. I usually feel quite resourceful. I don't feel I have to stick with the crowd for fear of being lonely or isolated when I'm learning.
- *Community-oriented (vs. dislocated)* I have access to adult sources of support and guidance in my home and community, and I am ready to draw on these when it seems helpful. I feel that I live within a supportive social context.

Strategic Awareness Versus Powerlessness

- *Planning (vs. automatic pilot)* I tend to think about my learning at the outset and to plan how I will go about it. I usually have a fair idea how long something is going to take me, what resources I will need, and how successful I am likely to be.
- *Articulate about learning (vs. inarticulate)* I am able to talk about the process of learning, how I go about things; and about myself as a learner, what my habits, preferences, strengths, and weaknesses are.

Deakin-Crick, Broadfoot, and Claxton 2002

Using these characteristics as goals for student learning will help teachers develop instructional strategies that will strengthen students in weak areas and lead them into lifelong learning. Individual students, of course, will respond to these teaching strategies in different ways. Some students—those with particular learning disabilities and even some who read well—find it easier to learn from sources other than reading. We must not confuse becoming an effective lifelong learner or thinker with becoming an avid reader. Among the many famous people who have been diagnosed as dyslexic are Winston Churchill, David Boies, Tom Cruise, Leonardo da Vinci, Albert Einstein, Anthony Hopkins, John Irving, and Agatha Christie. I have heard people speak of the "gift of dyslexia" because it allowed and even forced them to think in new and creative ways. Certainly these people can be characterized as lifelong learners in spite of their reading or spelling difficulties.

All students should come to understand the important place learning must have throughout their lives. Students who develop skills for lifelong learning will carry with them the resilience, creativity, critical curiosity, learning awareness, and interdependence they will need in order to continue to grow in knowledge about the world God has given us.

I have taught children and young people at many different grade levels from grade one through university. It may be that at the end of my days on this earth, I will stand before the throne of Grace and be asked, "Think of those whose lives you have been allowed to touch. How are my children, Gloria?" And I will have to answer … truthfully!

About the Author

Gloria Goris Stronks, who recently retired as professor of education at Calvin College, is currently serving as an educational consultant. Dr. Stronks is also chair of the board of directors for Worldwide Christian Schools.

Strengthen Your Foundations

1. Consider each of the six insights we have gained from brain research. How will knowledge of each of these influence teaching and learning activities in your classroom? For additional reading about the brain and education, see Patricia Wolfe's *Brain Matters: Translating Research into Classroom Practice* (ASCD, 2001).

2. Describe ways in which you will encourage your students to respond to each of the responsibilities that grows from the relationships in which they live.

3. Go to the following website: http://www.thomasarmstrong.com/multiple_intelligences.htm. Read Thomas Armstrong's explanation of the eight intelligences. Next, download chapter 6 of *A Vision with a Task* (Stronks and Blomberg 1991) http://www.calvin.edu/academic/education/vision/6learn.htm. Read the following sections: "Providing for Diversity: Unwrapping Different Ways of Knowing" and "Providing for Diversity: Affirming Learning Styles." What examples can you give to show evidence that you as a staff recognize and celebrate different ways of knowing? Which of the ways of knowing need more attention in your school? For additional reading about intelligences see David Lazear's *The Intelligent Curriculum: Using Multiple Intelligences to Develop Your Student's Full Potential* (Zephyr Press, 1999).

4. Is it important to teach students about the four kinds of consciences described in this chapter? If so, identify ways in which they are taught in your school and classroom. How might you plan different places in the school's curriculum where students encounter heroes of the past and present? For additional reading concerning the development of consciences, see Julia Stronks and Gloria Stronks' *Christian Teachers in Public Schools: A Guide for Teachers, Administrators, and Parents* (Baker, 1999, pages 34–42).

5. Identify places in your school's curriculum where one or more of the lifelong learning characteristics might be emphasized.

6. Give evidence that your school and classroom are places of *shalom,* places where the distress of others makes one feel compassion and long to take action so that justice will prevail. Plan a survey that might be completed by students in your school to determine whether they perceive their school and classroom as places of caring or whether certain students are being teased inappropriately. For additional reading on this topic see "Great Expectations, Great Challenges: Is This How Middle School Students Are Supposed to Act?" in *Reaching and Teaching Young Adolescents,* Stronks and Knol (ACSI, 1999).

References

Bloom, Benjamin S., and David R. Krathwohl. 1956. *Taxonomy of educational objectives:* Book I: *Cognitive domain.* New York: Longmans.

Caine, Renate, and Geoffrey Caine. 1997. *Education on the edge of possibility.* Alexandria, VA: Association for Supervision and Curriculum Development.

Deakin-Crick, Ruth, Patricia Broadfoot, and Guy Claxton. 2002. *Developing an effective lifelong learning inventory: The effective learning profile (ELLI).* Center for Assessment Studies, University of Bristol. Unpublished manuscript.

Fowler, James. 1992. Character, conscience, and the education of the public. In *The challenge of pluralism: Education, politics, and values.* Edited by F. Power and D. Lapsley. Notre Dame, IN: University of Notre Dame Press.

Gardner, Howard. 1984. *Frames of mind: The theory of multiple intelligences.* New York: Basic Books.

Greene, Albert. 1998. *Reclaiming the future of Christian education.* Colorado Springs, CO: Association of Christian Schools International.

Stronks, Gloria, and Nancy Knol. 1999. *Reaching and teaching young adolescents.* Colorado Springs, CO: Association of Christian Schools International.

Sylwester, Robert. 2000. *A biological brain in a cultural classroom: Applying biological research to classroom management.* Alexandria, VA: Association for Supervision and Curriculum Development.

CHAPTER SEVEN

The Nature of Learning

Barbara Bode

How do people learn? What is the teaching/learning process? What motivates and enhances learning? How do people remember what they have learned? How do individual differences affect learning? To help the reader understand some basic facets of learning, this chapter will explore Christian education, brain-based education, and neurological systems. In addition, it will examine the relationship of memory, emotional influences, gender differences, and individual learning differences to the teaching/learning process.

Christian education learning theory stands in stark contrast to most other theories of learning. Although twenty-five different words are used in the Bible for the teaching/learning process, the focus is always on "teaching them to observe all things that I [Christ] have commanded you" (Matthew 28:20). This emphasis on acquiring knowledge that results in obedience to God's Word is unique to Christian education. Students are seen as image bearers, made in the image of God, responsible for His commands to establish dominion over the creation and to occupy the earth. The students are also seen as bearers of Adam's image as a sinner, and as such they are responsible for the re-creative commands of God for their salvation and sanctification. Our chief aim in education is to bring students into a right relationship with God based on His Word. Learning involves both head and heart. With the head, students can learn God's Word as a revealed body of information. They can learn the wisdom and information gained by humankind through the centuries, and they can even develop the skill to design new paradigms of knowledge. With the heart, students can develop and maintain right relationships with God, others, and themselves (Chadwick 1982). Developing a Christian worldview through Bible-centered instruction, learning to think with the mind of Christ, and behaving in a godly manner are foundational in Christian education.

Brain-based learning is anchored in observations of how children develop and hypotheses about how the brain functions. It focuses especially on how they acquire, organize, store, and use information. *Learning* is defined as the insight gained when new relationships are identified, resulting in meaningful configurations.

Another developmental approach, called *neurological systems*, posits eight systems of learning, each having many subcategories. According to this approach, every child can learn if his or her learning systems are analyzed and evaluated to identify strengths and weaknesses. The basic method used in this approach is to understand how each brain works and teach through a child's strengths. This new perspective on learning involves recognizing neurodevelopment and its relation to the way children learn.

Distinctives of Learning Theory in Christian Education

A Biblical Psychology of Learning: How Your Mind Works (Beechick 1982) provides both the focal point of learning and the framework from which other learning theories can be understood. The author makes a clear case that the Bible is the source of understanding oneself and provides the basis for a biblical learning theory. Psalm 139:14 tells us that we are "fearfully and wonderfully made." Many theorists offer explanations of the nature of learning but fall short of providing a full understanding because such explanations simplify human nature.

Ruth Beechick's work provides a foundation for defining the learning processes. Knowing the human heart is the key to understanding learning. The heart is the seat of spiritual life (Ephesians 3:17), moral life (Romans 2:15), emotional life (1 Timothy 1:5), motivations (Ecclesiastes 1:13), and thought life (Proverbs 15:28). The heart and its interaction with the head are critical to learning. To fully understand the nature of learning, we must recognize the spiritual dimension of human beings.

Students need direction in spiritual formation and transformation, and that direction is absent in all the secular theories of learning. Dallas Willard (2002, 13, 18) hits the mark: "We live from our heart" and "Science misses the heart.... For the spiritual simply is our life, no matter what grand theories we may hold or what we may say when trying to be 'intellectual,' 'well informed,' and 'up-to-date.' "

Beechick suggests that children's learning begins with the loving discipline of parents. The family sets the stage for children to understand that the fear of the Lord *is* the beginning of wisdom. It is important to note that this parent-child relationship operates primarily at the level of heart knowledge, not head knowledge. As a child matures, self-discipline begins to emerge, and a healthy respect for parents expands to include teachers and ultimately God. "The human heart, will, or spirit is the executive center of a human life. The heart is where decisions are made for the whole person. That is its function" (Willard 2002, 30).

Parental love and discipline—and later, each teacher's love and discipline—enable children to acquire information and build concepts through self-discipline and a heart-set (attitude toward learning) that determines whether or not learning is going to take place. As children learn facts, develop concepts, and express themselves creatively, their self-discipline increases, allowing their learning to increase.

A breakdown in learning happens if the heart-set is opposed to learning. As the heart shuts down, learning and creativity are hindered. Therefore, in their children's early years, parents are responsible to disciple them lovingly toward a heart-set that encourages a positive attitude toward learning. The parents' relationship with their young children is the key to learning. Thus, educators must actively build partnerships with parents. Parents have a powerful influence on student motivation, will, purpose, and determination because these attributes are all related to the heart.

But Michael Peterson (2001, 178) warns that "today's students will learn differently from the way past generations learned" and "we will need to teach them differently too." Educators must compete with media productions that are "brief, amusing, and sensational.... Youth have to do little cerebral work and seem to be getting habituated into a passive state of mind in which they expect everything they encounter intellectually to be quick, easy, and entertaining" (182). He further says, "Clearly, children are receiving less emotional support from parents.... A number of trends in contemporary life strongly suggest the serious effect of parental absence and inattentiveness throughout childhood and teenage years" (180). The partnership with parents is more important than ever.

Educators along with parents have a responsibility to nurture the student's heart toward becoming God's image bearer. "Keep your heart with all diligence, for out of it spring the issues of life" (Proverbs 4:23). "The spiritual formation for the Christian basically refers to the Spirit-driven process of forming the inner world of the human self in such a way that it becomes like the inner being of Christ himself" (Willard 2002, 23).

No one understood the human heart more clearly than Jesus Christ. Lois E. LeBar (1958) acknowledged this in her classic book

Education That Is Christian. The primary characteristic of Jesus' teaching methods was His focus on the person. He always responded to personal need, and His response to others guided His interaction with them. He did not ask people to repeat what He said, but He related to people and asked them questions on a personal level. This personal focus is the key to Jesus' teaching. Many times He answered a question with a question to help others analyze and learn from their own activities. If they could not give an answer, He would give another example. The first chart summarizes basic learning principles used by Jesus.

Explanations from known to unknown	Nicodemus	John 3:1–15
Questions for critical thinking	Parables	The Gospels
Concrete examples	Bread of Life Feeding 5,000	John 6:43–59 Matthew 14:15–21
Learning by doing	Disciples sent forth Seventy sent forth	Matthew 9:36–11:1 Luke 10:1–24
Students actively involved	Samaritan woman	John 4:1–42

The Scriptures provide other examples of God's instruction to His people, showing how He used the spontaneous vitality of actual life rather than artificial stimulation. The second chart summarizes teaching methods in the Old Testament.

Repetition with variety	God will supply: manna, water (at Rephidim and Elim), sacrifices
Individual differences	Offerings of sacrifices varied
Diagnostic testing	Spiritual test where God might prove them: i.e., food and water
Direct instruction	Law given on Mt. Sinai
Projects	Building the Tabernacle
Natural life situation	Moses and the children of Israel relate to deepest daily concerns
Using the senses	Sight: manna, cloud/fire signals to stop or travel Hearing: trumpet to announce travel Touch: sin offerings Taste: manna, bitter water/sweet water Smell: fragrant incense

Lois LeBar (1958, 118) aptly summarizes the essence of God's dealing with His people as "beginning His lessons where people are." He starts with our needs and problems, helps us to gain an understanding of His truth as it pertains to our problems, and then relates His truth to everyday living so that we can impart wisdom through both knowing and doing the Word of God. How can this best be adapted to the classroom? That is the bigger question.

Brain-Based Educational Strategies

Psalm 139:14 tells us that humans are "fearfully and wonderfully made." Brain research supports this principle and challenges simplified approaches to learning and teaching. Teaching to separate domains—cognitive, affective, psychomotor—to attain certain behavioral objectives ignores many functions of the brain. In general, by being overly specific about facts to be learned and outcomes to be produced, educators can prevent students from gaining a full understanding of certain concepts.

Renate and Geoffrey Caine (1991) note how brain research relates to educators. They propose that much classroom instruction is brain antagonistic because it focuses on acquiring surface knowledge. To improve instruction, teachers need to move to brain-compatible education as proposed by Leslie Hart (1975). Hart's approach recognizes the complexity of the brain, saying that it operates according to a basic set of rules for meaningful learning, organizing instruction to accommodate those rules.

Brain-based learning recognizes that the brain is equipped with a set of exceptional features:

- the ability to detect patterns and to make approximations
- a phenomenal capacity for various types of memory
- the ability to self-correct and learn from experience by analysis of external data and self-reflection (metacognition)
- an inexhaustible capacity to create

The human brain has a need to find deeper meaning than what is presented in most classrooms. The brain seeks to organize information by constantly making connections on many levels simultaneously. It is therefore important for educators to orchestrate experiences from which students learn efficiently. Caine and Caine (1990, 66–70) developed twelve principles for brain-based learning that are worthy of consideration by Christian educators. They are at the right and on the next page.

Principle	Implication for Educators
The brain is a parallel processor.	Use a variety of methods and approaches.
Learning engages the entire physiology.	In your teaching, incorporate stress management, nutrition, health, and emotional concerns. Learning is influenced by development.
The search for meaning is innate.	Use with all students the creative teaching styles that are typically used for gifted students.
The search for meaning occurs through "patterning."	Present information so that it allows the brain to extract patterns: for example, use integration, thematic teaching, whole language, life-relevant approaches.
Emotions are critical to patterning.	Provide a supportive emotional climate. Use cooperative, metacognitive approaches.

Principle	Implication for Educators
Every brain simultaneously perceives and creates parts and wholes.	Introduce parts in the context of the whole: for example, vocabulary within reading and writing experiences, scientific principles within living science.
Learning involves both focused attention and peripheral perception.	Organize materials outside the focus of students' attention: e.g., charts, illustrations, set designs, art, and music. Teachers' subtle "body language" should signal enthusiasm.
Learning always involves conscious and unconscious processes.	Use metaphors, analogies, reflection, and metacognitive activities to make the material personally meaningful.
There are two types of memory: a spatial system and a set of systems for rote memory.	Avoid an overemphasis on rote memory, which inhibits transfer of learning and effective functioning of the brain.
The brain understands and remembers best when facts and skills are embedded in natural spatial memory.	Utilize experiential learning, classroom demonstrations, projects, field trips, metaphors, drama, and interaction of subjects. Include lectures only as part of a larger experience.
Learning is enhanced by challenge and inhibited by threat.	Strive to create a state of relaxed alertness in students: i.e., low threat, high challenge.
Each brain is unique.	Provide multifaceted teaching to allow students to express visual, tactile, emotional, and auditory preferences.

Learning and Memory Theory

Brain-based education recognizes the characteristics of learning and accommodates them in the instructional process. The reason these orchestrated experiences enrich learning is related to memory processes.

Two kinds of memory are important for instruction. The first is called *taxon memory*, which focuses on taxonomies, or lists of items that are not initially meaningful. Information is transferred from short-term memory to long-term memory by practice, rehearsal, and repetition. The second kind of memory is known as *locale memory,* or *spatial memory*. Human beings experience life in a physical environment that provides the context for learning. They constantly construct internal spatial maps that operate within the locale memory system. Locale memory is used when one remembers events and places without making a deliberate attempt to memorize them. Field trips rely heavily on locale memory. Relationships to facts previously memorized are integrated quickly within this memory system. It is the whole experience that allows almost instant learning to happen.

The learning that involves memory is highly complex, but teaching in accordance with these two memory systems enhances higher order thinking. Both systems should be used in classrooms. Taxon memory should be used when necessary, but the focus should then turn to locale memory, which is activated by experiences and a thematic organization of the curriculum. There is a need "to deliberately embed new taxon content in rich, lifelike, and well-orchestrated experiences that require genuine interactions" (Caine and Caine 1991, 47). This process requires a master teacher who enhances traditional methods with brain-based activities that activate locale memory. Educators need to move from simple memorization strategies to meaningful learning by making their schools "real world" communities where students are involved in real experiences, such as participation in school newspapers and chapels. These methods, which are similar to those Jesus used, fall mainly in the category of locale memory.

Taxon and Locale Memory Systems

Taxon Memory Systems	Locale Memory Systems
Memorization procedures and categories	Natural memory
Requires repetition, practice, and rehearsal	Effortless—assimilated as part of experiences with environment
Static, context-free facts and lists—isolated items not initially meaningful	Exists in relation to where a person is in space
Linked to extrinsic motivation: future reward or potential punishment	Linked to intrinsic motivation: novelty, curiosity, expectation
Information processing model of short-term memory feeding long-term memory	Builds internal relationships; enhances memory through sensory acuity, emotions, long-term memory
Focuses on parts	Uses parts to construct whole
Behavioral objectives—performance outcome model	Thematic teaching—focuses around stories, metaphors, celebrations, imagery, music, cooperative learning
Lecture, textbooks	Inquiry learning, critical thinking analysis, creative and group processes
Formal testing, paper and pencil tests, multiple choice	Evaluation integrated into instructional process; complex, open-ended, meaningful, unique to individual: portfolios, performances, projects
Quick, recognizable results	Transference of results to other contexts and areas of life
Student participation—short-lived	Student participation—longer periods of time

Learning and Individual Differences

Modalities. Brain-based education includes teaching to students' learning strengths. Walter Barbe and Raymond Swassing (1979) helped educators understand the concept of teaching through modality strengths. A modality is any sensory channel through which a person receives and retains information. Visual learners learn by seeing. Auditory learners learn from verbal instruction. Kinesthetic learners learn by doing, using their large and small muscles along with their sense of touch.

Heredity and environment shape a person's modality strengths. The sensory channel through which a student processes information most efficiently is called a dominant modality, and it is observed most readily in early childhood. As students mature, they are more able

Teacher Characteristics of Dominant Learning Styles		
Visual	**Auditory**	**Kinesthetic**
Physical organization very clear; neat teacher's desk, student desks face teacher, several bulletin boards colorfully decorated, materials neatly organized, posters and pictures around room	Vague physical organization of classroom, but teacher is near students; neat, unorganized desks and shelves, chalkboard opposite teacher's desk, one bulletin board	No physical organization to classroom, desks have wide aisles, an open space in room, untidy and unorganized shelves, room organized by activity, much student artwork displayed
Learning centers identified by artwork	Learning centers present	No learning centers
Teacher use of filmstrips, overhead projector	Listening stations	Three-dimensional models
Workbooks, worksheets	Verbal discussions and lecture	Gesturing, acting, drama
Students must have permission to talk or move around room	Student talk encouraged	Talking tolerated if it doesn't interfere; students move freely
Student reading, sight words	Reading aloud, phonics	
Math drills, flashcards, worksheets	Verbal math problems	Going to board to do math problems
Two-dimensional art activities	Student small-group interaction	Hands-on experience methods

to integrate information from various modalities. A secondary modality is less efficient and supplements a dominant modality. Some students have a mixed pattern with no dominant style.

Teachers should be aware of their own modality strengths and guard against forcing their own styles on their students. Instruction should take advantage of students' modality strengths while seeking to strengthen their weaker modalities. They should make minor adaptations to accommodate various learners. The charts listing teacher and student characteristics of dominant learning styles will assist educators in making these adaptations as they evaluate themselves and their students. An awareness of strong and weak modalities in their students will allow teachers to respond appropriately to individual needs.

Multiple Intelligences. As mentioned earlier, Howard Gardner provides research on multiple intelligences as they relate to learning. Gardner posits eight discrete intelligences, and possibly a ninth called *existential intelligence,* which recognizes a spiritual dimension to the mind (Nicholson-Nelson 1998). The first two, verbal/linguistic and mathematical, are the primary ones used in schools. By recognizing others, educators can expand their instructional practices and become responsive to their students' varied ways of thinking and learning.

The Eight Intelligences

by Howard Gardner

- *Verbal/linguistic:* language, grammar, writing
- *Mathematical*: scientific thinking, numbers, geometry

- *Visual/spatial:* visual arts, architecture
- *Bodily/kinesthetic:* eye-hand coordination, sculpting, physical games
- *Musical/rhythmic:* instruments, rhythmic and tool patterns, "hearing" written music
- *Interpersonal*: cooperating in groups and having ability to "read" people
- *Intrapersonal:* understanding self
- *Naturalist:* understanding nature
- [*Existential:* pondering nature of existence; spiritual realm—being investigated]

Student Characteristics of Dominant Learning Styles

	Visual	Auditory	Kinesthetic
Learns by:	Seeing, taking notes, visualizations, planning, lists, illustrations	Listening, auditory repetition, talking, subvocalization, dialoguing	Doing, moving, touching, feeling; likes action stories
Distracted by:	Visual disorder	Sounds	Nonmovement; environment, impulsive
Uses words like:	*see, look*	*listen, hear*	*get, take*
General description:	Quiet: doesn't like to listen long, likes visual, uses facial expressions that denote emotions	Enjoys listening and talking, likes music, very verbal when expressing emotions	Gestures: doesn't like to listen long, likes performing arts, fidgets, appears disheveled, very physical when expressing emotions
Ways to teach spelling:	Films, written word, spelling flashcards	Students chat back and forth, spelling bees	Tracing and writing spelling words

Temperament and Learning. Personal temperament is important in understanding how a child learns. Hippocrates identified four basic temperament types: sanguine, choleric, melancholic, and phlegmatic. People can be a mixture of several temperament types with one or two predominating. The Myers-Briggs Type Indicator is an assessment instrument that evaluates personality types according to Hippocrates' original categories. David Keirsey and Marilyn Bates (1984) report research using this instrument to identify percentages of people in the general population reflecting each temperament as well as the temperaments of those who are attracted to a career in teaching. An understanding of one's own temperament and that of one's students is important for effective instruction, enabling teachers to facilitate the learning of different types of students.

As discussed by Otto Kroeger and Janet Thuesen (1988), Myers-Briggs elucidates four major dimensions or preferences based on the following personality dichotomies:

Information-gathering function	S —	Sensing: uses senses to focus on facts and specific details
	N —	iNtuition: sees global view, big picture
Decision-making function	T —	Thinking: head, objective
	F —	Feeling: heart, subjective
Source of energy: how and where a person gathers information and makes decisions	E —	Extrovert: expressive, outgoing
	I —	Introvert: reserved, internal
Lifestyle orientation: preference for information gathering (S or N) or decision making (T or F)	J —	Judging: rapid decision making, organizes data, prefers structure
	P —	Perceiving: searches for information, creative, prefers spontaneity

Four major temperament types result: SP, SJ, NT, NF. Each of these temperaments has a unique learning style, and each has four variations. A description of the sixteen types is not within the scope of this discussion. However, the charts on the previous two pages summarize student and teacher responses in an educational context for each of the four main types (Keirsey 1998, Brightman 2002, Kroeger and Thuesen 1988).

A major conclusion can be drawn from this chart. More than 50 percent of teachers are SJs or NFs. Teaching attracts people who perpetuate the educational practices in which students like themselves prosper. However, approximately 50 percent of students have temperaments unlike those of their teachers, and thus it is important for teachers to understand the needs of students unlike themselves. Teachers need to expand their instructional techniques beyond what comes naturally to include activities that meet the real needs of their students. Once teachers have crossed that bridge and are willing to try new things, they will be less frustrated with students whose temperaments differ from their own.

Neurodevelopmental Systems

Dr. Mel Levine, a pediatrician, has devoted his life to understanding learning. He has developed a comprehensive model of learning based on eight neurodevelopmental systems that are dependent on each other: attention control, memory, language, spatial ordering, sequential ordering, motor, higher order thinking,

Teacher/Student Personality Types

Type	SP Sensing/perceiving	SJ Sensing/judging	NT Intuitive/thinking	NF Intuitive/feeling
% student population	38%	38%	12%	12%
% teacher population	4%	56%	8%	32%
Length of service	Short stay	Long stay	Medium stay	Long stay
Student descriptors	Likes freedom, spontaneity; is active, fun-loving, uninhibited; performer, player, adventurer	Has sense of belonging, duty, responsibility, service	Has competency, intellectual curiosity	Has increasing sense of self in relation to others; dramatic, idealistic, empathetic
Instructional issues	Likes hands-on activity, risk-taking, performing, media presentations, interviewing, films, drawing, constant change, sound, color, action; shuns homework, avoids paper and pencil; worst fit in regular classroom; most likely to drop out of school	Has good study habits, learns well with teacher, likes workbooks, textbooks, lectures; completes homework; does not like to invent or improvise; best fit in regular classroom, likes step-by-step sequential teaching, interviewing, memorizes well	Independent learner, loves ideas, discussion with teachers and intellectual peers, long-term projects, research, collecting, reading, giving a lecture, debating; may not always do homework	Enjoys discussion, role playing, dramatic play, fiction, small-group instruction, cooperative learning, global learning, speaking, reading, writing letters and reports
Preferred curriculum content	Arts: music, drama, crafts; mechanics, construction; physical education	Sports, agriculture, social sciences, clerical work, business, accounting, teaching, nursing	Philosophy, technology, communications, math, science, building, architecture, inventing	Language arts, humanities, social science, writing, theology, speech, foreign content
Student responses to schooling	Likes practical subjects with immediate rewards; wants feedback on performance; enjoys dialoguing; rebels against class supervision, may be disruptive with noise and movement; dislikes lecture format	Desires feedback on product, wants to please teacher; thrives on stability, responds to physical punishment, likes awards, such as stickers, values report card; less open to learning new things	May be a loner, may need help, delayed social development, needs priorities (tries to do everything); self-doubting; likes lectures, responds to verbal, logical, well-reasoned dialogue, not physical punishment; expects teachers to be competent	Enjoys democratic process, thrives on recognition, caring, personal attention; sensitive to rejection; responds to physical closeness; does not respond to physical punishment; a pleaser
Teacher descriptors	Teaching practical, hands-on skills, industrial arts, vocational-technical, music, crafts, coaching, preschool, elementary; lesson plans bane of existence	Procedures important, punctuality and neatness as important as content, organized; pre-K to grade 12 teachers, school administrators, librarians, speech pathologists; teachers of business, social sciences, sports	Subject-oriented; enjoys conceptual, problem-centered discussions; loves challenges from students; teachers of science, philosophy, math, technology, communications; university professors	Ability to make all students feel important and cared about; media specialists, teachers of English, art, drama, social science, foreign language, speech
Favored instructional techniques	Projects, contests, games, demonstrations, shows	Recitation, drill, tests and quizzes, composition, demonstrations	Lectures, tests, reports, compositions, projects	Group projects, interaction, discussion, shows, simulations, games

and social thinking. There are almost eighty subcategories that make up the eight systems. It is not within the scope of this chapter to elucidate them fully, but a comprehensive study of this seminal research can be found in Levine's book *A Mind at a Time* (2002).

Understanding these neurological systems as they relate to learning is valuable for parents and educators as it enhances their understanding of cognitive functions, helping them unravel the complexity and uniqueness of each child's mind. Many students' learning patterns do not fit well with their educational setting. Identifying each child's profile for learning can impact the choice of teaching approach, allowing teachers to choose techniques that will strengthen strengths and bypass weaknesses. (Note that Levine's eight systems partially overlap Gardner's eight intelligences.) Levine's learning model offers opportunities for in-depth study of each system as it relates to the aims of education. Levine offers practical information for dealing with each system as well as a developmental continuum for each one. For example, long-term memory can be enhanced by long-term projects that last a year or more. Mentors from the community or school can serve as resources for students, who can delve into an area of special interest, thus becoming experts. Studying just before going to sleep helps to consolidate material into the long-term memory. In addition, reviewing material for ten minutes at the close of a period of instruction enhances memory. Block scheduling also works in favor of long-term memory, especially when a final review is added.

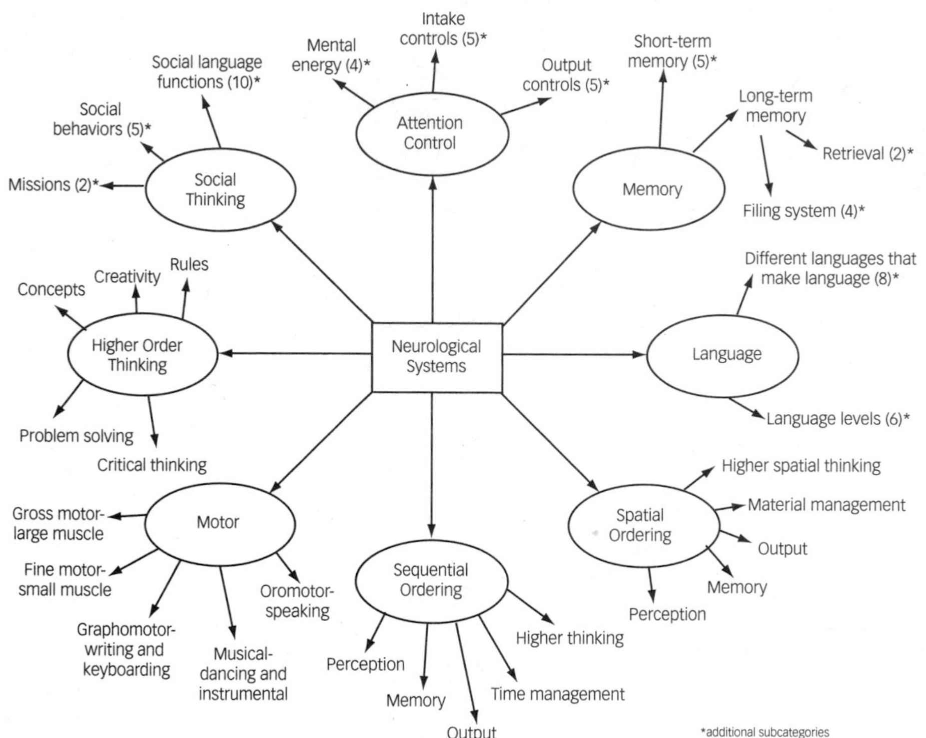

Compiled from M. Levine. 2002. *A Mind at a Time*. New York: Simon and Schuster.

Emotional Influences on Learning

Four states of mind that can frustrate the learning process are motivation, feelings and moods, self-esteem, and behavior. Students will do well in school if they are able to succeed in their learning tasks. Success breeds success. Sensitive teaching can enhance a student's motivation by making the educational goal more attractive, attainable, and effortless. Capitalizing on areas of student interest can also increase motivation.

Performance anxiety interferes with learning because stress alters the neurotransmitters of the brain that control memory and attention (Minirth 2002, 5). It is important to help students cope effectively with their stress before it leads to depression. Parents play an important role by loving their children unconditionally, helping them feel good about themselves, providing a biblical perspective on how important they are, and modeling a healthy perspective on reality. Building a strong sense of self-esteem within the context of the family is essential. Ruth Beechick's explanation of this, described at the beginning of this chapter, strengthens the discussion.

Mel Levine also suggests that an underlying system deficiency can cause misbehavior. Students with weak attention controls can get into trouble in a classroom setting. Others with expressive language problems cannot use language to monitor their own behavior with appropriate self-talk. Low social-thinking capacity may impede a child's ability to resolve conflicts and relate well with peers. Saving face to mask their weaknesses causes some children to become the class clown or troublemaker.

Robert Sylwester (cited in D'Archangelo 1998, 20–25) puts it another way: "Our profession has paid little attention to emotion. And yet, our emotional system drives our attention system, which drives learning and memory and everything else that we do." In addition, Geoffrey Caine offers insight into emotional influences on learning:

> Because ours is a social brain, it's important to build authentic relationships in the classroom and beyond. Complex learning is enhanced by challenge and inhibited by threat. We want to deeply engage learners with their purposes, values, and interests. Thinking and feeling are connected because our patterning is emotional. That means that we need to help learners create a felt meaning, a sense of relationship with a subject, in addition to an intellectual understanding. Once educators and parents grasp that complexity, they begin to function differently in their lives and in their classrooms.
>
> (cited in D'Archangelo 1998, 20–25)

Eric Jensen (also cited in D'Archangelo) suggests specific activities to engage students' emotions: productive debates, storytelling, and projects that include public demonstrations so that emotional experiences are tied to the presentation. Students whose emotions are not engaged will feel a void.

Gender Differences

James Dobson (2001, 181), in his book *Bringing Up Boys,* develops some thought-provoking insights into educating boys. He says, "Elementary classrooms, especially, are designed primarily by women to fit the temperament and learning styles of girls."

Boys typically excel in math, science, logic, reasoning, problem solving, visual and spatial skills, and gross motor skills. Full of energy, boys like adventure and are risk takers. Classroom accommodations that recognize gender differences will greatly enhance the learning and achievement of boys. With boys it is important to utilize the locale memory systems previously discussed. Boys need to move, build projects, and connect concepts with visual tools such as mapping (exemplified in Levine's chart). When boys learn to read, they are attracted to stories with a fast pace and lots of action, such as stories about sports and adventure, and nonfiction books focusing on such topics as insects, reptiles, and airplanes (Hales 2000).

God made boys and girls different. Research has shown that gender differences exist, and girls need gender-specific support as well. Their strengths help them begin the schooling process: earlier development, good verbal skills, ability to read (usually a year earlier than boys), intuition, power of concentration, and fine motor skills. On the other hand, girls tend to have weaknesses that hinder them from reaching their potential: aversion to risk, lack of confidence in math, undiagnosed learning difficulties, fear of failure, less desire for adventure, avoidance of confrontation, and less techno-literacy. Strategies to help girls succeed include thinking out of the box, providing experiences (such as LEGOs) that build spatial skills, teaching them to praise themselves, and stressing computer skills.

The strengths of boys lie in spatial skills, hands-on approaches to learning, self-reliance, goal orientation, competitiveness, individualism, and math skills. Their weaknesses can put them at risk in schools that are not gender sensitive: developmental lag, lack of verbal skills, restlessness, slower mastery of fine motor skills, pencil anxiety, tendency to rush to the bottom line, and more learning problems. Strategies to help boys succeed include understanding their developmental lag, recognizing their shorter attention span, engaging them in fun verbal activities, providing opportunities to write with a pencil, encouraging the use of computers for writing, and orchestrating hands-on and other activities that allow them to move around (Hales 2000).

Summary

The relationship of all these theories to Christian educational philosophy illustrates that there are kernels of truth that are discoverable through a study of general revelation. The Bible recognizes the importance of instructing children in the way they should go. At the same time, the goal of all Christian school teaching is for students to come into right relationship with Christ and seek to be conformed to His image.

Perhaps the best scriptural word about maintaining this balance is Ephesians 6:4, where parents (including their teacher surrogates) are commanded to bring up children "in the nurture and admonition of the Lord" (KJV). The verse suggests a balancing of two important concepts. First, *nurture* is a gardening term that implies structure, organization, and stability. Such an environment implies recognizing learning differences and teaching accordingly. Second, *admonition* refers to encouraging and building up; we are to be "teaching and admonishing one another in psalms and hymns and spiritual songs, singing with grace in your hearts to the Lord" (Colossians 3:16). Admonition balances nurture with the love and belonging that gives students a good concept of themselves, their value as persons, and their potential for serving the Lord and humankind. Teaching in this balanced atmosphere conveys a proper level of self-esteem and frees students to achieve at the level of their God-given potential.

Final Thoughts

Psalm 139:14 says that humans are "fearfully and wonderfully made." Christian educators who begin with this premise know that teaching is complex and demanding. The more we learn about children and their culture, the motivations of their hearts, and the functions of their brains as they learn, the more challenging the task of teaching them becomes.

About the Author

Barbara Bode is currently head administrator of Tampa Baptist Academy in Tampa, Florida. Her experience includes several years of teaching in public schools as well as serving at the academy as a teacher, a principal, and a curriculum specialist.

Strengthen Your Foundations

1. Evaluate your own teaching style. Make a list of changes you would like to implement in your classroom, basing your ideas on what you have learned in this chapter.

2. Develop a lesson that activates both the taxon and locale memory systems. Identify lesson components as they relate to each system.

3. Look at conventional teaching practices and evaluate whether they are brain-compatible or brain-antagonistic.

4. Evaluate yourself to identify your preferred learning style and temperament type, basing your conclusions on the limited information presented in this chapter. Develop a lesson that includes activities to enhance learning for students whose learning styles and temperament are unlike yours.

5. How does brain-based education relate to learning styles and temperament types?

6. Extend a lesson already taught to include another kind of intelligence as outlined by Gardner.

7. Experiment with similar classes that are taught the same content. Vary the way the content is taught by using different brain-based educational principles. Have the students evaluate the activities. Evaluate the content learned in each class.

8. Develop a lesson that includes activities appropriate for different learning modalities or personality types. Allow your students to choose an activity. Evaluate.

9. Develop an instructional plan for students based on their dominant and secondary modalities (visual, auditory, kinesthetic) and the three strongest of the eight (or nine) intelligences. Develop a class profile describing those modalities and intelligences. From this information develop a thematic integrated unit.

10. Develop a list of activities that would help students connect emotionally.

11. Discuss how an awareness of gender learning differences could impact your attitudes, class rules, and lesson planning.

References

All Kinds of Minds: www.allkindsofminds.org.

Barbe, Walter Burke, and Raymond H. Swassing. 1979. *Teaching through modality strengths: Concepts and practices.* Columbus, OH: Zaner-Bloser, Inc.

Beechick, Ruth. 1982. *A biblical psychology of learning: How your mind works.* Denver, CO: Accent Publications, Inc.

Brightman, H. J. 2002. Student learning and the Myers-Briggs type indicator. Retrieved August 3, 2002, from Georgia State University, Master Teacher Program: www.gsu.edu/~dschjb/wwwmbti.html.

Caine, Renate, and Geoffrey Caine. 1990. Understanding a brain-based approach to learning and teaching. *Educational Leadership* (October): 66–70.

——. 1991. *Making connections: Teaching and the human brain.* Alexandria, VA: Association for Supervision and Curriculum Development.

Center for Applications of Psychological Types. 2000. http://www.capt.org.

Chadwick, Ronald P. 1982. *Teaching and learning: An integrated approach to Christian education.* Old Tappan, NJ: Fleming H. Revell.

D'Archangelo, M. 1998. The brains behind the brains. *Educational Leadership* (November): 20–25.

Dobson, James. 2001. *Bringing up boys.* Wheaton, IL: Tyndale House.

Gardner, Howard. 1984. *Frames of mind: The theory of multiple intelligences.* New York: Basic Books.

Hales, D. 2000. Teaching boys, teaching girls. *Parents* (September): 202–8.

Hart, Leslie. 1975. *How a brain works.* New York: Basic Books.

Hyerle, David. 1996. *Visual tools for constructing knowledge.* Alexandria, VA: Association for Supervision and Curriculum Development.

_____. 2000. *A field guide to using visual tools.* Alexandria, VA: Association for Supervision and Curriculum Development.

Keirsey, David W. 1998. *Please understand me II: Temperament, character, intelligence.* Del Mar, CA: Prometheus Nemesis Book Company.

Keirsey, David W., and Marilyn Bates. 1984. *Please understand me.* Del Mar, CA: Prometheus Nemesis Book Company.

Kroeger, Otto, and Janet M. Thuesen. 1988. *Type talk: The 16 personality types that determine how we live, love, and work.* New York: Dell Publishing.

LD Online: www.ldonline.org.

LeBar, Lois. 1958. *Education that is Christian.* Old Tappan, NJ: Fleming H. Revell.

Levine, Mel. 2002. *A mind at a time.* New York: Simon & Schuster.

Minirth, Frank B. 2002. A brief digest on everything you ever wanted to know about the chemistry of emotions: Thirteen medication types that can change brain chemicals and emotions. Retrieved August 2, 2002, from www.minirthclinic.com/digests.html.

Nicholson-Nelson, Kristen. 1998. *Developing students' multiple intelligences.* New York: Scholastic Professional Books.

Palladino, Lucy Jo. 1999. *Dreamers, discoverers, and dynamos: How to help the child who is bright, bored, and having problems in school.* New York: Ballantine Books.

Peterson, Michael L. 2001. *With all your mind: A Christian philosophy of education.* Notre Dame, IN: University of Notre Dame Press.

SchwabLearning.org: www.schwablearning.org.

Spears, Dana Scott, and Ron L. Braund. 1996. *Strong-willed child or dreamer?* Nashville, TN: Thomas Nelson.

Willard, Dallas. 2002. *Renovation of the heart: Putting on the character of Christ.* Colorado Springs, CO: NavPress.

Zemelman, Steven H., Harvey Daniels, and Arthur Hyde. 1993. *Best practice: New standards for teaching and learning in America's schools.* Portsmouth, NH: Heinemann.

CHAPTER EIGHT

Teaching Methodologies

W. Philip Bassett and Eddie K. Baumann

Imagine that a carpenter shows up on the job site where you are building a new home. He opens his toolbox, and you realize he has only a hammer. As he pounds nails, you recognize that he is quite good with a hammer. However, you are worried because you know he will soon have to cut boards to length, put in screws, and level the dirt for the walkway. In teaching, a commonly used metaphor is the teacher as a builder whose toolbox contains a variety of tools, or methods of teaching. Just as the builder who has only a hammer would be considered almost useless (treating every task as a nail to be hammered), similarly ineffective is the teacher who relies almost exclusively on one method of instruction. A common perception of a good teacher is one who draws on a varied repertoire of teaching strategies in order to teach knowledge and skills in the way most appropriate for students.

In this chapter it is assumed that the teacher's goal is to develop a varied repertoire of teaching methods, and that all teachers have a lifetime professional goal of adding new methods while refining those they currently use. Although teachers do not develop teaching skills solely by reading about them, knowledge gained by reading is a starting point. The purposes of this chapter are (1) to present two organizational frameworks for teaching methodology in order to increase the reader's awareness of the wide range of teaching methods that exist, (2) to discuss professional, biblical, and philosophical considerations for choosing certain methods, and (3) to describe some methods that can yield excellent dividends in student learning.

Organizing Models of Instruction

One way of understanding teaching methods is to develop a sensible schema for organizing the various models of instruction. One of the most common in recent years is the four "families of models" developed by Bruce Joyce in the 1970s (Joyce and Weil 2000). This practical approach differentiates models and develops clearly the theoretical underpinnings of the *Models of Teaching* approach. More recently, the *Dimensions of Learning* model delineates five types of thinking in which students engage as part of the learning process (Marzano et al. 1988; Marzano and Pickering 1997). Fairly complex models of teaching are organized along with classroom management techniques, simple instructional techniques, and strategies for approaching instruction. The *Models of Teaching* and *Dimensions of Learning* approaches are explained briefly below.

Joyce's Families of Models

In the late 1960s, Bruce Joyce had already begun identifying effective models of teaching. He developed a fairly extensive collection of models based on four criteria: (1) a sound theoretical base, (2) a long history of successful use, (3) adaptability to the needs of a variety of learners and the nature of various content, and (4) evidence that the model worked based on experience and formal research. Joyce organized the models into four categories or families of models. The book *Models of Teaching,* first published in 1972, identifies four families of models: the personal, information processing, behavioral, and social families. Joyce's book, now in its eighth edition, has been used to train thousands of teachers and to inform research in teaching methodologies.

Joyce and Weil (2000) consider the school as a center of inquiry and a community of learners. This view of what schools should be considers the implications of research in brain-based learning, learning styles, and the role of culture in learning and teaching. They view instruction as learner-centered, and thus they see models of teaching as really "models of learning." Consequently, the goal of schooling should be to help students become "powerful learners"—providing a variety of strategies for how to learn.

Personal Family. The personal family is based on the notion that reality resides in the mind of each individual. Because this view denies much of the Christian belief in absolute truth, this family of models is not one to pursue aggressively. However, some of the goals of this family are compatible with biblically based goals: for example, that students need to understand themselves better, take on more responsibility for their own learning, and strive to grow and become stronger people. Carl Rogers' nondirective approach to teaching and Abraham Maslow's enhancing self-esteem are the two models Joyce and Weil have included in this family. The work of both Maslow and Rogers is based on very powerful insights into human nature, and study of these models can yield ideas for improving education.

Information-Processing Family. The information-processing family is based mainly on cognitive psychology. The models here take advantage of humanity's God-given drive to make sense of the world around us (Genesis 1:28). Many of the models are more teacher-directed than others and are designed to help students master content, organize data, develop concepts, generate creative thinking, and commit material to memory.

Concept attainment is one of the more widely disseminated information-processing models. Joyce and others adapted the model on how people think and understand concepts using research of the late Harvard psychologist Jerome Bruner (1960, 1966). Students view data sets made up of pictures, sentences, word pairs, formulas, shapes, and so forth that are designated as examples or nonexamples of a concept the teacher has in mind. By comparing the two sets—examples and nonexamples—students identify essential attributes and arrive inductively at a definition of the concept. The teacher then tests students' understanding by having them identify other examples or develop an example of their own.

Table 1: Concept Attainment Chart

Phase	Teacher Activities	Student Activities
Phase One: Presentation of the Data Set	• Presents data set of 15 to 20 exemplars of each, indicating which are and which are not examples of the concept • Provides students with a focus and guides thinking with questions if necessary • Helps students examine attributes and develop definition • Names concept	• Hypothesize which are and which are not examples of the concept. • Identify attributes of the positive examples • Develop a definition based on attributes
Phase Two: Testing Students' Attainment of the Concept	• Presents additional examplars, some of which are more difficult • Has students identify or develop examples of the concept	• Identify more teacher-generated exemplars as examples or nonexamples • Develop or identify more examples or nonexamples independently
Phase Three: Analysis of the Students' Thinking Processes	• Have each student talk with one or more partners about his or her thinking process • Discuss some student insights with the class • Avoid lecturing about "how" to think	• Describe his or her own thinking process to other student(s) • Reflect on how to improve inductive thinking

Advance organizers are one of the most widely researched of the information-processing models. Their development and use is based on work done by David Ausubel (1963, 1977) for the purpose of helping students get more out of lectures, reading, and films.

Table 2: Advance Organizer	
Phase	**Teacher Responsibilities**
Phase One: Presentation of Advance Organizer	• Clarify aims of the lesson • Present organizer: identify defining attributes, give examples or illustrations as appropriate, provide context; repeat previous steps; prompt awareness of learner's relevant knowledge and experience
Phase Two: Presentation of Learning Task or Material	• Present material to be learned • Make logical order of learning material explicit • Link material to organizer
Phase Three: Strengthening Cognitive Organization	• Use principles of integrative reconciliation to integrate new material with students' existing cognitive structure • Elicit a critical approach to subject matter • Clarify ideas • Apply ideas actively

Before lecturing or assigning reading, teachers present students with a schema for organizing the information (hence the name "advance"). The organizer should be based on how the "experts" have organized the major concepts being taught. How the mind processes information must also be taken into account. The organizer is presented, the content is taught, its organization is made explicit, and after the presentation or reading, students strengthen their own mental organizer by relating the new material to the organizer that was presented.

The mnemonic model is based on the work of several theorists and practitioners who have developed popular applications (Lorayne and Lucas 1974, Pressley, Levin, and Delaney 1982). The model goes beyond repetitious rote learning, and teaches students principles and techniques for memorizing important concepts and information. Users of this model recognize that memorizing and recalling factual information is an important academic skill with numerous real-life applications. Besides helping students to recall information they are studying, the use of the memory model teaches them how to memorize better and enjoy it more. The model is based on three general principles and six specific techniques. (See table 3.) Using the model, teachers and students work through four phases: (1) identifying and attending to key material by underlining, listing, or reflecting, (2) making connections using specific techniques (e.g., key words, substitution, or linking systems), (3) using imagery to expand or make associations or develop richer connections, and (4) practicing recall until the material is learned.

Behavioral Family. The behavioral family is based on the work of B. F. Skinner and his theory of operant conditioning. Most behaviorists view human beings as self-correcting organisms who use the consequences of their actions to modify their behavior. Central to behavioral models is the idea that human beings are passive, waiting for the environment to act on them before responding. This principle violates the biblical view of humans as active agents responsible and accountable to God. Despite this contradiction with the biblical view, behavioral psychology has been highly influential in American schooling (both public and Christian) because of its historic roots and its insistence on measurable outcomes to learning. Some of the models in this family (e.g., mastery learning, direct instruction) seem to be preferred by more conservative educators. While one may disagree with the philosophical foundations of behaviorism, the models it has inspired are highly effective for certain learning objectives.

Table 3: Mnemonic Model

Three General Principles	Six Specific Techniques
1. *Association:* You can remember anything if you can associate it with something you already know. This is the basic memory rule. 2. *Activity:* You have to be actively involved with something to remember it. The more senses or parts of the brain you involve, the better and more easily you remember. 3. *Practice:* The more you practice or review something, the better and longer you will remember it. Practice should be more frequent at first.	1. *Awareness:* Pay close attention to what you want to memorize, and highlight or make lists. You can't remember something if you aren't aware of it. 2. *Linking:* Using word associations that link facts together like a chain, each item reminding you of the next, or linking facts together in a whole, such as a picture or acronym, helps to you remember a lot of information efficiently. 3. *Association:* Develop associations with mental pictures, things already very familiar, or facts already known. 4. *Substitute words:* Use words that sound like what you are trying to remember, a specific kind of association: "D'you know the capital of Alaska? It's Juneau." (D'you know—Juneau) 5. *Key words:* Choose and memorize key words to remember material more effectively. Each item in this table begins with one or two key words. If you memorize them, you more easily remember the information that goes with them. 6. *Ridiculous:* The more unusual or ridiculous an association is, the easier it is to remember.

Mastery learning, also called programmed learning, was first developed by Skinner and later Benjamin Bloom. In this model, material is organized into units ranging from simple to complex. Students generally work individually on material presented through an appropriate medium under the guidance of the instructor. After each unit, students are tested, and they do not proceed to the next unit until they have mastered the material in the current one. This approach has been used for many subject areas and at grade levels from kindergarten to graduate school.

In the direct instruction model, students are given unambiguous objectives, and they participate in activities clearly related to the objectives. Students are carefully monitored, and they receive feedback on how well they are doing and how they can improve. One of the most exciting models in this family is simulation. In simulations students practice skills and use information in settings that approximate real-life situations to some degree. Students are given feedback and coaching as to how to improve until the skill is mastered. In some simpler applications, students may practice arithmetic skills while simulating a shopping trip, or geography skills while planning an imaginary journey. "Oregon Trail" and "Flight Instructor" are well-known computer simulations.

Social Family. Models in the social family are based on the idea that when students work together the whole is indeed greater than the sum of its parts—that a collective energy, or synergy, is created when people work together. The goal of models in this family is to develop a community of learners built on a school culture that promotes cooperative relationships among teachers and students. Though there are other models in this family, the ones most widely used fall under the rubric of what is commonly called "cooperative learning" and what Joyce calls "partners in learning."

Cooperative learning refers to a range of models and techniques for structuring classroom environments so that at times students have the opportunity to work together in groups of two to five to accomplish a common goal. Everyone should be involved and should share in responsibilities and rewards. Cooperative learning models and techniques vary widely in complexity. Some, like "Turn to Your Partner," take as little time as fifteen to thirty seconds for two students. Others, like "Expert Jigsaw," have students work in two different groups over two or more class periods.

Over the past twenty years, one widespread and often controversial change in classroom practice has been the growing use of cooperative learning. In general, cooperative learning has been criticized for two reasons. Ideologically, it violates the strongly held American ideal of individualism. Methodologically, it has been viewed as ineffective because few teachers implement cooperative learning strategies well. Space does not permit a full discussion of the issues, but two questions may suffice to make a point. First, is it biblical that those in the body of Christ (including students) learn to work together toward a common goal? Second, is it biblical that those who are intellectually or academically gifted use their gifts to help those not so gifted? If the answer to these questions is yes, then Christian teachers should learn to use cooperative learning techniques effectively.

Research of cooperative learning techniques began in 1898, and cooperative learning is one of the most thoroughly researched educational innovations in the United States. The great majority of the studies show positive outcomes, including gains in academic achievement, improved social skills, increased use of higher level thinking, improved race relations, and positive attitudes toward the teacher and the school—compelling reasons for using cooperative learning in some form. Another reason is the opportunities it offers for students to put into practice Christian character qualities related to interpersonal relations that are biblical and should be highly valued.

Most of the current theory, research, and development in cooperative learning has been done since the mid-1970s. Among these is the work of Roger and David Johnson, who, with their colleagues at the University of Minnesota, developed the "Learning Together" approach. They have also conducted, overseen, or analyzed hundreds of research projects based on their approach (Johnson and Johnson 1994). At Johns Hopkins University, Robert Slavin (1995) also conducted research and developed cooperative learning approaches and associated curriculum materials. Many of these models focus on the mastery of specific content, and some include a certain level of competition to encourage teamwork. Slavin emphasizes the need to rely on research-proven methods that teachers can learn to use with a reasonable amount of time and effort.

Table 4: A Structural Approach to Cooperative Learning

Basic Principles	Types of Structure	Samples
1. *Positive interdependence:* Students need the group to complete the task successfully; it is not easier to do it alone. A gain for one is a gain for all.	1. *Team building:* Promotes good working relationships among teammates	Team interview Lost on the moon
2. *Individual accountability:* Students must be held accountable for meeting their responsibilities or playing specific roles, and for learning the information or skills the group has worked on. They learn together and test alone.	2. *Class building:* Similar to team building structures, but the focus is on the whole class rather than the team	Inside-outside circle Fact or fiction Find someone who ...
3. *Equal participation:* Care should be taken that everyone in the group gets a chance for input and participates in the work of the group. Nobody should be "hitchhiking" while others do the work, and nobody should be "chauffeuring" the group so that everything is done his or her way.	3. *Mastery structures:* help students learn content knowledge or prepare for exams	Numbered heads together Inside-outside circle Jigsaw
4. *Simultaneous vs. sequential interaction:* Teachers should ask themselves, What percentage of the class is actively involved at any one time? When one student at a time is called on to answer a question, the answer is 4 to 5 percent. When students answer their partner's question, the answer is 50 percent.	4. *Communication builders:* promote the development of communication skills	Blind hand Jigsaw Think–Pair–Square
	5. *Thinking skills:* promote higher level thinking skills like categorizing, analyzing, and generating ideas	Build-what-I-write Think–Pair–Square
	6. *Information sharing:* helps students learn to develop, analyze, and share information effectively	Round table Rotating review Three-stay-one-stay

More recently Spencer Kagan (1994) has developed the structural approach to cooperative learning. A cooperative learning "structure" is a way of structuring the interaction in a classroom so that students work together to learn material or accomplish a task. Since the structures are flexible, teachers can use them for various content areas at a range of grade lev-els. The structural approach is built on four basic principles and organizes dozens of structures into six categories according to their function. Several of the structures fit into more than one category because they can be used to meet different goals and thus are considered multifunctional. Table 4 lists the four basic principles and the six types of structures and gives examples of each.

Table 5 briefly describes some of the structures that have been found useful and that are fairly easy to implement.

Table 5: Easily Implemented Cooperative Learning Structures
(adapted from Kagan 1994)

Structure	Directions
Think–Square–Share	Students think on their own about a topic assigned by the teacher, then share their responses with their small group. The teacher then calls on students at random to share with the entire class.
Team Statements	Each student writes a short statement about an assigned topic (could be a summary of what the teacher has been teaching). Groups of four then get together to write a team statement that includes ideas from each person's individual statement. The team statement is often much different from any of the individual statements and of high quality.
Think–Pair–Square	Students think on their own about a topic assigned by the teacher, then share their ideas with a partner from their small group of four. Pairs then share with the other pair in their small group. In a variation, students explain their partner's idea to the small group.
Turn to Your Neighbor	Each student turns to an assigned "neighbor" sitting nearby and discusses a topic assigned by the teacher, reviews a list, works a problem, gives an opinion or … you get the picture! Usually the teacher calls on a few students at random to tell the class what they discussed with their partner.
Inside–Outside Circle	Half the class members form an "outside" circle facing inward, about an arm's length apart. The other half form an "inside" circle facing a person in the outside circle who becomes their partner. This structure works with most ages and for many purposes. When it is used as a mastery structure, students each have two flash cards with number facts to review questions or information they have been studying. After doing their flash cards, students trade one card and the teacher has one of the circles rotate 2 to 4 students, and the process is repeated with a new partner. When Inside-Outside Circle is used as a class-building structure, students share the answer to an assigned question such as, "At what historical event would you like to be present, and why?"

The Dimensions of Learning

Robert Marzano and his colleagues (Marzano and Brandt 1988; Marzano and Pickering 1997) have developed the *Dimensions of Learning* (DOL) approach to teaching and learning. DOL is not a linear, five-step process of teaching, but a way of organizing what is known about the teaching and learning process. The five "dimensions" are based on an analysis and synthesis of the educational research from the 1960s to the present as to the types of thinking students are typically asked to engage in at school. The five dimensions are developing Positive Attitudes and Perceptions (dimension 1), Acquiring and Integrating Knowledge (dimension 2), Extending and Refining Knowledge (dimension 3), Using Knowledge Meaningfully (dimension 4), and Productive Habits of Mind (dimension 5). The accompanying graphic organizer shows that the heart of schooling is the acquisition, development, and use of knowledge and skills, while in the background the attitudes and perceptions of students are always affecting their acquisition of knowledge, and students are always developing mental habits. An important precept is that all learning is thinking and that the focus of education should be students and what they learn, not teachers and what they teach.

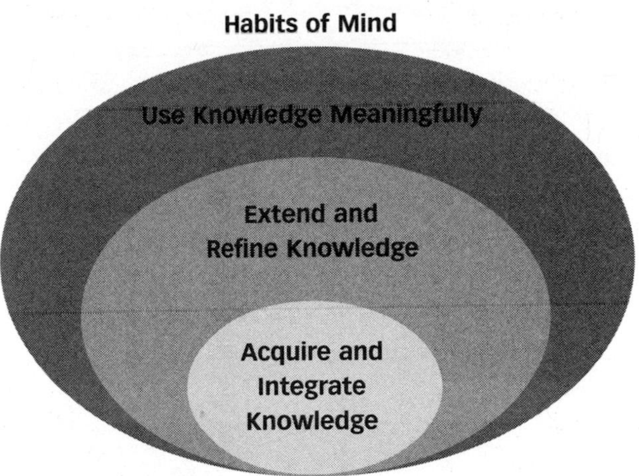

In studying the *Dimensions of Learning,* it is important to realize that while it includes viewpoints of both behavioral and cognitive psychology, the dimensions have a decidedly constructivist perspective. At the risk of oversimplifying, constructivist psychologists generally believe that meaning is "constructed" by the learner through his or her learning and experiences. Many would say the same about truth—it is a human construct individually developed and understood. Those looking at learning from a biblical perspective believe that truth is objective and that God puts meaning into the universe. While a constructivist might say a learner "builds meaning" as he learns, a biblical Christian would be more comfortable saying that the learner "*discovers meaning*" or "*builds understanding*" of truths that already exist. This basic philosophical distinction is important; however, it is also important not to dismiss the excellent work by which the *Dimensions of Learning* approach has contributed to better understanding of the teaching and learning processes.

Following are brief descriptions of the each five dimensions including some of the teaching methods that belong to each:

Positive Attitudes and Perceptions. This dimension is better understood as "helping students develop *positive* attitudes and perceptions" about learning. The honest student will readily admit that what is learned in any class usually depends on the learner's attitude toward the class and the teacher, and a perception of the importance

Table 6: Dimension 1: Positive Attitudes and Perceptions

About Classroom Climate: Students are always developing and filtering their learning through their attitudes and perceptions. Teachers can influence these attitudes and perceptions positively to help enhance the learning process.

Critical Considerations	Techniques to Use
Acceptance by the teacher Acceptance by peers Sense of emotional and physical comfort Sense of order	• Establish a personal relationship with students • Monitor your own attitudes and perceptions about students • Clearly communicate classroom rules and procedures • Stop malicious teasing • Respond positively to students' incorrect responses or lack of responses • Greet students daily

About Classroom Tasks: Student success on classroom tasks is highly influenced by their attitudes and perceptions regarding the tasks they are asked to do. Teachers can influence these attitudes and perceptions positively to help enhance student performance.

Critical Considerations	Techniques to Use
Perceived value of tasks Clarity of expectation Perceived ability to be successful Availability of necessary resources	• Connect tasks to students' interests • Connect tasks to students' goals • Identify expected behavior during the task and at its completion • Provide positive feedback • Break complex tasks into smaller steps

Adapted from R. J. Marzano and D. J. Pickering. 1997. *Dimensions of Learning Teacher's Manual,* 2d ed. Alexandria, VA: Association for Supervision and Curriculum Development.

of what is being taught and how it is taught. Attitudes and perceptions are divided into two major categories: those related to classroom climate and those related to classroom tasks. Teachers need to address the following questions when seeking to help students develop positive attitudes and perceptions: *Do students feel acceptance from their teacher and their peers? Do students feel a sense of comfort and order? Do students understand the value of the tasks they will be engaged in, and are expectations clear? Do students believe they have the ability and the resources to complete the tasks successfully?*

Some techniques for promoting a positive classroom climate are listed in the *Dimensions of Learning Teachers' Manual* (Marzano and Pickering 1997). The teacher establishes a relationship with each student in the class, monitors his or her own attitudes, establishes and communicates classroom rules and procedures, is aware of malicious teasing or threats in or out of the classroom and takes steps to stop it, and responds positively to students' incorrect responses or lack of response. Some techniques for promoting a positive perception of classroom tasks are linking classroom tasks to student interests and goals, providing positive feedback, identifying and articulating specific behaviors expected during and after completion of tasks, and breaking complex tasks into small steps or parts.

A teacher's attention to students' attitudes and perceptions can greatly influence learning in the classroom. Teachers can choose to influence attitudes and perceptions in an active and positive way, or just let them happen.

Acquiring and Integrating New Knowledge. This dimension is, perhaps, the central focus of most schooling. It involves the ability to understand new knowledge, integrate it with what is already known, and then recall it for use. An important distinction made in the DOL approach is that there are two kinds of knowledge that should be taught differently. *Declarative knowledge* is factual knowledge, or what might be called "head knowledge." One understands declarative knowledge when he or she can explain or "declare" it. *Procedural knowledge* deals with skills—knowledge that results in "doing" and often takes place in steps. For example, it is not enough to be able to talk about doing long division, or even to list the steps; one must be able to do it to say he or she has learned long division. There are three activities for teaching each of the types of knowledge and several techniques, models, or strategies for each. Teachers will usually choose one or two techniques or strategies from each type of activity to accomplish the goals for that activity. Please see table 7 for a concise listing of these activities and related methods.

There are three important insights that are not obvious from the table. The first is that teachers must determine what type of knowledge they are attempting to teach. This may not always be as straightforward as it seems. When acquiring declarative knowledge, or working on tasks that require the use of declarative knowledge, students often must use skills or procedural knowledge such as reading or writing. On the other hand, when

Table 7: Dimension 2: Acquiring and Integrating New Knowledge

Procedural Knowledge (Skills)

Activity	Sample Strategies or Techniques
Construct a Model	• Demonstrate the new skill or process, talking your way through it. • Give students a written set of steps to guide them. • Have students mentally rehearse the steps involved.
Guided Practice	• Demonstrate and provide practice in the important variations of the skill or process. • Point out common errors and pitfalls. • Provide a variety of situations in which students can use a specific skill or process.
Internalizing (Not all skills or processes should be taught to the point that students have internalized them.)	• Help students set up a practice schedule. • Have students chart their accuracy when practicing new skills or processes. • Have students chart their speed when learning a new skill or process.

Declarative Knowledge (Facts and Information)

Activity	Sample Strategies or Techniques
Constructing Meaning or Understanding	• Help students experience content using a variety of senses. • Use K-W-L charts. • Use concept attainment or other inductive thinking models. • Use reciprocal teaching techniques. • Use active learning techniques.
Organizing Information	• Have students create physical and pictographic representations of information. • Have students use graphs and charts. • Have students use organizational patterns and their graphic representations. • Provide students with advance organizer questions. • Present note-taking strategies that employ graphic representations.
Storing or Memorizing Information	• Teach students the link or peg word method. • Teach students to make mnemonic devices.

Adapted from R. J. Marzano and D. J. Pickering. 1997. *Dimensions of Learning Teacher's Manual,* 2d ed. Alexandria, VA: Association for Supervision and Curriculum Development.

learning procedural knowledge, students often must first learn some declarative knowledge on which the skill or its use is based. Though it is not always a "clean" decision, the teacher can decide what type of knowledge is being taught by looking at the core activities and the outcomes desired.

The second insight relates to the amount of time spent in each type of activity for each type of knowledge. When teaching declarative knowledge, most of the time should be spent on helping students "discover meaning" or "build understanding." The least time should be spent on helping students store or memorize the information. This is true in part because if students understand what they are learning and can see how it is organized, it will be much easier to memorize it. Is it any wonder that a classroom teacher fails when she asks students to memorize poorly organized information that they do not understand? When teaching procedural knowledge, the teacher should spend more of the allotted time on internalizing the skill and less on presenting or constructing models. Should we be surprised that students get bored when watching their teacher or classmates demonstrate a skill over and over, or get frustrated when they are given skills practice for homework before they have had a chance to "shape" the skill by working on it when they can have appropriate feedback?

Finally, one must consider how the three activities interact when teaching declarative and procedural knowledge. When teaching a skill (procedural knowledge), the teacher usually focuses on only one activity at a time—constructing a model, giving guided practice (shaping), or giving extended practice for learning the skill until the student can do the procedure almost automatically (internalizing). These three activities are fairly discrete and do not usually overlap. However, when teaching declarative knowledge, a teacher may be doing all three activities at the same time. For example, as students work on a graphic organizer for new knowledge, they may be building understanding and beginning to memorize the new information as they see how it is organized and fits in with what they already know. Many declarative knowledge methods address two or even three of the activities at a time.

Extending and Refining Knowledge. While acquiring and integrating knowledge in dimension 2 may be the primary focus of most schooling, many teachers wish to take their students to dimension 3, the extending and refining of knowledge. In dimension 3 learners begin to examine and analyze knowledge in ways that help them make new connections, discover or rediscover meanings, gain new insights, and clarify and correct misconceptions (Marzano and Pickering 1997).

In the DOL model this dimension comprises eight complex reasoning processes, and these are often considered fundamental to developing critical thinking skills. The eight processes are outlined in table 8. While the authors of the *Dimensions of Learning* model say that all these processes are used unconsciously by people every day, students can be taught to use them more deliberately and rigorously, and to consider the knowledge and concepts of the disciplines we are teaching in school.

Table 8: Dimension 3: Extending and Refining Knowledge

Reasoning Process	Description
Comparing	Identifying and articulating similarities and differences in items
Classifying	Grouping things into definable categories on the basis of their attributes
Abstracting	Identifying and articulating the underlying theme or general pattern of information
Inductive reasoning	Inferring unknown generalizations or principles from information or observations
Deductive reasoning	Using generalizations and principles to infer unstated conclusions about specific information or situations
Constructing support	Building systems of support or assertions
Analyzing errors	Identifying and articulating errors in thinking
Analyzing perspectives	Identifying multiple perspectives on an issue and examining the reasons or logic behind each

Adapted from R. J. Marzano and D. J. Pickering. 1997. *Dimensions of Learning Teacher's Manual,* 2d ed. Alexandria, VA: Association for Supervision and Curriculum Development.

Using Knowledge Meaningfully. The focus of dimension 4 is applying knowledge to solve problems or develop ways of gathering additional information. While knowledge need not always have practical utility to be worth learning, most teachers want their students be able to apply their classroom learning to their lives away from school. The processes identified in dimension 4 are complex, build on the skills learned in dimension 3, and require students to complete meaningful, long-term tasks. Six processes are identified with dimension 4, and they are outlined in table 9 on the following page.

Productive Habits of Mind. "Habits of Mind" refers to the approach to learning that students develop in school and will carry into their adult lives. While schooling inevitably teaches some habits (and not always the most productive ones), the DOL model encourages teachers to engage students explicitly in developing productive habits of mind. The habits identified in the DOL model fall into three categories—creative thinking, critical thinking, and self-regulation. Table 10 lists several thinking skills.

While doing an excellent job of addressing thinking skills and even some character qualities, dimension 5 does not address qualities of a spiritual nature. For example, shouldn't students be developing the

Table 9: Dimension 4: Using Knowledge Meaningfully

Reasoning Process	Description
Decision making	Generating and applying criteria to select from among seemingly equal alternatives
Problem solving	Overcoming constraints or limiting conditions that are in the way of pursuing goals
Invention	Developing unique products or processes that fulfill perceived needs
Experimental inquiry	Generating and testing explanations of an observed phenomenon
Investigation	Identifying and resolving issues about which there are confusions or contradictions
Systems analysis	Analyzing the parts of a system and how they interact

Adapted from R. J. Marzano and D. J. Pickering. 1997. *Dimensions of Learning Teacher's Manual,* 2d ed. Alexandria, VA: Association for Supervision and Curriculum Development.

Table 10: Dimension 5: Productive Habits of Mind

Critical Thinking helps us make our actions more reasonable and logical while remaining sensitive to the opinions and feelings of others. One way to help students develop these specific habits is to have them engage in debate with a focus on developing them.

Being clear and seeking clarity

Being open-minded

Taking a position when the information warrants it

Being sensitive to others' feelings and level of knowledge

Creative Thinking helps us think more flexibly and without constraints, leading to improved creativity and problem solving. One way to help students become better creative thinkers is to have them engage in problem solving to highlight and develop these thinking skills.

Engaging intensely in tasks even when answers or solutions are not immediately apparent

Pushing the limits of one's knowledge and abilities

Generating, trusting, and maintaining one's own standards of evaluating

Generating new ways of viewing a situation outside the boundaries of standard conventions

Self-Regulated Thinking involves more conscious self-control of our actions. One way to help students develop these habits is to have them identify and pursue long-term goals relative to specific habits.

Being aware of one's own thinking

Planning

Being aware of necessary resources

Being sensitive to feedback

Evaluating the effectiveness of one's actions

Adapted from R. J. Marzano and D. J. Pickering. 1997. *Dimensions of Learning Teacher's Manual,* 2d ed. Alexandria, VA: Association for Supervision and Curriculum Development.

habit of kindness as part of their education? Character-quality development should be one of the foremost goals for education. The Christian teacher might rename this dimension "Habits of Mind and Heart."

Table 11 presents a simple but effective five-step model for teaching habits of mind and heart. It is suggested that a teacher introduce no more than two habits at a time and that students focus on a habit for one to two weeks before another is introduced.

Table 11: Five-Step Model

1. Introduce the habit in a high-interest way by telling a story, doing a role play, reading a children's book, watching a video, or hearing a special speaker.
2. Have students identify and briefly discuss the importance of the habit. Then brainstorm with students and list specific situations in which they might find the habit useful in their current lives. Encourage specific situations.
3. Help students identify strategies for developing, using, or remembering to use the habit over the next few days. Often Bible verses and prayer can be incorporated in this step.
4. Help students develop specific long-term goals for using the habit over the next few days or weeks. These can be "private" or "public" goals.
5. Give students the opportunity to evaluate themselves, be evaluated by a small group of peers, or receive your feedback on their progress toward their long-term goals.

—Adapted from Marzano et al. 1988; Marzano and Pickering 1997.

This simple method for teaching habits of mind and heart can pay long-lasting dividends for students. Many schools, especially Christian schools, state that developing good character qualities and forming good thinking practices are among their goals for their students. Fewer schools actually have a system for teaching and evaluating students in this dimension of learning.

It should be noted that, as one considers teaching methods for each dimension, the emphasis shifts from teacher-centered to learner-centered instruction. This is especially noticeable as one moves from dimension 2 to dimensions 3 and 4. Teachers who desire to align their curriculum goals with the goals for these dimensions will need to be cognizant of that need as they choose their instructional strategies. In the next section we will look at some considerations for selecting teaching methods.

Selecting Teaching Methods

Let's return to the story of the builder. Suppose you fire the carpenter whose only tool is a hammer and hire a builder who has a full toolbox. You watch as he begins work and find out that he is pretty good with all of his tools. However, after about a week you realize you've never seen him consult a blueprint or any other kind of plan. When asked, he simply replies that he does what seems right to him at the time and trusts it will all work out in the end. Justifiably, you might be a bit nervous about what the finished product will look like, and whether it will function in any recognizable way.

Teachers must also have a plan for what they seek to accomplish, and they need to choose the methods of instruction that are best for reaching their goals. Deciding on our goals allows us to choose methods of instruction that will best accomplish them. Without such a plan most teachers find themselves in a pattern that can be described as "teach, test, and hope for the best."

In this regard, the best teaching is developed via "backward design" (Wiggins and McTighe 1998). Most teachers try to develop instructional techniques, simulations, thematic units, and other activities that will be fun and will raise student interest. However, they should always choose their methods in the context of an overall plan that the teacher and school have for the student.

Teachers also need to consider whether they are choosing methods that are teacher-centered or student-centered. We have already discussed how teaching methods can be organized by "families" (Joyce and Weil 2000) or by their function related to the *Dimensions of Learning* (Marzano and Pickering 1997). The classifications of teacher-centered and student-centered instruction are discussed below.

Teacher-Centered Instruction

Teacher-centered approaches to instruction are those "in which the teacher's role is to present the knowledge to be learned and to direct, in a rather explicit manner, the learning processes of the students" (Shuell 1996, 731). As cognitive views of learning have become more prominent in educational literature, teacher-centered instructional methods have been criticized as being too behavioristic (Stoddart et al. 1993). However, effective teacher-centered instruction can enhance cognitive processing and the development of both declarative and procedural knowledge. Teacher-centered instruction models and techniques are included in both Joyce's *Models of Teaching* and Marzano and Pickering's *Dimensions of Learning*.

Teacher-centered methods can be effective for reaching a number of objectives in the curriculum. They

Table 12: Direct Instruction Model

Direct Instruction Step	Information Processing Element
Introduction and Review	• Attract and focus learner attention • Activate background knowledge
Presentation	• Input information into working memory
Guided Practice	• Begin encoding into long-term memory
Independent Practice	• Complete encoding • Develop automaticity

From P. Eggen and D. Kauchak. 2001. *Educational psychology: Windows on classrooms.* 5th ed. Upper Saddle River, NJ: Prentice-Hall.

are effective for developing basic skills in students that can later be used in more student-centered activities such as problem solving. Teacher-centered techniques such as lecture or expository instruction can provide students the background knowledge necessary to participate in learner-centered activities such as discussions. Effective teacher-centered instruction transmits information to students in ways that are meaningful and that encourage effective retention. Often such methods are the most efficient for delivering curriculum content in the limited time available.

Table 13: Active Response Activities

Thumbs Up or Down Have all the students indicate their response to a question with a thumbs up or a thumbs down or another hand signal.

Choral Response (1) The teacher repeats the material to be memorized. (2) The teacher and class recite together. (3) Partners or small groups look at each other and recite to each other at the same time.

Turn to Your Neighbor Each student turns to an assigned "neighbor" and discusses a topic assigned by the teacher, reviews a list, works a problem, gives an opinion, or ... you get the picture! All students are responsible to have an answer ready if called on by the teacher.

However, teacher-centered methods have downsides that need to be considered. If an instructional goal is to develop students' ability to think critically, solve problems, demonstrate discernment, or integrate biblical principles with new situations, the teacher will need to move beyond teacher-centered activities to those that are more learner-centered. Also, Eggen and Kauchak (2001) point out that teacher-centered methods are often cited as creating passivity in students because they are so firmly based in behaviorist theory that they rely almost exclusively on lecture and explanation, thus minimizing student thinking. The authors also point out that these problems may have more to do with poor implementation of teacher-centered methods, not strictly the methods themselves. Teachers can avoid many of these potential pitfalls by engaging students in the some of the active response activities suggested in this chapter (see table 13).

Learner-Centered Instruction

Learner-centered instruction includes those methods in which learners, under the teacher's guidance, are made responsible for constructing or discovering their own understanding, knowledge, and insights. Such instruction is most appropriate when the goals of instruction include such things as developing inquiry or problem-solving skills and a deeper understanding of the topic, identifying relationships between new and previously learned content, and developing skills associated with critical thinking, such as comparison, abstraction, inductive or deductive reasoning, constructing support, analyzing errors.

The advantages of learner-centered instruction are noted in the instructional goals that these techniques are designed to promote. Most Christian educators want their students to learn to think critically, become more self-directed and self-regulated in their learning, relate new information to what they already know, solve problems well, and relate biblical truths to daily living as well as to their school subjects.

Despite these important benefits, learner-centered instruction has several potential difficulties that may discourage teachers from its use. First, the methods it involves tend to require the teacher to have greater flexibility and to manage a wider range of instructional resources. Also, learner-centered techniques can easily become the goal of instruction rather than a tool to meet the intended goal. For example, if the teacher decides to use cooperative learning as a tool, cooperative learning groups may become the curriculum instead of serving a broader curriculum goal, such as learning to analyze the ideas of others. Also, learner-centered teaching, to be effectively connected to curriculum goals, may result in learning that genuinely reflects what we want students to be able to do but proves difficult to assess. (See chapter 12, "Christian School Assessment: Philosophy and Practice.")

Perhaps the single biggest reason some teachers shy away from learner-centered methods is time. Simply put, most of these techniques take more time to develop and implement than do teacher-centered methods. The process of learner-centered instruction takes time, the cognitive processes can be time-consuming, and in general the higher the level of cognitive functioning we desire from students, the more time we must allocate to allow them to do it. The evolution of curriculum in the United States has not been friendly to such cognitive functioning. In general, curriculum can be designed either to cover fewer topics in greater depth or to cover many topics briefly. Most often curriculum design (including that of Christian designers) has taken the latter approach. However, the research on the development of thinking strongly suggests that an emphasis on the former develops greater retention and the ability to use content more effectively (Sizer 1984, 1992; Sternberg and Spear-Swerling 1996). Thus teachers and schools that hope to develop their students' critical thinking skills must often break from close alignment with generic curriculum packages.

About the Authors

W. Philip Bassett joined the education faculty at Cedarville University in 1991 and became chair of the department in 1998. Dr. Bassett is also an adjunct professor at Philadelphia Biblical University and Columbia International University. He has worked with national and international Christian school teachers in several countries.

Eddie K. Baumann, who holds a Ph.D. from the University of Wisconsin, is an associate professor of education at Cedarville University in Cedarville, Ohio. Dr. Baumann teaches courses in philosophy of education, educational psychology, and methods of teaching thinking. He also serves on the graduate faculty of Columbia International University in Columbia, South Carolina.

Conclusion

Like good carpenters, expert teachers possess a number of tools, are competent in their use, and select those that are best designed for the particular tasks that need to be accomplished. While all teachers have preferences in the techniques (tools) they use and how they use them, expert teachers (like expert carpenters) know that in certain situations there is a "right tool for the job." This knowledge comes from learning about available techniques and becoming comfortable in their use through practice. Through acquiring such knowledge and applying it in our classrooms, we can better fulfill our calling to educate the students that God has entrusted to us.

Strengthen Your Foundations

1. Try to develop a simple advance graphic organizer to introduce a unit of instruction (cf. Joyce and Weil, chapter 13; Marzano and Pickering, Dimension 2) and use it to introduce, present, and review the content of the unit with your students. For upper elementary through high school students, a blank organizer can be used to serve as a means of helping them take notes and review for the unit test.

2. Read the *Dimensions of Learning Teacher's Manual,* 2d edition (available from the ASCD website. www.ascd.org). Then do the following:
   - Pick one skill or procedure from each dimension and implement it in your classroom.
   - Develop or revise an existing unit of instruction (typically two to three weeks long) that addresses each of the five dimensions. Models for developing a unit are provided in the chapter, along with a sample unit entitled "Putting It All Together."
   - Choose one or two dimension 3 skills (Extend and Refine Knowledge) and make the development of those skills the focus of instruction for a semester or school year. Dimension 3 skills are normally associated with higher level thinking.

3. Study the cooperative learning techniques or structures that focus on students' working in pairs (Kagan, especially chapters 8–13, or see table 5 of this chapter), and implement a few of these in your classroom. Keep a log or journal of the results (both positive and negative) and some things you would do differently in subsequent uses of the technique. Be sure to review your journal before each use of the technique.

4. Browse Joyce and Weil, and consider each of the families of models. Develop two or three lessons from each family using the models, and implement these lessons in your classroom. Be sure to try a model at least three times so that you start to become comfortable in its use.

References

Ausabel, David. 1963. *The psychology of meaningful verbal learning.* New York: Grune & Stratton.

——. 1977. The facilitation of meaningful learning in the classroom. *Educational Psychologist* 12, 162–78.

Bigge, Morris L., and S. Samuel Shermis. 1998. *Learning theories for teachers.* 6th ed. New York: Addison Wesley Longman.

Bruner, Jerome. 1960. *The process of education.* Cambridge, MA: Harvard University Press.

——. 1966. *Toward a theory of instruction.* New York: W.W. Norton.

Clark, Gordon H. 1981. *A Christian view of men and things.* Grand Rapids, MI: Baker Book House.

Eggan, Paul, and Don Kauchak. *Educational psychology: Windows on classrooms.* 5th ed. Upper Saddle River, NJ: Prentice-Hall.

Fenstermacher, Gary D., and Jonas F. Soltis. *Approaches to teaching.* New York: Columbia University, Teachers College Press.

Johnson, David, and Roger Johnson. 1994. *Learning together and alone: Cooperation, competition, and individualization.* 4th ed. Needham Heights, MA: Allyn & Bacon.

Joyce, Bruce, and Marsha Weil. 2000. *Models of teaching.* 6th ed. Needham Heights, MA: Allyn & Bacon.

Kagan, Spencer. 1994. *Cooperative learning.* San Juan Capistrano, CA: Resources for Teachers.

Lorayne, Harry, and Jerry Lucas. 1974. *The memory book.* Ballantine Books, reissued 1996.

Marzano, Robert J., Ronald S. Brandt, Carolyn Sue Hughes, Beau Fly Jones, Barbara Z. Presseisen, Stuart C. Rankin, and Charles Suhor. 1988. *Dimensions of thinking: A framework for curriculum and instruction.* Alexandria, VA: Association for Supervision and Curriculum Development.

Marzano, Robert J., and Debra J. Pickering. 1997. *Dimensions of learning trainer's manual.* 2d ed. Alexandria, VA: Association for Supervision and Curriculum Development.

Pressley, M., Levin, J. R., and Delaney, H. D. 1982. The mnemonic keyword method. *Review of Educational Research* 52, no. 1, 61–91.

Shuell, Thomas J. 1996. Teaching and learning in classroom context. From D. Berliner & R. Calfee, eds. *Handbook of educational psychology.* New York: Simon & Schuster, 726–64.

Sizer, Theodore R. 1984. *Horace's compromise: The dilemma of the American high school.* Boston, MA.: Houghton-Mifflin.

——. 1992. *Horace's school: Redesigning the American high school.* Boston, MA: Houghton-Mifflin.

Slavin, Robert E. 1995. *Cooperative learning: Theory, research, and practice.* 2nd ed. Needham Heights, MA: Allyn & Bacon.

Sternberg, Robert J., and Spear-Swerling, Louise C. 1996. *Teaching for thinking: Psychology in the classroom.* Washington, DC: American Psychological Association.

Stoddart, T., M. Connell, R. Stofflett, and D. Peck. 1993. Reconstructing elementary teacher candidates' understanding of mathematics and science content. *Teaching and Teacher Education* 9, 229–41.

Wiggins, Grant, and Jay McTighe. 1998. *Understanding by design.* Alexandria, VA.: Association for Supervision and Curriculum Development.

CHAPTER NINE

The Teacher

Ellen Lowrie Black

Teaching in a Christian school is a calling and a ministry that results from knowing God well and following His direction. Being an educator is a vocation; being a Christian educator is a spiritual ministry that has passion and purpose.

Christian education is based on a worldview consistent with the Word of God, which is absolute truth. It is the centrality of the Bible in education that distinguishes everything that happens in the Christian school. This centrality is non-negotiable. It is not up for discussion or a popular vote. Roy W. Lowrie Jr., a founding president of ACSI, said:

> A Christian school teacher must believe, with no mental reservation, that the Bible is the Word of God. It is essential to hold to the inerrancy, the infallibility, and the authority of the Bible. Any lesser view cannot be tolerated in the school.
>
> The Bible is the key to the Christian philosophy of life and education. If it is not accepted as God's Word, the teacher has lost the key and has nothing truthful to offer the students. To be strong, the school must not hire or must dismiss any teacher not holding this view of the Bible. (1978, 13)

The teacher's primary responsibility in the Christian school is twofold, to be both the spiritual leader and the academic leader. Teachers who do not embrace a biblical worldview are incapable of teaching the whole child, for God created humankind with a mind, body, and soul.

Children are made in the image of God. They are not the result of an evolutionary process that denies the existence and power of God. The Christian teacher demonstrates love and respect for the person that the learner is in God's eyes rather than in human eyes.

The exciting—and, yes, critical—responsibility of a Christian teacher requires a clear understanding of who we are, why we are here, and where we are going. A teacher who knows God well has the opportunity to teach as a proxy for Jesus Christ. The requirement to teach according to biblical guidelines is clearly presented in the book of Deuteronomy:

> Only take heed to yourself, and diligently keep yourself, lest you forget the things your eyes have seen, and lest they depart from your heart all the days of your life. And teach them to your children and your grandchildren. (4:9)
>
> You shall teach them to your children, speaking of them when you sit in your house, when you walk by the way, when you lie down, and when you rise up. (11:19)

Christian school teachers, in partnership with the home and church, play an integral role in obeying the command to teach all day long the truths found in the Scriptures. Academic and spiritual truths go hand in hand.

The Teacher as Spiritual Leader

Teachers are spiritual leaders who daily impact the development and growth of their students. All students are in the process of becoming … something. The spiritual influence of a teacher helps determine what that "something" will be. Tony Campolo puts it this way: "We are unfinished creations. God is still at work trying to bring us into the fullness of our potentialities. A primary instrument for enabling us to become all that God wants us to be is education. We must develop our gifts and expand our understanding of how we can serve our Lord" (2000, 126).

Christian school teachers recognize the spiritual dimension of their work. That work is actually a ministry with eternal implications. God has created and wired each student in a unique manner. Teachers who truly embrace this fact work diligently to provide experiences and opportunities for growth. This growth comes as students integrate the talents and interests God has given them into the very essence of their personhood.

Christian teachers recognize the work of the Holy Spirit in the lives of their students. As Roy Lowrie writes,

> This morning I taught my Bible class for the last time.... It was nostalgic for me, for I've enjoyed my hours with them in the Word. It has been good for me—and I hope for them.
>
> We accomplished a lot this semester, but I'm conscious that there is so much more to do. Yet I think that is always the way it is when it comes to teaching Bible. By the very nature of the Book, you never feel that you are done. I look forward to having them again next year....

> I wasn't just teaching the class for the term. My objective was to affect them for the duration of their lives. The Spirit has to do that, I realize, but I approach each class with that desire, that God would be the teacher. (1980, 33)

Christian teachers whose students are born again have the blessing and privilege of teaching their own younger brothers and sisters in the Lord. The work of the Holy Spirit influences both the teacher and the students.

As a spiritual leader, the Christian school teacher accepts the authority of God's Word, and God's Word is relevant for all aspects of school life. It alone is absolute truth and is the standard against which all things are measured. It is impossible to be a Christian educator without an unwavering commitment to the authority of Scripture. Through the Bible, God's truths are made clear. These truths are the lens through which education is viewed. They provide the core assumptions, as Ron Chadwick notes:

> The first basic assumption, therefore, for the Christian educator is that the Bible, verbally inspired and inerrant in its entirety, is the final authority in all areas of Christian education. [We recognize] that the Word of God is "alive and powerful and sharper than any two-edged sword." [What the Bible says] is not what God would say if He *were* here but what God is saying because He *is* here.
>
> The second major assumption for the Christian educator is that all truth is God's truth. Although there usually exists a dualistic concept of sacred and secular truth, it is assumed here that all truth is from the hand of God and is intended for man's use. God is the source, the *Quelle* of all truth that ever was, or is, or yet will be. (1990, 10)

The Teacher as Biblical Role Model

Teachers are role models every moment of every day. Students watch very carefully and process what they see and hear—right, wrong, or indifferent. Being a role model is a serious thing. The apostle Paul, in writing to Timothy very near the time of his own execution, develops the idea of teachers as role models. He admonishes Timothy to continue in the things he has been taught because he knew his teachers (2 Timothy 3:14). Timothy was taught by Paul as well as his own mother and grandmother, and he was exhorted to follow the example of his spiritual mentors.

Being a biblical role model is a calling of the Christian teacher. It is not an option or an afterthought. Fundamental to everything a teacher does is the biblical challenge to be a role model. Students

Students on teachers: Elementary school

In third grade Mrs. Short always singled me out but in a good way. She thought I was adorable. I guess I was a teacher's pet but not because I tried to be. She sat me up in front and really made me feel special.

—Chad

One of my favorite elementary teachers was Mrs. Shoemaker. She was really sweet and cared about us. I went to see her last year and she still cared about what was going on in my life.

—Robin

My favorite elementary teacher was Mrs. Wenger in fifth grade because she treated us with respect but maintained good discipline. We had fun but knew when we had crossed the line.

—Kerry

My favorite elementary teacher was Ms. Freeman because she allowed us to earn extra credit points. She had a treasure box with toys and things that were worth different point values. The extra credit points that we earned could be used toward those toys and things.

—Jennifer

should be exhorted to follow the path established by their teachers. Paul says, "In all things showing yourself to be a pattern of good works; in doctrine showing integrity, reverence, incorruptibility" (Titus 2:7).

Because we are spiritual role models, our students will be very much aware of our spiritual condition and our enthusiasm toward the things of God. David Elkind says, "Teachers are important role models for children. When teachers are no longer excited about what they are teaching and have lost their commitment to young people, their effectiveness as role models is lost or diminished" (1984, 153).

The Teacher as Reflection of Christ

In the Gospels, the model of Christ as a teacher provides insight and direction for the Christian school teacher and has direct application in the classroom. Of primary interest is the fact that Jesus understood His audience, and He adapted His teaching strategies to the understanding and needs of those He sought to teach.

Jesus met the physical needs of His learners as demonstrated in the feeding of the five thousand. He knew that physical comfort and health directly impacted their ability to listen to Him and wrestle with His words. Any experienced teacher will tell you how difficult it is to teach challenging content just before lunch hour. A teacher who recognizes and attends to the students' physical needs follows Jesus' lead.

It is interesting to observe how Christ interacted with differing groups of learners. He was patient and kind with people who came to Him with broken lives. He encouraged them to take responsibility for their actions. He did not condone sin but rather provided a chance to live a new way. He never embarrassed or shamed people into the kingdom of God.

Jesus spoke very differently to those in positions of authority who should have known better. He did not let the Pharisees and Sadducees off the hook but rather confronted them more rigorously as time passed. Teachers have the right to expect more from students who are more mature, or who have greater gifts. Jesus was tough on those who wanted to use their power to oppress and control others. A Christian teacher who is "fair" does not treat all students in exactly the same manner. Fairness requires discernment, and discernment demands the use of varying strategies.

Christ went out of His way to protect the hurting and disadvantaged. His example compels those who teach to intercede on behalf of those who are not as strong as others, including those who are picked on physically or emotionally. A Christian teacher cannot tolerate behavior that belittles and hurts others. Schools and classrooms should be places of love, acceptance, and nurturing.

Christian school teachers need to be growing continually in their understanding of students and the issues that impact their lives. Such growth requires prayer and insight. Teachers who are good shepherds know their "sheep."

The Teacher as Mentor

The Christian teacher has the unique opportunity to mentor and disciple students, and thus enable them to grow in ways much deeper than would be possible in a typical classroom. One part of Jesus' mission on earth was to mentor the apostles and prepare them for their ministry following His return to heaven. To accomplish this purpose, Jesus spent His days living among His brethren. He did not have them sit down for "class time" but taught them all day long. One can imagine how exhausting that must have been. Yet the apostles could never have turned the world upside down had the goals of their instruction been simply academic or cognitive growth and not the development of a practical faith.

Mentoring is a shepherding process. In *Shepherding a Child's Heart,* Ted Tripp says the following:

> This shepherding process is a richer interaction than telling your child what to do and think. It involves investing your life in your child in open and honest communication that unfolds the meaning and purpose of life. It is not simply direction, but direction in which there is self-disclosure and sharing. Values and spiritual vitality are not simply taught, but caught. (1995, 15)

Because Christian teachers have a calling and a mission, it is imperative that they model Christ as they interact with their students. If we educate people intellectually but fail to touch their souls, we have not achieved our mission as Christian teachers.

Mentoring takes time, and it depends on relationships. One engaging trait of the generation now in our schools is that they are relational. For students today, relationships are central. They are not impressed with the degrees and titles their teachers hold. They are, however, impressed when teachers spend time with them, attend their games

Students on teachers: High school

My favorite teacher was Mr. Hill. Everyone knew teaching was more than just his job. We were a part of his life, and he cared what we became and how we served Christ. He sacrificed so much to teach at our small Christian school, and he invested time into our individual lives.

—Curry

In high school Mr. Scorsone was our P.E. teacher. He was awesome at creating TEAM UNITY. Our classes were serious at times, and fun and entertaining at other times. He was a friend, not just a teacher.

—Chad

One of my favorite high school teachers was Mr. Rushing. He was a people person and related with people, but he did not take any whining from them.

—Robin

Mrs. King was an encourager and an example of a dedicated Christian woman.

—Joelle

and concerts, eat with them, and show a genuine interest in what is important to them. Relationships count.

Teachers today earn the right to be heard by spending time and investing in the lives of students. Only then are students open to the life-changing input that they long for but sometimes resist. It's true that mentoring is exhausting, and it is also true that students will sometimes disappoint us. Because mentoring is exhausting, Jesus modeled for us the need to get away and spend time with the Father. Teachers who want to stay the course and touch lives over two generations do well to heed Christ's example and build time with the heavenly Father into their schedules.

While we teach a salvation based on faith in Jesus Christ, it is easy to get caught up in a life of works. Teachers need to learn to say no. They need to allocate time for physical and spiritual renewal. This is the only way to continue to be energized to teach the exciting, challenging, and exhausting children and young people that God brings us each day. Mentoring will wear you out … you wouldn't want it any other way!

The Teacher as Academic Leader

The second major area of leadership for teachers is academic. Academic commitment is not made at a spiritual cost. Rather, the spiritual ministry of Christian teachers demands that they be strong in their academic commitment.

Tension between the spiritual and physical has led to a disconnect between the spiritual and the academic, a split that unfortunately has undermined the development of a Christian mind. Hundreds of years ago, Galileo acknowledged the connection between the two. He declared, "Holy Scripture and Nature are both emanations from the divine word: the former dictated by the Holy Spirit, the latter the observant executrix of God's commands" (Sobel 2000, 64).

Learning and cognitive growth are to be pursued vigorously, but with a difference: In the Christian school, the purpose for academic pursuits is not personal gain; rather, the focus is to advance the kingdom of God. Knowledge is valuable when men and women, boys and girls, use it to follow God's will. Excellence in Christian education implies that all students are challenged to develop their gifts from God.

Harry Blamires expresses his concern regarding the demise of mental development consistent with God's Word:

The Christian mind surveys the human scene under the illumination of the fact that God became man, taking upon himself our nature, and thereby exalting that nature for all time and for eternity. Thus the Christian's conception of the human person is a high one, his sense of the sacredness of human personality being deeply grounded in revealed theological truth. (1963, 156)

How teachers view their role as educators greatly influences their curriculum choices. Harro Van Brumelen (1994) lists three key points that Christian school teachers must remember as they do their academic planning:

1. They must boldly initiate their students into their cultural and Christian heritage.
2. They must encourage students to grow in normal rational autonomy (i.e., in being able to think critically and discerningly, recognizing that such thinking must always take place within the bounds of faith commitments).
3. They need to teach *with* commitment if they are to teach *for* commitment. (p. 260)

Commitment to Learning

Teachers who enjoy their ministry and have an enthusiasm for the learning process tend to have enthusiastic students. Attitudes are contagious and are directly linked to motivation, and teachers benefit from monitoring their own attitudes carefully. A commitment to learning can be sensed when teachers exhibit wholesome positive attitudes. Robert Marzano writes:

Good teachers have always tried to foster positive attitudes and perceptions about learning. In a well-run classroom, many of the ways they do so seem to be simply a part of the natural flow of activity. But seemingly transparent behaviors are usually the result of conscious decisions, of teacher planning. Because attitudes and perceptions do play such an important role in learning, teachers must overtly plan and carry out behaviors to ensure that they are reinforced. (1992, 27)

A commitment to learning implies that Christian school teachers will continue to grow professionally. The notion that Christian schools are not about the education of the mind is false. Mediocre education that is Christian is still mediocre education. Failure to grow personally as a Christian educator diminishes one's ministry. Failure to challenge students cognitively marginalizes the fact that God created humankind with a cognitive ability that is unique and powerful. To be satisfied with minimal preparedness devalues students and teachers alike.

Students on teachers: High school

My favorite high school teacher was Mrs. Aberie. She taught advanced composition and literature. She was a teacher who cared, and she taught with passion. I loved her class because it challenged me. She used examples from other subjects, from personal experience, and from topics relevant to my own life to stretch my critical thinking and writing abilities. I learned to appreciate learning.

—Kerry

My favorite high school teachers were Mr. Barry and Mr. Searl. Mr. Barry taught my calculus class of six. He just clicked with us, and we had fun together. He let down his guard a little and joked around with us. Mr. Searl didn't make us sit in chairs. We could sit on our desks or in the windows.

—Jennifer

The Christian teacher is preparing the learner for a future that will bring many questions that cannot be answered. We cannot predict the future. We can, however, ascertain that our students need to develop certain skills in order to be ready for what God has planned for their lives. These include:

- biblical knowledge
- a life consistent with that knowledge
- strong reading skills
- effective oral communication
- mathematical competence
- technical skills
- higher order thinking and reasoning skills
- discernment
- social skills

Christian school teachers should be lifelong learners, committed to personal growth. While resources may be limited, all teachers have access to conventions, books, personal mentors, faculty in-service training, professional journals, and the Internet with its vast resources. In addition, many teachers can and should pursue graduate school.

A specific area that needs much attention today is technology. Many primary-age children have more advanced computer skills than their teachers. Administrators and teachers alike need to enhance their own technology skills and then integrate them into the curriculum.

Cognitive Development

Cognitive development happens when the learner participates in higher level thinking processes. While there is a place in education for some rote memorizing of facts, the ability to apply facts and to think critically and creatively is essential. Academic leadership implies that teachers plan and teach for cognitive growth.

In the Christian school it is sometimes the case that students are rewarded for conformity but are not challenged to think for themselves and solve problems independently. Effective Christian school teachers are those who carefully nurture and challenge students to develop their critical thinking skills. As previously stated, it is impossible to know or predict all that a student will need to know, so teachers do well to focus on developing higher level thinking skills. Jacobsen, Eggen, and Kauchak have said:

> Teachers can promote critical thinking in their classrooms by involving students in cognitive activities such as identifying main ideas,

> fostering and monitoring comprehension, constructing and representing meanings, analyzing text structures and constructing spatial networks. (1999, 138)

Teachers committed to cognitive development are also committed to ongoing assessment, which provides information that directs future lesson structures and learning activities. Educators spend much time assessing and evaluating the learners' progress. Though there is often a resistance to evaluation of instruction, such evaluation is essential if teachers are to continue their own cognitive growth.

The trust and respect that historically was given to teachers is no longer the norm. The accountability of teachers for instruction and results continues to be a primary concern in many communities. Public awareness of educational issues continues to increase. John Silber (1989), chancellor and interim president of Boston University, says:

> Accepting standards and demonstrating competence in meeting those standards is one way for teachers to regain intellectual respect and public support for taxes to finance salary increases. In addition, they must also regain the respect that, as individuals of outstanding moral integrity, they once enjoyed. Most adults can think back to the times when teachers were greatly respected and revered in the community for the quality of their lives. The notion that today's teachers will command respect from the community and from their students without similar qualities is unrealistic. (p. 21)

Although teachers are being more closely scrutinized today, there are great opportunities for them to model and promote a strong commitment to learning. Christian school teachers are strategically positioned to demonstrate competence both academically and spiritually.

Students on teachers: High school

Mrs. Letourneau taught in a public school, and she had the guts to stand up for what she believed. She set biblical guidelines in her class and put up with no less. She was very strong-willed.

—Dana

The teacher who had most impact on me in my high school experience was Mrs. Kokozka. She was my French teacher for three years. Her energy, enthusiasm about learning, and willingness to take time out of class to listen to students' concerns set her apart from her colleagues. She was literally excited to be in class with us every day. If there was one lesson she instilled in us, it was to learn for the sake of learning.

— Kristen

Characteristics of Effective Teachers

Academic leadership and effectiveness are manifest in the things teachers do to manage their classrooms. Good intentions alone do not lead to effective instruction and enhanced student learning. The teacher must do many things to be effective, and the art of teaching comes into play.

There are numerous definitions of effective instruction and lists of the qualities it entails. While these qualities may appear self-evident, teachers benefit by reviewing their performance and assessing personal practice. Robert MacDonald has found the following characteristics of effective teachers:

- Willingness to be flexible, to be direct or indirect as the situation demands
- Ability to perceive the world from the student's point of view
- Ability to personalize one's teaching
- Willingness to experiment, to try out new things
- Skill in asking questions (as opposed to seeing oneself as a kind of answering service)
- Knowledge of subject matter and related areas
- Provision of well-established examination procedures
- Provision of definite study helps
- Demonstration of appreciative attitudes (evidenced by nods, comments, smiles, etc.)
- Use of conversational manner in teaching—informal, easy style (1991, 230–31)

The book of Nehemiah illustrates effective instruction. After the walls were restored, everyone gathered to hear the reading of the scrolls. "Also … the Levites, helped the people to understand the Law; and the people stood in their place. So they read distinctly from the book, in the Law of God; and they gave the sense, and helped them to understand the reading" (Nehemiah 8:7–8).

Effective teaching responds to the needs and understanding of the learner. Ezra was reading the Scriptures while the people stood. We are also told that there were teachers and scribes who were teaching, and there was understanding because the teachers and scribes brought sense to what the people heard.

Common Mistakes of Beginning Teachers

New teachers face unique challenges, and recognizing some common mistakes can be useful in avoiding them. Kellough and Roberts cite many, including these:

- Lack of or inadequate long-range planning
- Sketchy lesson planning
- Emphasis on the negative
- Spending too much time with one student or one group
- Beginning a new activity before gaining student attention
- Sitting while teaching
- Too serious, no fun
- Using the same teaching strategy or combination of strategies day after day
- Inadequate use of silence (wait time) after asking a content question

- Not requiring students to raise their hands and to be acknowledged before responding
- Settling for less when you should be trying for more
- Using threats
- Too slow in intervening during inappropriate student behavior
- Reading student papers only for correct answers and not for process and thinking
- Failing to do frequent (every few minutes) comprehension checks
- Wanting the students to like the teacher
- Taking too much time to give verbal directions for a new activity
- Overusing punishment for classroom misbehavior
- Introducing too many topics simultaneously (1998, 141–45)

Conclusion

All education is based on a philosophy or worldview. Christian school teachers educate from a worldview framed by the Word of God, so their responsibilities must focus on spiritual formation and academic preparation. Although academic pursuits are sometimes viewed as unspiritual or self-serving, academic integrity demands a commitment to developing the mind in preparation to serve God. Again, the purpose of all pursuits in the Christian school is to develop students' skills and knowledge in order to benefit the kingdom of God.

Jesus' life provides the model for teaching and mentoring. A teacher who spends much time with students understands them and touches their lives. In order to be effective over time, teachers have the responsibility to be lifetime learners. New strategies and new technologies enhance the teacher's effectiveness. The Christian school teacher, who is indwelt by Holy Spirit, impacts lives for time and eternity. The challenges are many. So are the rewards and blessings.

About the Author

Ellen Lowrie Black, Ed.D., serves as an educational consultant to schools and universities as well as many other organizations in the areas of strategic planning and leadership. She has nearly two decades of experience in higher education as a professor, dean, and vice president.

Strengthen Your Foundations

1. Teaching in a Christian school is a spiritual and vocational calling. Write a one-page summary of God's calling in your life. Share this with your students and/or colleagues.

2. Compare and contrast selections from Christian and secular textbooks that deal with the origin of life. With your students, utilize biblical references to discuss the selections. Regularly share with your students from your own reading and studying how a worldview not consistent with Scripture is presented as truth.

3. Teachers often struggle with balancing the many demands on their time. Jesus modeled the practice of personal retreat and spiritual renewal. Identify those people, places, and things that are restoring to you. Develop a six-month personal renewal plan. Now implement your plan! You may want to share your plan with a close friend to develop a level of accountability.

4. Ask three educators the most important books they have read this year. Read at least one of them. Reread a book you have studied in the past. Use a pen and/or highlighter.

5. After identifying an area of instruction that you want to enhance, go to the library or the computer, and identify specific strategies you might implement. Give yourself a time line for implementation. Allow yourself the freedom to make mistakes.

References

Blamires, Harry. 1963. *The Christian mind.* Ann Arbor, MI: Servant Publications.

Borich, Gary D. 1999. *Observation skills for effective teaching.* 3d ed. Upper Saddle River, NJ: Prentice-Hall.

Campolo, Tony. 2000. *Let me tell you a story: Life lessons from unexpected places and unlikely people.* Nashville: Word Publishing.

Chadwick, Ronald P. 1990. *Christian school curriculum: An integrated approach.* Winona Lake, IN: BMH Books.

Cochran, Leslie H. 1989. *Administrative commitment to teaching: Practical, research-based strategies to strengthen college teaching effectiveness.* Cape Girardeau, MO: STEP UP, Incorporated.

Dick, Walter, Lou Carey, and James O. Carey. 1996. *The systematic design of instruction.* 4th ed. New York: HarperCollins.

Elkind, David. 1984. *All grown up and no place to go: Teenagers in crisis.* Reading, MA: Addison-Wesley.

Hendricks, Howard G. 1987. *Teaching to change lives: Develop a passion for communicating God's Word to adults or children—in the church, in the home, in Bible study groups, or in schools.* Portland, OR: Multnomah Press.

Jacobsen, David A., Paul Eggen, and Donald Kauchak. 1999. *Methods for teaching: Promoting student learning.* 5th ed. Upper Saddle River, NJ: Prentice-Hall.

Jarolimek, John, and Clifford D. Foster Sr. 1993. *Teaching and learning in the elementary school.* 5th ed. New York: Macmillan.

Joyce, Bruce, James Wolf, and Emily Calhoun. 1993. *The self-renewing school.* Alexandria, VA: Association for Supervision and Curriculum Development.

Kellough, Richard D., and Patricia L. Roberts. 1998. *A resource guide for elementary school teaching: Planning for competence.* 4th ed. Upper Saddle River, NJ: Prentice-Hall.

Kozol, Jonathan. 2000. *Ordinary resurrections: Children in the years of hope.* New York: Perennial.

Lowrie, Roy W. Jr. 1978. *To those who teach in Christian schools.* Colorado Springs, CO: Association of Christian Schools International.

——. 1980. *Inside the Christian school.* Colorado Springs, CO: Association of Christian Schools International.

MacDonald, Robert E. 1991. *A handbook of basic skills and strategies for beginning teachers: Facing the challenge of teaching in today's schools.* White Plains, NY: Longman.

Marzano, Robert J. 1992. *A different kind of classroom: Teaching with dimensions of learning.* Alexandria, VA: Association for Supervision and Curriculum Development.

Moreland, J. P. 1997. *Love your God with all your mind: The role of reason in the life of the soul.* Colorado Springs, CO: NavPress.

Silber, John. 1989. *Straight shooting: What's wrong with America and how to fix it.* New York: HarperPerennial.

Sobel, Dava. 2000. *Galileo's daughter: A historical memoir of science, faith, and love.* New York: Penguin Books.

Sweet, Leonard. 1999. *Aqua church: Essential leadership arts for piloting your church in today's fluid culture.* Loveland, CO: Group Publishing Incorporated.

Tripp, Ted. 1995. *Shepherding a child's heart.* Wapwallopen, PA: Shepherd Press.

Van Brummelen, Harro. 1994. *Steppingstones to curriculum: A biblical path.* Seattle, WA: Alta Vista College Press.

Waldron, Peter W., Tani R. Collie, and Calvin M. Davies. 1999. *Telling stories about school: An invitation.* Upper Saddle River, NJ: Prentice-Hall.

Wiggins, Grant, and J. McTighe. 1998. *Understanding by design.* Alexandria, VA: Association for Supervision and Curriculum Development.

Wilkinson, Bruce H. 1991. *Teaching with style: What your students wish you knew about teaching but were afraid to tell you.* Atlanta: Walk Thru the Bible Ministries, Incorporated.

SECTION THREE

Instructional Foundations

Sections 1 and 2 have presented the biblical, philosophical, and psychological foundations for Christian school education. This section will cover some applications of those principles with the purpose of helping educators develop an educational framework that is thoroughly biblical.

The focus is on the student. Any teacher's main responsibility is to enable students to learn. However, Christian education has a more demanding assignment. The Christian teacher plans carefully so that lives can be transformed. The biblical goal for each student is to know Christ and grow more like Him. Note the progression in the topics:

The section will consider first the *instructional philosophy* that serves as the basis of the school's total educational program and each teacher's instructional approach. Second, to provide a quality Christian education, the teacher must understand *curriculum design* and how curriculum planning is unique in the Christian school. Third, *assessment* provides a basis for grading, sets the tone of the learning experience, and tells the teacher whether the lessons were successful. A biblical approach to assessment is vital. Fourth, the classroom becomes a natural setting for *moral and character development*. Lives are transformed in the daily routine of a well-planned educational system. Finally, a classroom that welcomes students to a happy learning experience is critical, so *discipline* techniques are necessary. Learning and life change can take place only when classes are well managed. The Christian teacher's assignment is to help students learn how to think, reason, and evaluate.

Of course, not all instructional needs can be covered exhaustively in an introductory text. It is hoped that the concepts, principles, and practical ideas presented here will serve as catalysts for developing an educational approach that is distinctively and dynamically Christian.

CHAPTER TEN

Instructional Philosophy

Marti MacCullough

This chapter introduces the process of developing overall approaches to teaching derived from three learning models, all based on the underlying nature of human learning. The Christian educator must examine his or her biblical beliefs about learning before selecting an overall approach to instruction. The answer to the key question *How do humans learn?* forms the foundation for an instructional philosophy.

What is an instructional philosophy?

How do I develop a teaching approach, or model, that is consistent with my philosophy of education?

Once I am committed to an instructional model, how do I use it effectively in real-life classroom teaching?

Take a minute to read carefully the conversation below. The setting is the teachers' lounge at lunch break, and three teachers are discussing their views on instruction. Which teacher do you agree with most, and why?

CECILIA: Look, Bob, there are many approaches to teaching, and a good teacher can use any or all of them! Teachers use a variety of approaches depending on the subject matter and the students' age level. They lecture and use discussion, hands-on materials, activities, group work, and the like. Teaching is variety!

BOB: You're right about variety. But an overall approach is settled when you decide which philosophical perspective you will adopt. Logically different approaches are not really compatible. For example, a humanistic theorist might never dictate exact information for the students to copy and commit to memory. A behaviorist, on the other hand, would almost never plan an activity that leads to a discussion.

CECILIA: Are you saying that teachers should pick one overall approach to teaching and use it always? Isn't that a bit narrow and impractical? Besides, how could it be illogical to use all kinds of methods! Come on, teachers should be practical and creative! They should pick and choose for the occasion.

BOB: Practical and theoretical do not have to be opposites. *How should I teach?* is the most fundamental question a teacher can ask and answer. It is both theoretical *and* practical! You can't dodge the issue by shouting "practical"! We can't be random; we need to do our work out of a sound philosophical framework.

CECILIA: Don't you think a teacher can see the value of different approaches and use them for different situations? Look, I use a myriad of strategies and activities to help kids learn. I use what the subject and the developmental level of the students dictate, don't you?

BOB: Well that sounds good, but I think your overall approach comes from a set of educational beliefs that frame all you do. To use an eclectic approach is like saying one can be a Christian sometimes, a Moslem sometimes, and a Jew sometimes depending on the situation. Approaches to teaching require fundamental commitment to beliefs and values related to the student, the teacher, and the purpose of education.

CECILIA: Now you sound like my philosophy professor. She was into thinking more than doing. I'm a doer. I teach!

LOUIS: Hey, you two, there's no need to argue! The two of you are talking about different things. Bob, you're talking about an overall approach or plan to promote learning that comes from your philosophy of education. And Cecilia, you're talking about methods that are the tools to work out the plan. You two need to get on the same page! Don't be so serious!

BOB: Cecilia, maybe he's right! Let's discuss how our two concepts* might work together. How about over dinner tonight? We can leave from here after our faculty meeting.

CECILIA: Deal!

—Adapted from Fenstermacher and Soltis 1998

* What two concepts are being confused in this conversation?

Like Cecilia, many teachers consider themselves eclectic in their approach to classroom instruction, and they view their eclecticism as a positive pedagogical principle. However, one of the biggest misconceptions held by teachers today is that *methods*, of which there are myriads, are the same as *overall approaches*, or learning models, of which there are basically three. In the conversation above, Bob was also clouding the issue by using the terms *approaches, models,* and *methods* in unclear ways. Confusion on this issue leads to ineffective results. Teachers either find the method they personally prefer and use it almost exclusively, or they use a lot of variety and pat themselves on the back for their creativity. Neither practice leads to effective, consistent teaching and learning. What is needed is a well-thought-out overall approach to instruction, a blueprint or pattern based on how human beings learn. An instructional philosophy is the set of beliefs that undergirds the instructional approach.

Models and Methods

Models of learning that lead to overall instructional approaches are different from, but related to, methods of teaching. One's underlying philosophical framework results in the selection of an instructional approach, which in turn leads to a particular pattern or model for instruction. Methods, which are the activities and strategies used in implementing the model, are selected on the basis of the subject matter, the developmental level of the students, and the objective of a particular lesson. The process of developing a learning model that leads to an instructional plan moves like this. One examines his:

philosophy of life (root philosophy) ➔
➥philosophy of education ➔
➥nature of the learner ➔
➥theory of learning ➔
➥**learning model** (the focus of this chapter) ➔
➥teaching model ➔ lesson plan ➔ methods

The first section of this book reviews broad underlying philosophies of life, that is, the several root philosophies that undergird both ancient and current educational theories and practices. The development of a working *educational philosophy* demands first the examination of one's *root philosophy* and second a commitment to those beliefs that frame the chosen view of life so that beliefs will inform educational practice. An aging, dusty document written for a course in philosophy of education is not the goal. Informed practice is!

For the Christian, the biblical instruction is clear. Our philosophy should be "after Christ," that is, "rooted in Christ," in whom "are hidden all the treasures of wisdom and knowledge" (Colossians 2:3). Does this mean that we throw off all study of other root philosophies? Certainly not. There is of course something in almost every root philosophy that is compatible with biblical truth. Should we therefore select the view closest to our own and add the descriptor "Christian" to say what we are, as in "Christian realist" or "Christian existentialist"? While some Christians use that approach, it may be better to simply answer the issues of philosophy—the metaphysical, epistemological, and axiological questions—from a biblical perspective and then systematically develop a Christian theistic philosophical outlook or worldview as the foundation for a strong Christian educational philosophy. This has been done in previous chapters of this book.

An educational philosophy, which is narrower than a philosophy of life or a root philosophy, deals specifically with the elements of education: the aims of education, the nature of the learner and human learning, the role of the teacher and teaching, and the nature and character of the curriculum, including the plans, delivery, and learning context. Educators in popular culture often refer to their overall perspective as "traditional" or "progressive" instead of using one of the labels for educational philosophies or theories reviewed in chapter 3. Many arguments related to education are fought out of these two broad camps.

Take a minute and decide which of the two broad labels, traditional or progressive, you agree with most and why.

American education tends to swing back and forth between these poles. As you read journal articles or study the history of American education, you may agree with the *traditionalist* that there are eternal truths (absolutes), objective knowledge, and reality that exists outside the human mind and prior to human experience. However, you may agree with the *progressivist* that the active participation of the learner is essential in the learning process. And there are other aspects of teaching and learning that cross between the traditional and the progressive views. Certain elements of each are appropriate for "biblically rooted" educators. Selection, however, is not arbitrary. Once the underlying philosophy of Christian (biblical) theism has been firmly established, its tenets are used to evaluate, appreciate, and use knowledge in other areas. The Christian educator brings to the study of instructional philosophy or learning theory his root philosophy. Within the boundaries of his beliefs, he is free to choose from among the practical options that fit with the Christian worldview. In that sense, he can be eclectic, but eclecticism at the level of root philosophy is never a good idea!

Instructional philosophy, the subject of this chapter, therefore comes from somewhere. There are underlying beliefs that inform decisions about overall approaches to teaching. To be a good practitioner, one must first be a "philosopher." I think that Bob (in the opening dialogue) is right! *Why not reread the dialogue before you continue?* Teachers who are serious about building their work on a solid foundation will not be satisfied with choices and practices that contradict their beliefs.

Beliefs Matter!

With which option (a, b, or c) under each category (1, 2, and 3) do you most agree, and why?

1. Do you believe that a *teacher* is more of (a) a dispenser of knowledge, (b) a guide to the learning process, or (c) a knowledgeable person who structures, dispenses, and facilitates learning?
2. Do you believe that a *student* is more of (a) a passive receiver of knowledge, (b) an active creator of knowledge, or (c) an interactive processor and user of knowledge?
3. Do you believe that the *curriculum* should be (a) separate subjects, with the "basics" and the great books committed to memory, (b) that which interests the student and can be arranged around a theme or project, or (c) solid subject matter from all areas of human inquiry, integrated among and across content areas and with real life and values?

Those holding different educational philosophies will answer the above questions very differently. Select your view and try to defend it on the basis of your underlying belief system.

Foundational Beliefs

What are the key beliefs (philosophical questions) that inform instruction? The following are key questions about human nature and learning that help to build the foundation for instruction:

1. What is the actional nature of the human being?
2. What is the moral nature of the human being?
3. What is the developmental nature of the human being as it affects learning?
4. What are human differences, and how do they affect learning?
5. What is the nature of knowledge and knowing?
6. What knowledge is the most worth knowing?

These six questions are addressed, to some degree, elsewhere in this book by various writers. Here we will consider primarily question 1, which most clearly addresses the character of an overall approach to instruction. In their book *Learning Theories for Teachers,* Morris Bigge and Samuel Shermis frame the issue this way:

> Each theory of learning, especially as it is applied in schools, is closely linked to a conception of the basic innate moral and actional nature of human beings. Hence when teachers seriously consider how they are going to teach children and youths, they inevitably formulate some assumptions about the essential moral and actional natures of students as human beings. (1998, 14)

Three Views

There are three basic views of the actional nature of human beings: passive, active (or proactive), and interactive. Theorists and philosophers use the term "actional nature" to refer to the relationship between humans and their environment or to the source of human motivation as inside, outside, or both inside and outside. Those who hold that humans are *active* in their actional nature believe that underlying psychological characteristics are inborn, and that learning comes from *within.* The environment is simply a location for natural unfoldment. Those who hold the view that humans are basically *passive* believe that human characteristics are determined primarily by the environment, or forces *outside* the person. Those who hold that humans are *interactive* in their actional nature do not equate learning with the simple unfoldment of inner urges alone. Nor do they equate learning only with the conditioning process that works on the human being from without. Interactionists believe that psychological characteristics arise as human beings take in information from an outside world and try to make sense out of it by processing the information using their innate capacity to know and to learn.

Learning theories differ on this issue. Historically, the actional nature has been viewed as either passive or active, and the following beliefs or elements in instruction have been pitted against each other:

passive	*versus*	active learner
rote memory	*versus*	conceptual learning
intrinsic	*versus*	extrinsic motivation

Since the appearance of cognitive science on the educational scene, new evidence and applications for human learning and a new actional label have entered official educational terminology. That label is *interactive*. The term connotes more than a mix or balance of passive and active (sometimes passive and sometimes active). It refers to a new way of looking at the nature of the student. It describes the way the mind works in the learning process.

The interactive nature of the learner has been confused at times with simple social interaction (talk) and cooperative learning, or the use of technology in learning, or the allowing of questions during class or at the end of class. All of the above strategies may be a part of interactive learning; however, the concept of the interactive actional nature describes the way the human mind learns using inner and outer factors.

Behaviorism, the instructional theory that dominated much of the twentieth century, claimed to be the only scientific learning theory because it measured observable behaviors only. Behaviorism holds that the human is *passive* in relation to the environment and that learning happens primarily because of outside elements (the teacher, the text, a video). The learning model derived from this belief is one of outside stimuli soliciting a response or reaction. Future responses (the learning) are determined by the skilled conditioner-teacher and environmental reinforcement. The teacher is everything! The model for teaching is teacher-centered!

Humanistic theorists that follow the views of the romantics, such as Rousseau and Froebel in the eighteenth century and the existentialists of the 1960s, usually adopt natural unfoldment as part of their underlying belief systems. Thus they believe that humans are *proactive* and that learning happens primarily because of inside factors unfolding naturally. The environment is simply a location for learning, and learning is autonomous and developmental. The student is everything. The model for teaching is student-centered!

Twentieth-century cognitive interactionists hold that the human being is neither a passive receiver of information from the environment nor an autonomous creator of knowledge but rather one who comes equipped with the capacity to know and learn. The world around provides something to know. Both inside and outside factors are vital. The learning process involves the student, the curriculum, and the teacher in dynamic interplay. The model for teaching is learning-centered!

How might a Christian determine which of the three views above fits best with the view of humanity that the Scriptures reveal? A close examination of God's Word shows us that humans are made in the image of God with the capacity to seek and to know truth. We find also that the One in whose image we are created has provided something outside ourselves to know—His Word, His world, and Himself. Christian philosopher Gordon Clark, writing about epistemological issues, puts it this way, "God has fashioned both the mind and the world so that they harmonize" (1981, 316). The biblical view declares that truth exists *outside* the knowing mind and that knowledge (truth) is possible because the mind (*inside*) has been created to know truth. Reason would inform us, then, that learning requires both inside and outside elements.

While it is recognized that the Bible is not a textbook on learning theory, it portrays by precept and example a clear picture of humans that helps us select the interactive actional approach as the one most closely aligning with a biblical view of the actional nature of humans. It is a view that also preserves truth that exists outside the knowing mind. For example, in the teaching ministry of Jesus, one may readily see His expectations related to the *inside* processing of information and the receptivity of His teachings from *outside*. On one occasion a lawyer, wishing to trap Jesus, asked Him about eternal life. Jesus questioned the lawyer about his current knowledge of the law. The student gave the right response: "Love the Lord your God with all your heart, with all your soul, with all your strength, and with all your mind"; and love "your neighbor as yourself" (Luke 10:27). Wishing to justify himself, the lawyer asked, "Who is my neighbor?" Jesus did not lecture, but instead He told the story of the Good Samaritan. Afterward, Jesus asked the lawyer-student which of the three in the story he thought was neighbor of the man in need. In other words, the Teacher was saying, I'll give you some information, but *you* need to process it and draw a conclusion! His overall approach was interactive. He challenged the mind (inside) with outside information. On this occasion He used several ***methods:*** questioning, storytelling, discovery from the story, listening-to-find-out, and direct instruction.

On another occasion (Matthew 16), Jesus asked, "Who do men say that I am?" The disciples responded that some believed He was John the Baptist, Elijah, or some other prophet. Jesus asked, "Who do you say I am?" Perhaps speaking for the group, Peter declared, "You are the Christ!" Now Jesus knew that the answer given by stimulus *(who am I?)* response *(the Christ)* was right. However, He also knew that Peter did not have complete understanding. The teacher, Jesus, arranged a field trip several days later. He took Peter, James, and John to the mountain (often called the mount of transfiguration), where God the Father allowed Moses and Elijah to appear with them. Now Peter, revealing a misconception in his learning, said, "If you wish, I will put up three shelters, one for you, one for Moses, and one for Elijah." In what he said, Peter the student revealed his misconception, a failure to understand that Jesus was the Christ, the Son of God, and in a different category from the others. God the Father covered over Moses and Elijah, and Jesus appeared in His glorified form. The Father spoke (direct instruction), saying, "This is my son..., listen to Him." Both inner and outer factors were considered as methods to *impress* (put in) information and to *express* (draw out) thinking and learning.

Jesus was always concerned with the inner processing of the student as well as with the truth He was presenting. He often used a student's prior knowledge and experiences to get the mind actively processing His words. Check out the parables in this regard. He was also concerned about the person's stage of development and readiness to learn. He did not ask the question "Who do men say that I am?" until many months after He began His ministry with the disciples. The disciples needed more experience. When they were ready, He presented new information to facilitate and promote their learning.

In the past, Christian educational philosophers have tried to portray the concept of the interactive nature of human beings by including active and passive as well as inner and outer elements in their educational theories. While that approach helped teachers to design curricula, it also left the door open for them to favor one, perhaps active, over the other. The same teacher might pay the other lip service only. There was no overall approach to teaching that could really be labeled "interactive." As a young teacher of teachers, I developed a model I called "directed inquiry" to try to depict the concept of outer (directed) and inner (inquiring mind) elements. The concept of the interactive actional nature, with its applications to learning and teaching, now opens the door to a framework for teaching that clearly takes into account a biblical view of humans. We owe a debt of gratitude to cognitive science for this new paradigm built on experimental evidence that answers the question *How do humans learn?* Let's see how this works to help develop an approach to teaching. How might the three views of the actional nature lead to different models for learning and teaching?

Characteristics of the Three Broad Learning Models

1. Behaviorist Learning Model

The actional nature of the human being is *passive.*

Description. The teacher communicates both knowledge and conclusions, and reinforces student responses.

Curricular label. Content- or subject-centered. The source of motivation is *outside* the learner.

Teaching model. Telling, testing, reinforcing.

Teacher. Thinks, organizes, tells, draws conclusions if any, and is mentally active; reinforces student learning, usually with grades.

Student. Listens, takes notes, gives back encyclopedic responses (facts) or memorized notes in the exact form given; does not have to process content mentally in order to pass; may be conditioned in class to be mentally passive.

2. Humanistic Learning Model

The actional nature of the human being is *active.*

Description. The teacher provides materials and guides thinking, but communicates neither knowledge nor conclusions.

Curricular label. Process- or experience-centered. Content is not a major issue; thinking is. The source of motivation is *inside* the learner; it unfolds naturally.

Teaching model. (Sometimes called the *autonomous developmental model.)* Discovery-oriented.

Teacher. Encourages, provides materials (such as texts and films), pulls together divergent thinking through discussion; does little structuring based on objectives; content is *not* a major goal; feeling good about thinking and learning *is.*

Student. Theoretically, self-motivated to explore in search of knowledge or to come up incidentally with a question or problem to pursue; researches and draws conclusions; creates knowledge; engages in self-assessment. The model assumes mental activity.

3. Cognitive-Interactionist Learning Model

The actional nature of the human being is *interactive.*

Description. The teacher provides structure and information for each instructional objective. Concepts, principles, and conclusions are the results of teacher input *and* student thinking prompted by teacher-prepared activities and questions related to the information provided.

Curricular label. Learning-centered; content *and* process are emphasized. Assessment involves retrieving information in the words and understanding of the student. The source of motivation is *inside* but is often triggered by *outside* elements in the learning process, or the interplay between inner and outer elements.

Teaching model. The interactive model, directed by the teacher but continually involves the student in the mental work (processing); uses both exploratory (discovery, inquiry) and explanatory (directed, expository) methodology.

Teacher. Organizes learning for each objective; provides questions and arouses thinking related to a problem to be solved, an issue to be examined, or some structured content; provides input (lecture, research, resource persons, films, modeling, text material); prepares student activities to relate new knowledge to prior knowledge; provides activities designed to cause students to manipulate (process) information, classify, categorize, draw conclusions, or use information in a true-to-life situation.

Student. Listens purposefully, takes notes, talks, writes, reads "to find out," researches to solve a problem or issue, or to understand a generalization; draws conclusions under the guidance of the teacher and based on the input given. Active thinking and mental effort in class are essential as a part of the lesson. Methods are both impressive (reading and listening) and expressive (writing and talking). Students must express what they have processed to check accuracy and receive feedback for continued learning.

Designing a Model or Plan

Look at the following elements of a lesson, which are typically addressed in educational texts and pedagogy classes. For each of the three views, think about the underlying beliefs concerning the actional nature of the student. Determine which of the four elements might be a part of a teaching model (lesson plan) under each actional nature. Place a check mark in front of those you select:

Passive	**Proactive**	**Interactive**
Motivation activity	Motivation activity	Motivation activity
New content or skill	New content or skill	New content or skill
Processing activity	Processing activity	Processing activity
Assessment	Assessment	Assessment

Your selections should look like these. Explain why to review the characteristics of each model.

Passive Model	**Proactive Model**	**Interactive Model**
Motivation activity	Motivation activity	✓Motivation activity
✓New content or skill	New content or skill	✓New content or skill
Processing activity	✓Processing activity	✓Processing activity
✓Assessment	Assessment	✓Assessment

Reinforcement activity. Take a lesson you have taught or will teach in the future and lay it out, using each of the above models. With at least one other person, discuss differences and similarities, and draw conclusions.

Developing the Interactive Model

In developing an instructional model, one might think like this:

- If something inside matters in the learning of new information, I must plan to activate that inside something in order to motivate toward the learning at hand.
- If something outside matters, I must study and organize content and skills to deliver these in light of the students' prior experiences and current knowledge.
- If learning occurs as information is taken in and processed by the individual, I must create student processing activities, both group and individual.
- If learning occurs inside and I am a teacher who needs to assess learning, I must create ongoing assessment activities that provide feedback to the teacher by answering the question *Are they getting it?* and to the student by answering the question *Am I getting it?*

A learning model based on the interactive nature of the human is not just passive telling and testing; nor is it just unguided activity or simply drawing out. Rather, it is an orchestration of the following four elements:

- *Engaging the mind* (inside) using an activity planned by the teacher (outside)
- *Providing new information* by giving it (outside the student) or creating a student activity that requires the student to get the new information from some source
- *Creating student activities* to help the student make sense out of new material or skill, form closure, make connections, generalize, draw conclusions, or practice and use a skill
- *Assessing learning* by using student feedback to see whether students are getting it

Definition of Interactive Learning

Interactive learning is the process whereby the learner takes in new information from his or her surroundings and uses prior categories, vocabulary, and understandings to begin to process, make sense of, and store the information for retrieval and use.

True or false (according to the definition)

▲ Subject matter (content) is vital.
▲ Prior knowledge of the learner is important.
▲ Student processing activities are not optional.
▲ Memory (storage) is essential.
▲ Understanding is a key to learning and transfer.

All are true!

What About Instructional Objectives?

Do I really need instructional objectives? Proponents of all three views of the actional nature of human beings—active, passive, interactive—write objectives. Those who hold the behaviorist (passive) view use behaviorally stated objectives specific to each skill or piece of data that is to be learned. They may give a list of five or more objectives for one lesson. The behavior (what the teacher observes) *is* the learning, so each desired behavior must be targeted. Those with humanistic (active) theories may have objectives, but they are usually written in affective terms or in process (not content) terms. Proponents of cognitive interactive theory will have one broad objective for each lesson, and they will state it behaviorally. The teacher views what the student can demonstrate in class as evidence of learning. To assess learning, the teacher must see something the student has written or hear something the student has said. The objective keeps the big idea in focus so that related facts can be connected to it in a meaningful way. The objective for the interactionist is the target concept, skill, or "big idea" of the lesson.

Back to Methods

What about methods? If both inner and outer elements are vital to learning, then methods must be both impressive and expressive. Many methods or strategies are available to the teacher.

Make a list of as many methods as you can think of right now. Did you list ten, twenty, or more? While there are only three basic models of learning based on the actional nature of the student, there are many methods.

In choosing methods, the teacher is guided by understanding the subject, knowing the purpose for each lesson element, and being aware of the students' developmental level and individual differences. However, choosing an overall learning approach is a philosophical matter that requires a commitment to the answer to the question, *How do humans relate to their environment in the process of learning—passively, actively, or interactively?* Methods are used to carry out the instructional plan or model. For example, the lecture method might be used almost exclusively in the passive model and frequently in the interactive model but almost never in the active model. The discussion method might be dominant in the active model but excluded (at least in the lesson plan) in the passive model. A myriad of methods may be used in interactive teaching, methods that will sometimes feature the teacher or outer elements, and other times the students' mental processing (in groups and as individuals).

Methods for Interactive Teaching

Methods for Information Acquisition*	Methods for Processing and Constructing Meaning*
stories	discussion
monologues	cooperative groups or pair share
lectures and mini-lectures	question and answer (write and speak)
research	role play
reading ("to find out")	drama
field trips	creative and response writing
video or films	charts to compare and contrast
Internet search	art (draw or diagram)

*These are just samples.

A tool box of fifty items without a blueprint will not get the house built. Likewise, a blueprint or plan without tools is useless. Teachers who are serious about promoting learning must not only study methodology and equip themselves to use various methods for various purposes and age levels; they must also know where they are going, that is, have a blueprint for their overall approach. An instructional philosophy and the overall teaching approach derived from it are vital links to effective teaching. You now have enough information to begin to develop an instructional philosophy that will inform your practice.

Practical application. Below you will see a model for instruction that fits the interactive nature of the learner. Lesson plans using this model will vary significantly, depending on the methods used for the different content areas and on the developmental level of the learners. Methods—the activities used to carry out the plan—can vary, but the elements of the plan, or overall approach, remain the same.

Lesson Plan: Interactive Learning

I. Concept or subconcept to be taught
II. Instructional objective, based on the "big idea" of the lesson
III. Lesson outline (four elements)

A. Motivation

Purpose: to activate or engage the student's mind toward the concept or skill to be learned

Set up a question to answer, an issue to examine, a skill to develop, or a problem to solve. Use the students' prior knowledge or past experience. Make it "student friendly."

Keep the lesson objective in focus. Describe the activities and methods to be used.

B. Development of the concept or skill
Purpose: to promote new learning and connect it with previous learning
Carefully organize new and relevant information. Use hands-on, minds-on materials as much as possible for science and math. Use demonstrations and modeling in all subject areas. Use advanced organizers of relevant information to aid concept development unless the use of these will squelch curiosity or interfere with problem solving. Make sure you have *mastered* the concept or skill. Study. Practice. Describe the methods to be used.

C. Student processing activities (closure)
Purpose: to guide the student in the process of making sense out of the new knowledge or skills; to use it; to fit it in; to store it
Write out questions and/or describe activities in which students are guided to organize, relate, connect, and use information and instruction from B above to answer a question, solve a problem, or practice a skill introduced in A. This element requires the student to process information and to make sense of new learning. Describe the methods to be used.

D. Assessment of Learning
Purpose: to provide an opportunity for the student and the teacher to know whether or not learning is happening
Use at least one question and/or activity to determine learning. Does the learner *understand* what he or she has said and discussed or memorized? Can the student use the new information or skill? This element may be graded, but it is *not* necessary to grade all individual assessments, especially in the formative stage.

Sample Science Lesson Outline Using the Interactive Model

Concept: Refraction of light

Instructional objective: The student will be able to solve a real-life problem using the concept of refraction of light.

1. Motivation activity

   Method: Demonstration

   The teacher provides an aquarium two-thirds full of water and placed at eye level on a table for the students to observe. As she lowers a doll into the water, keeping the head above the water, students will observe a "headless doll," an illusion caused by the bending of light as it travels through two different media, air and water.

   (*Oohs* and *ahs* are followed by the questions, *How did you do that? Why does that happen?* to which, the teacher replies, *Let's find out.*)

2. New information

   Methods: Hands-on activities in teams of four or five (five stations with experiments that use refraction)

   Students discover what happens when light travels through different media and record their observations.

3. Student processing activities

   Methods: Drawing conclusions in writing for each experiment

   Sharing conclusions with their team

   Using the information to define *refraction of light* in their own words

   Checking their definition against the text

   Solving a problem given to each team:

   Sample problem: *You are in a swimming pool with a friend who drops a hair clip into the water. You see it on the bottom. You reach down and it is not there; it moved. Explain what you think happened.*

4. Assessment activity

   Method: Question and answer; writing

   Sample question: *Can a spear fisherman successfully practice his craft on dry land? Why or why not?*

About the Author

Marti MacCullough currently serves as the dean of the School of Education at Philadelphia Biblical University, where she also teaches philosophy of education, learning theories, and educational psychology. Dr. MacCullough has a passion for informed teaching and for excellence in education for God's glory.

References

Bigge, Morris L., and S. Samuel Shermis. 1998. *Learning theories for teachers.* 6th ed. New York: Addison Wesley Longman.

Clark, Gordon H. 1981. *A Christian view of men and things.* 2d ed. Grand Rapids, MI: Baker Book House.

Fenstermacher, Gary D., and Jonas F. Soltis. 1998. *Approaches to teaching.* New York: Columbia University, Teachers College Press.

CHAPTER ELEVEN

Understanding Curriculum Design

Harro Van Brummelen

Key questions:

What are the aims and worldview foundations of Christian school programs?
How do you plan a yearly overview?
How do you design and adapt unit plans for your classroom?
How do you select suitable classroom resources?
How do you implement curriculum change effectively?

All school programs have a worldview basis. Every curriculum guide, every course outline, every textbook, and every unit plan makes assumptions about what students should know about society and what values they should adopt.

A science curriculum may take for granted that technology can solve society's problems—or show that scientific problems also have moral and social dimensions. A social studies course may avoid faith as a vital aspect of culture—or highlight it. Algebra may stress theory—or emphasize how algebra solves real-life problems. In all these cases, educators use their worldview, explicitly or implicitly, to make curriculum decisions.

So how does a biblical worldview affect curriculum? Amanda Boyce sums it up as follows:

> Curriculum can be viewed as a take-off for evidencing God's love. All humans are created by God and for God. Therefore, the aim of all teaching and learning is to reveal to students the reality of their identity. However, humanity's identity includes recognition of the reality of sin and the consequent need of redemption. The outworking of curriculum therefore strives to be redemptive by guiding students to the only source of redemption—Jesus Christ. God is Truth; truth was created by God and comes from Him. Furthermore, God's truth informs His reality. The goal of curriculum is to make this truth known to students, thus enabling them to respond to God and impact the world and those around them for God.

> The beginning of knowledge is the fear of the Lord. Therefore, teaching and learning should be focused on God's truth and reality. Once gained, the knowledge of God's truth—whether revealed in His Word or in His creation—will allow us to interpret our culture and our God-given calling. Values such as love, justice, and integrity are God-ordained, being interwoven into the fabric of His reality. Therefore, we encourage and reward commitment and adherence to such values as we implement the curriculum.
>
> The curriculum should evidence humanity's purpose in life to our students—that of loving God above all and our neighbors as ourselves. By God's grace, curriculum can offer teachers the opportunity to help students recognize their calling to engage as Christians in our secular society. Ultimately, we want curriculum to cause students to become passionate about living and sharing the truths about God's reality. (2002, 1)

Aims of the Christian School Curriculum

The aims of the Christian school curriculum are rooted in a biblical worldview. Figure 1 shows a set of curriculum aims with matching questions that help justify curriculum choices. Not all of these aims and questions apply to all curriculum topics. However, each year's program can contribute significantly to each aim.

We can use these aims and questions to develop a responsible Christian orientation to curriculum design. Unlike traditionalists, who see curriculum as just conveying information and concepts, we see it as the reflective unfolding, interpretation, and application of God's truth. Unlike behaviorists, who see curriculum as just a controlled and efficient process, we see it as fostering students' positive response and responsibility to God, their fellow humans, and society. Unlike constructivists, who see curriculum as a quest for constructing personal meaning and personal truth, we see it as a journey that deepens understanding of God's revelation, both in His Word and in His world, and its implications for life. In a Christian approach to curriculum, students learn about God's creation and how humans have unfolded it, and how God calls us to respond as disciples of Jesus Christ.

Figure 1 Aims of the Christian School Curriculum and Related Questions

Aims of the Curriculum	Questions for Justifying Curriculum Choices
Overall aim: To become committed to Jesus Christ and to a Christian way of life, able and willing to serve God, neighbor, and society	*Does the curriculum:* • Teach content from a perspective that is faithful to Scripture? • Enhance understandings and abilities for exercising responsible and responsive discipleship? • Consider biblical values and encourage students to form dispositions and commitments based on them?
To unfold the basis, framework, and implications of a Christian vision of life	*Does the curriculum:* • Help students know and experience a Christian worldview and its implications for life in society? • Encourage students to choose and commit themselves to a biblical way of life?
To learn about God's world and how humans have responded to God's mandate to take care of the earth	*Does the curriculum:* • Familiarize students with our Christian and Western cultural heritage? • Address meaningful and significant current issues? • Show the wonder of God's creation? Show how humans have unfolded as well as abused His world? Show what it means to live according to God's intent for His creation?
To develop and apply the concepts, abilities, and creative gifts that enable students to have a transformational impact on culture for Jesus Christ	*Does the curriculum:* • Develop students' diverse abilities, taking into account their stages of development and their different learning styles? • Ask students to create products, procedures, and theories that unfold God's reality and develop their insights, abilities, and dispositions? • Encourage students to use their learning to contribute to life both inside and outside of school? Help them to become servant leaders who support each other to promote the lordship of Christ in all areas of life?
To discern and confront the idols of our time: materialism, hedonism, scientism, relativism, and other "isms" in which people place their faith in something other than God	*Does the curriculum:* • Make students aware of, and able to critique, the shared meanings of our culture? • Foster understanding and discernment of key trends and issues in society? • Help students promote the positive and confront the negative characteristics of our culture?

Christian Worldview as a Basis for Curriculum Design

Figure 2 shows the key elements of a biblically based worldview. The history of the world can be described in four main epochs, each with a special God-given injunction and each with particular implications for curriculum design:

Figure 2 Elements of a Biblical Worldview

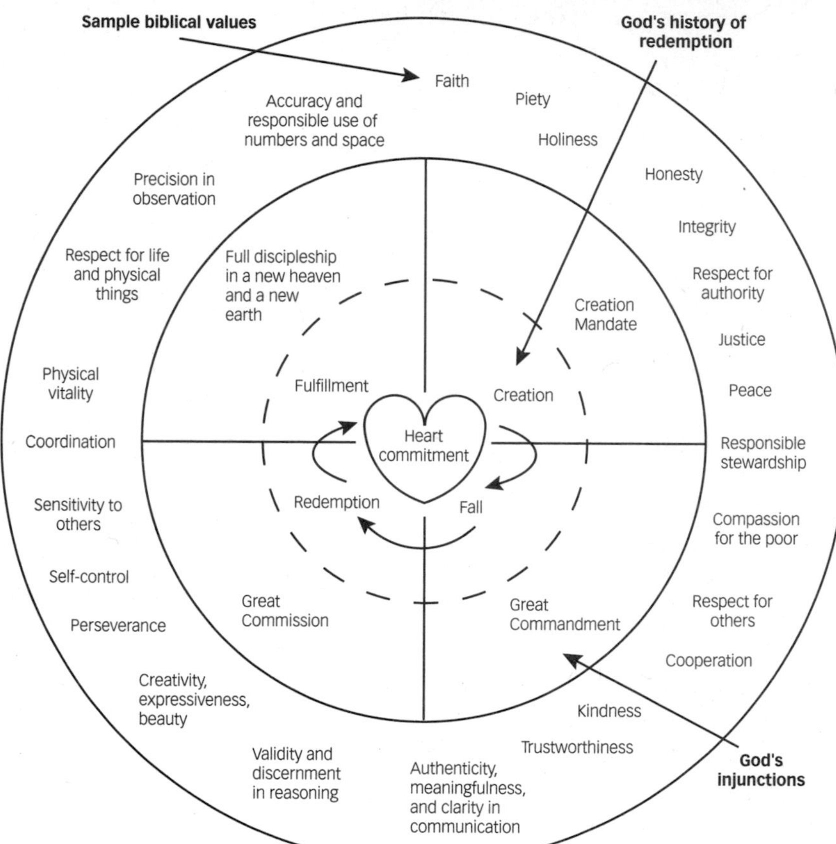

1. God's creation of the world, including humans in His image

God saw everything that He had made, and indeed it was very good (Genesis 1:31).

At creation, God gave humans His Creation Mandate, also called the Cultural Mandate. God told Adam and Eve to be fruitful, to rule over the earth, and to tend and take care of God's garden (Genesis 1:28 and 2:15). Thus God called humans to develop the possibilities of His creation, to be stewards of His creation. They were to enable everything in God's world to fulfill its intended function. God entrusted humans with His creation in all its complexity for the benefit of all creatures. The fall into sin did not negate that call, even though sin will continue to undermine human efforts until Christ's return.

What does the Creation Mandate mean for our curriculum? God calls our students to learn about, use, and value mathematical, physical, and biological entities and theories. He calls them to be involved in advancing civilization on the basis of biblical norms. They explore God's guidelines for family life, business, law, government, communication, the uses of technology, and aesthetics. They learn to advocate what is true, worthy, and upright. The curriculum helps them answer the question, *What is God's intention for the particular area of creation or culture that we are investigating?*

2. The fall into sin

Our sins testify against us (Isaiah 59:12).

Humans fell into sin. We are no longer able to fulfill the Creation Mandate. We live in a self-centered, not a God-centered, world. Therefore, our curriculum asks a second question: *How has human disobedience and sin distorted God's purpose? How have humans deviated from God's original intentions?"*

God promised that redemption from sin would be forthcoming. In the meantime, He gave us a mandate that Adam and Eve kept instinctively before the fall into sin: Love the Lord your God above all, and your neighbor as yourself (Matthew 22:37–39). Love is the key to being transformed by the renewing of our minds so that we no longer conform to the pattern of this world (Romans 12:2, 9–21). In other words, once we see how God's intent for His good creation has been warped by sin and evil, our response is to live lives of love for God and His world.

What are the implications for curriculum? Curriculum content deals with the effects of sin in society, but it also proclaims hope for the future because God is faithful (Psalm 146). Our curriculum helps students discern how personal and societal sin affects morality, government, crime, warfare, economics, interpersonal relationships, communications, the media, and our environment. But we don't stop there. The curriculum also encourages students to use their gifts in service to and love for God and neighbor, to develop the "mind of Christ" (1 Corinthians 2:16). We build praise and thanksgiving into the curriculum. We include content that deals with issues in our society where *agape* love can make a difference. We structure curriculum so that students use their diverse gifts to help and support each other, and where they apply their learning in service projects. The curriculum helps students lament the power of sin but also celebrate and bring about God's *shalom*—His peace and righteousness—where it is possible to do so.

3. God's redemption in Jesus Christ

This is indeed the Christ, the Savior of the world (John 4:42).

God provided the possibility of redemption through Christ's sacrificial death. So a third key curriculum question we may now pose is this: *How can we, through Christ's work of redemption, restore, at least in part, the love, righteousness, and justice that God intended for the world? How can the curriculum lead students into a deeper understanding of, experience in, and commitment to a Christian way of life?*

After His resurrection, Jesus added to the Creation Mandate both the Great Commission and the Great Commandment (Matthew 28:18–20). Christians often think of responding to the Great Commission as witnessing to those who do not believe in Christ. That is a crucial aspect of it! But there's more. Jesus enjoins us to make disciples (not just converts) of all nations (not just individuals). Disciples are people who base their thinking, words, and deeds on the principles Jesus taught us. And Jesus makes clear that we must teach people "to obey everything I have commanded you." So our curriculum leads students to cherish and promote humility, self-sacrifice, mercy, peace, justice, righteousness, truthfulness, faithfulness, and generosity—and to avoid legalism and hypocrisy. It explores responsible Christian responses to the influence of sin. It examines Kingdom norms that Jesus taught us, together with their implications. The curriculum helps students investigate, at an appropriate level, what it means to be Christ's ambassadors wherever God places them, using their insights, abilities, and value-based attitudes in God-glorifying ways.

4. Fulfillment of God's promise

And I saw a new heaven and a new earth (Revelation 21:1).

We can look forward to full discipleship in a new heaven and a new earth. We don't yet know what mandate God will give us then, but no doubt it will be one through which we can serve and praise Him fully. This leads to a fourth curriculum question: *How can we instill in our students a sense of hope, strength, and courage despite the many problems and struggles they face?*

We reject the idea of the innate goodness of human beings. The Bible makes clear that each of us and our whole society are tainted with sin. Still, our curriculum should leave students with a sense of hope. God's goodness is still evident in our world, and we look forward to full restoration of God's intent for His creation. So when we discuss broken family life, damaged ecosystems, or corrupt media, we can explore with students how they can still erect signposts to God's kingdom. They can still promote what is just and loving, both personally and together as a Christian community.

Embedding Biblical Values in the Curriculum

God also embedded in His creation values by which life can flourish. The outer circle of figure 2 shows some examples. The values we nurture in our curriculum, for instance, range from accuracy in mathematics to clarity in communications to holiness in the spiritual realm. In literature we choose selections that promote respect and compassion. In social studies we discuss questions of social justice, as well as value dilemmas faced by historical figures. In science we promote precise and truthful reporting of data. In mathematics we have students research and plot morally significant social trends.

Throughout the curriculum, we can explicitly plan to develop students' sense of responsibility, combining high expectations with love, encouragement, and support. We model biblical values, give reasons for them, and introduce cases that lead students to consider how such values apply in specific circumstances. In this way, we help students replace selfishness and faith in the autonomy of the individual with self-sacrifice, humility, and servanthood.

Planning the Curriculum

Schools make curriculum decisions at different levels. For instance, a school board may call for a revision of a school's science program to reflect updated mission and vision statements. The principal appoints a task force of teachers to work out a schoolwide scope-and-sequence chart and to recommend basic resources. Once these have been approved, teachers write a yearly outline for their science course and then develop or adapt unit plans. Later they plan day-to-day lessons. The success of curriculum implementation depends on teachers. Thus a teacher asks:

Does my curriculum:

- attain my school's vision and aims, and uphold a biblical worldview and vision?
- help students become responsive and responsible disciples?
- employ varied learning strategies suited for my class?
- meet the expectations of my school as well as other official standards?

Teachers usually prepare yearly course outlines on the basis of a school's overall scope-and-sequence map for the various subject areas. Figure 3 shows one possible format (for other more detailed ones, see Keenan 1998 and Van Brummelen 2002). All yearly overviews should list a schedule; topics, principal content, and goals; the main concepts, understandings, and values; key skills to be learned; and major student assessment strategies. The time allotment should reflect a balanced consideration of all topics, with no undue repetition between years. Also, each topic should contribute to the school's mission and aims.

Figure 3 Sample Yearly Overview Grid

Yearly Curriculum Overview					
Schedule	Topics and Goals	Concepts, Enduring Understandings, Values	Skills and Abilities	Student Assessment	Links to State Standards
September 3 weeks					
Sept./Oct. 4 weeks					

Designing and Adapting Unit Plans

The integration of a biblical perspective comes to the fore in the design and adaptation of unit plans. Jumping directly from a yearly outline to daily lesson plans usually results in a superficial hit-and-miss approach to implementing a biblical perspective, or in the inclusion of textbooks written from perspectives that are at odds with the school's vision and aims.

This section will suggest nine steps for teachers to take in planning a classroom unit. Often, of course, you will adapt existing units to fit your class. It is still important, however, to go through these steps, even if you use ideas from other sources. Whether or not you adapt other sources, you yourself should decide your theme, main concepts, enduring understandings, learning outcomes, suitable learning activities, and assessment strategies.

You will seldom do the steps in the exact order shown here. It is likely that you already have many good ideas for steps 4 through 8 even before you develop your thematic statement. But don't neglect the first three steps! They make it much more likely that your specific learning activities will contribute to your overall theme and approach.

1. Consider the significance and relevance of a topic. Whether or not you choose your own topics, consider how a topic can be significant to your students. Ask yourself:

- How can the topic contribute to my students' understanding of a Christian worldview, biblical values, and our Christian and cultural heritage?
- How does the topic expand students' previous knowledge and give them insight into significant issues?
- How can the topic meet students' learning needs and lead to worthwhile skill development?

Topics can be too narrow (apples) or too broad (progress); interesting but not that significant (kites); or unsuitable for a particular grade level (the French Revolution in grade 3). In this section I will use the example of a grade 8 unit on communication in the media developed by Amanda Boyce (2002). It is a topic that is significant for Christian students, for the media affect students on a daily basis. They have experienced the media but often have not analyzed how the media affect society and themselves personally. They need to discern what values the media promote and what a biblically based alternative would look like. Communication in the media is a topic of interest that lends itself to many types of student learning activities.

2. Brainstorm ideas. There are several ways of brainstorming, either by yourself or with other teachers. Some teachers like to begin with a web diagram. That technique is helpful for seeing what topics and concepts to include but less so for deciding on a biblically based approach. A good way to begin is to answer the four worldview questions posed earlier:

- *What is God's intention for the particular area of creation or culture that we are investigating?* The purpose of the media is to glorify God: to create and maintain positive relationships, to develop insights into culture and God's call on our lives, and to respond in step with God's plan in our expression of feelings, values, attitudes, and dispositions.
- *How has God's purpose been distorted by human disobedience and sin? How have humans deviated from God's original intent?* Communication is often used as a means to deceive and thus tear down rather than affirm others. The media also promote selfishness and indulgence, and they set up idols that replace God (e.g., hedonism).
- *Are there ways in which we can restore, at least in part, the love, righteousness, and justice that God intended for the world?* As

Christians we can make a difference as we become involved in the media through responsible and active participation. We can work to restore and maintain authentic, integral communication based on God's truth and biblical values. We can help students develop a biblical framework for judging media communication.

- *How can we instill in our students a sense of hope, strength, and courage despite the many problems and struggles they face?* We can empower students to evaluate culture and engage in it responsibly, and thus to have a positive impact on culture through positive media communication.

After answering these questions, you may want to consider some key values, skills, and activities you would like to incorporate in your unit. For your values consider what Paul wrote about the fruit of the Spirit (Ephesians 5). Go beyond personal ethics and morality, and consider such broad values as stewardship in economics; authenticity in communication; expressiveness and beauty in the arts; and accuracy and good judgment in observation, interpretation, and reasoning.

3. Formulate your unit theme and focus. A *thematic statement* describes the overall aim and approach of your unit, including the basic understandings, concepts, skills, values, dispositions, and commitments you want students to acquire. You also need to develop a set of *intended learning outcomes.* These emerge from your thematic statement but are more specific. They identify the desired results of classroom learning, and provide direction and balance. Outcomes include various emphases: content, abilities, values, and creative learning. Some teachers also formulate three or four *guiding questions* that help students focus on the unit's enduring understandings. They may post these and discuss them at the beginning and end of the unit. Figure 4 shows an example for a unit on media communications.

Figure 4 Sample Thematic Statement, Guiding Questions, and Intended Learning Outcomes

Lights, Camera, ACTION! A Grade 8 Unit on Media Communication
by Amanda Boyce, 2002

Thematic statement: The media both reflect and shape society. In this unit, students will study media as forms of communication. They will identify different kinds of media and the characteristics and effects of each kind. They will consider how the power of the media can be wielded both positively and destructively. They will explore how the media promote certain themes and biases, and how those affect both individuals and communities. The students will develop their skills in analyzing, discerning, and critiquing media communication as they distinguish between God's reality and the media's contrived "reality." They will reflect on their interaction and involvement with the media, and will participate in media communication. They will recognize their responsibility to engage in the media in a God-glorifying way. They will develop their media communication skills in order to begin to implement a Christian approach to media communication.

Guiding questions:

- How do the media wield their power in society?
- How do the media inform and affect the values of society and individuals?
- How has the role of the media changed over time?
- What is God's intention for media communication? How can the students contribute to fulfilling that intention?

Intended learning outcomes: *It is expected that students will:*

KNOW:

1. Define media and media communication.
2. Identify various types of media, their attributes and implications.
3. Investigate the characteristics, structure, emphases, and roles of media communication.
4. Identify and understand the positive and destructive influences of the media, both personally and on society.
5. Recognize the implicit and explicit biases in the media.
6. Investigate and justify a Christian orientation to media communication.

DO:

1. Analyze the role of the media in their everyday lives.
2. Evaluate the role, influence, and biases of media communication.
3. Compare and contrast media communication in different times and places.
4. Develop and justify a personal orientation to media communication.
5. Develop and demonstrate oral, written, and visual presentation skills in media contexts.
6. Design a form of media communication.

VALUE:

1. Appreciate the media as avenues for expressing God-given creativity.
2. Appreciate the media as a means of revealing and spreading God's truth.
3. Learn the importance of honesty, integrity, fairness, and clarity in communication.
4. Recognize their responsibility as Christ's disciples to engage in authentic and positive communication.
5. Demonstrate their commitment to glorify God in oral, written, and visual communication.

4. Design and choose learning activities. Steps 4 through 8 are best done simultaneously. For instance, your activities will depend to some extent on your resources. Also, if you design a learning activity related to one or more learning outcomes, you should decide at the same time how you will assess whether your students have attained those outcomes.

Check that:

- Each learning activity contributes to one or more learning outcomes. The whole set of activities should do justice to your overall theme.
- The range of learning activities is suitable for students with different ability levels and learning styles. All students should have opportunities for involvement and personal response.
- Your activities promote the learning of meaningful concepts and enduring understandings, worthwhile abilities and thinking skills, and important values and commitments.
- Your introductory activity is motivational, and your concluding activity reviews the main theme, understandings, and values.

5. Incorporate external standards. Many states and provinces expect Christian schools to follow specific guidelines or standards. In some instances we must reject such dictates (e.g., to teach a perspective in family life education that contradicts God's directives). Often, however, the standards help our students become contributing members of society.

6. Plan a schedule. Using your yearly outline as a guide, decide how many weeks the unit will take. Also decide how much time you will spend on the unit each day. Make a time chart to keep yourself on track.

7. Select suitable resources. Selecting textbooks and resources is an important step in curriculum planning. Resources are valuable learning tools. However, some of the available ones promote worldviews and values that are at odds with Christian ones. For example, some textbooks suggest that technology can solve humankind's problems. They may promote the view that human beings are autonomous and can choose their own values. They may imply that faith and religion are of little significance, and that Christianity has been a negative influence in culture. No resources are impartial, and they do have an influence on students.

It is important, therefore, that you and your school choose resources carefully. Here are some questions to guide your decisions:

- What commitments, values, priorities, and goals does the resource state or assume? Does it promote biblical norms for ethical, economic, aesthetic, and family life? Are there any overt or subtle biases?

- What topics and issues does the resource consider important? Do they match your priorities and goals?
- Does the resource support different types of learning activities, encouraging students to be thoughtful, responsive, and creative? Is the level of difficulty suitable?

If the perspective of the resource differs from yours, ask how you can still use it to meet your goals. If it is a Christian resource, check whether its perspective is well thought out without giving glib answers to difficult issues.

8. Plan student assessment. You use assessment activities to give your students feedback and improve their learning. Assessment also helps you make decisions about future teaching and learning strategies. Make it an integral part of your unit design, and use varied strategies. Align learning outcomes, learning activities, student products, and assessment strategies. Chapter 12 will discuss student assessment and evaluation.

9. Review the effectiveness of your unit. Once you have finished teaching the unit, spend a few minutes reviewing it. Did you realize the unit's intended outcomes? Did the students grasp the key themes and enduring understandings? Which learning strategies were successful? Which fell short of your expectations? Were the resources appropriate? Was the student assessment suitable and helpful? What can you celebrate? What should you change next time? Make some notes and put them with your unit file or box.

Implementing the Curriculum

Effective curriculum improvement requires the support of the whole Christian school community. A major innovation, such as a new language arts program, requires wide-ranging consultations to establish a climate of trust and to assure that the new program supports the school's mission. Teachers, administrators, parents, and students must understand and support the program's rationale, goals, and main features. They must also be convinced that the proposed program will benefit learning. Curriculum leaders—principals, department chairs, grade coordinators, and classroom teachers—need to be committed to the change.

Teachers are at the heart of effective curriculum change. They are involved in assessing programs, designing alternatives, evaluating resources, and implementing new programs. They need training and support—and adequate time. They must feel free to learn from their initiatives and make revisions to fit their own situation. A major change usually takes at least three years to implement: one year for discussion and planning, one for having some teachers pilot parts of the new program, and one or more years for general implementation.

Deliberation and assessment take place throughout the process as schools ask such questions as the following:

- Are the program content and learning strategies as well as the resources in harmony with the school's mission and vision?
- Are the teachers successfully implementing the program? Why or why not?
- What effects does the program have on students' knowledge, discernment, skills and abilities, values, dispositions, and commitments? What impact does the hidden curriculum have on the program?
- What are the program's strengths and weaknesses? Does it meet quality and quantity standards? Is it up-to-date? How do the results compare with those of programs in other schools?
- Do the results justify the cost in time, money, and emotional investment?

Principals as Curriculum Leaders

It is essential that principals take leadership in planning and implementing a Christ-centered curriculum. Principals continually ask whether the curriculum supports the school's purpose, vision, and values. They work at establishing a shared sense of mission throughout the school community. Also, they invest in, support, equip, and pray for their teachers. They use them in both formal and informal curriculum leadership capacities. They share responsibility and authority without seeking personal reward.

Principals build on teachers' strengths, celebrate their successes, and deal with setbacks. They are knowledgeable but understanding, purposeful but patient. Their authority comes from holding fast to the word of life (Philippians 2:16). Like Jesus, they testify to the truth in word and deed. They promote the lordship of Christ throughout the curriculum. In short, they build a sense of community in their school, and lead with insightful but compassionate authority.

Summary

No curriculum is neutral. Therefore, Christian schools need to carefully consider how their worldview basis, values, and aims affect their yearly overviews, unit plans, and choice of resources. All curriculum elements must support students in becoming committed to Jesus Christ and to a Christian way of life, able and willing to serve God, neighbor, and society. Those who design or adapt classroom units need to formulate a thematic statement, basic guiding questions, and intended learning outcomes. They should assess resources for their stated or assumed commitments, values, and priorities. Effective curriculum improvement requires that the entire school community understand and support proposed changes, and that the curriculum leaders establish a shared sense of mission in a supportive environment.

About the Author

Harro Van Brummelen is a professor and dean of education at Trinity Western University in Langley, British Columbia (vanbrumm@twu.ca).

Strengthen Your Foundations

1. Choose a grade level and a subject for which you have a curriculum guide available. Use the sample yearly overview grid (figure 3) to develop the beginning of a yearly course outline. Ensure that the outline reflects the mission and aims of your school.

2. Choose a textbook or other classroom resource. Answer the questions at the end of the section on selecting suitable resources to determine whether and how you would use the resource in your classroom.

3. With two or three other persons, consider why a particular unit topic would be a significant one to teach in a Christian school. Then answer the four worldview questions in this chapter, if applicable. Suggest some enduring understandings, basic skills, and central values for teaching the topic. List some key points that you would include in a thematic statement.

4. For a unit topic that you have taught or will teach in the future, develop a thematic statement, guiding questions, and intended learning outcomes. What types of learning strategies would support this unit focus?

5. Suppose your school wants to develop and implement a new social studies program. Your principal has asked you to lead a task force that will guide the process. List the steps you will take to ensure that the program supports your school's goals, has the support of the school community, and leads to meaningful student learning.

6. With a group of three or four other teachers in your school (if you currently teach), evaluate the program for one of your subjects. Use the questions in the "Implementing the Curriculum" section as a guide.

References

Boyce, Amanda. 2002. Lights, camera, ACTION! A unit on communication in the media. Unpublished curriculum unit. Trinity Western University.

Keenan, Derek. 1998. *Curriculum development for Christian schools.* Colorado Springs, CO: Association of Christian Schools International.

Van Brummelen, Harro. 2002. *Steppingstones to curriculum: A biblical path.* 2d ed. Colorado Springs, CO: Purposeful Design Publications.

CHAPTER TWELVE

Christian School Assessment: Philosophy and Practice

Timothy L. Heaton and Brian Coon

Developing a philosophy and practice of assessment is a crucial task for any educator. It is especially vital for Christian educators to know why they are doing what they are doing in grading the students entrusted to them. They also need to know whether there is a biblical foundation for their practices in assessment and grading.

A philosophy of assessment is not a new concept. John Blanchard wrote the following in *Christian Teacher* magazine:

> We teach in a day and age when many educators are abandoning the concept of grading and [with it] the concept of accountability. Our task as Christian educators, however, is not to avoid man's confrontation with responsibility, but to strengthen it by making it more meaningful, accurate, and consistent with our philosophy of Christian education. (1970, 27)

Several questions arise concerning the role of assessment in the Christian school:

- Can we as teachers accurately assess the knowledge, ability, and effort of the students in our class?
- Are students, as creations of God, too complex for us to make paper and pencil assessments of their effort, ability, and knowledge?
- Is there a biblical way to assess students that can be meaningful and can result in a valid grade?
- Why do we grade? What is the purpose of assessment?
- Is averaging or curving the grades a valid way to assess student learning?
- What role do learning styles and modalities play in assessment?
- Does assessment contribute to our students' becoming lifelong learners and biblical thinkers?
- How can we develop assessments that go beyond the knowledge level in Bloom's Taxonomy?
- Do we determine advancement in a way that is consistent with God's standards, or do we adopt a system developed by the secular schools that is based on a comparison of children's performance?

Any Christian school parent, teacher, or administrator is likely to agree that the Christian school should operate differently than one that is not Christ-centered. Because we as Christians believe that we should "do all for the glory of God," it seems that Christian schools should be superior to others—in content because every subject is examined in the context of a biblical worldview, and in educational practice because Christian teachers begin with the view that they are dealing not only with a student but with a child of our Creator. While we are quick to allow ourselves differences in philosophy and practice in areas such as content, discipline, and instruction, there are many areas of education, such as assessment, in which we blindly follow the standard practices.

If we truly mean to hold ourselves to a higher standard, we must scrutinize every classroom practice in the light of biblical principles. Unfortunately, the Bible leaves us with no instruction on how to assess our students: Christ didn't quiz His disciples on the Beatitudes. He recorded no percentages in the Lamb's Book of Life. We can, however, base our philosophy of assessment on the principles of God's Word.

First, because we understand that our students are children of God, we must give them first priority in our classrooms. Without this fundamental principle, any practice fails to reach the level of excellence expected of a Christian institution. And because our job is education, every effort we make in the classroom must further our students' education so that they may become lifelong learners.

Let us pause a moment to develop the subject of *lifelong learning,* as it is core to this philosophy of assessment. A teacher has either the laborious task of getting a student to learn all the content he will need to know or the noble task of teaching him to think critically. From Bloom's Taxonomy, we clearly see that encouraging students to memorize facts is not nearly as lofty a goal as teaching them to analyze facts critically in order to form their own unique and significant ideas.

This distinction is even more important for Christian teachers, who have the responsibility of developing in their students the ability to be biblically critical thinkers. Just as it is important that we teach our students to *analyze, synthesize,* and *evaluate* (higher levels of thinking in Bloom's Taxonomy), we must also teach them to use that same critical thinking ability to examine this world though the lens of the Word. In so doing, we are developing in them a Bible-centered worldview.

Assessment, if used correctly, can challenge a student to do that kind of thinking. With this in mind, Christian educators must acknowledge that assessment provides an opportunity for further education and perhaps is not simply a useful tool for instruction but the most powerful device in their arsenal.

Definitions of Terms (and the Implications)

Discussions of assessment are often accompanied by words such as *evaluation* and *grading*. These words are often used interchangeably, but their definitions have subtle differences. Webster defines *assessment* and *evaluation* synonymously as "determining, appraising, or judging the value of." To be a bit more precise, we will address *assessment* as the tool for evaluating and *evaluation* as the act of using the assessment tool. Grading, however, is "giving a mark or rating to." Although both evaluating and grading are part of the process of measuring a student, each has its own purpose and place. Think about shifting a car manually. The process of changing from first gear to second involves releasing the accelerator, pressing the clutch, moving the gearshift, releasing the clutch, and reapplying the gas. Although this series of acts is reduced to what we call *shifting*, each act individually serves a different function in the process. Similarly, for *assessment* we must first evaluate a student and then assign a grade to complete the process.

The purpose of evaluation is to allow the teacher to assess what learning has taken place and what changes in instructional methods need to be made. But when the student is the first priority and instruction is the focus, evaluation has much greater potential. Evaluation has the capability of furthering the process of instruction. Grading is a product, but evaluation is a process; a value or percentage recorded in a grade book teaches nothing, but a good assessment can teach.

In order to find a system of assessment that is able to continue the students' education, we must understand what assessment is and what it is not. Assessment is not a perfect system. As long as biases are involved in the processes of creating tests and grading them, we cannot eliminate the subjective nature of grading. All educators have some expectations and assumptions about a student's knowledge level that become evident when they make up a test and when they grade.

A teacher has no concrete means of determining what a student has learned over the course of an academic year any more than she can tell how much effort a student has put into an assignment. The work one student accomplishes in an hour may take an evening for another. While one student may need to study for hours to be successful at a test, another may need only a short review session. We must realize that no system of evaluation can account fully for every complicated facet of a student's learning process, and we ought not to trouble ourselves with searching for one. Instead, a teacher who truly has her students' best interest at heart will strive for an assessment technique that leaves the smallest margin of error possible. This form of assessment—although not flawless—must be a system that is ongoing, multifaceted, and both formal and informal.

The ongoing nature of assessment is of vital importance. As we have stated, assessment is not a product (as is grading) but a process. The process begins on the first day of class and extends until the last chance for instruction. Assessment must be incremental, taking advantage of many small opportunities to show the student's growth over time. These assessments need not be large, formal undertakings. (Nor should they be; it's difficult to say whether weekly "tests" would be more strenuous and agitating for the teacher or the student.) They need only be frequent.

It will be clear by now that this kind of assessment demands much of the teacher. Such a philosophy of assessment is not suitable for the teacher accustomed to using the same handouts year after year or pulling the same Scantron-graded multiple choice test for every unit. Instead, these proposals are for the teacher who is willing to bring time and creativity to the development of assessment tools that are capable of teaching students in ways that lectures or quizzes cannot. In such a classroom the teacher must take the time to know what the students are like as learners and how best to advance their education.

The concept that ongoing evaluation begins on day one of the class means just that. If we mean to base our assessment on a student's development instead of solely on achievement, we must know where that growth process begins. This approach requires that the teacher begin evaluating immediately. Again, formal testing is clearly inappropriate in the first days of a class, but a simple conversation with students (individually or in groups) can typically give an indication of what they know. Over time small evaluations like these can come together to show an attentive teacher what learning is taking place.

If a teacher plans to evaluate often, it is important that the assessment be multifaceted. In order to assess students fairly, we must give each student what he needs. This means that we do not assess all children in the same way but find the best way of assessing each one. Instead of repeatedly using tests that measure logical-mathematical or verbal-linguistic intelligences, we need to explore other ways of evaluating our students' learning. For example, having students create a concept map, make up a story, create an art project, or write their thoughts in a journal can indicate what learning has taken place while avoiding the monotony of standardized testing. We tend to teach and test the way we were taught and tested, but that may not be the best way for every student. Jesus recognized that Thomas was a skeptic and needed tangible evidence to prove that He was alive, so He told Thomas to touch Him.

It may be impractical for a teacher with twenty or more students to come up with an individual assessment plan for every child, but simply offering students some assignment choices allows them to choose the method that suits them best. Multifaceted assessment calls for using a different kind of assessment each time students are evaluated: for example, a short quiz, Socratic questioning, building a project, creating a skit. While the teacher may assess the whole class in the same way, over time each student will encounter different types of assessment.

Similarly, evaluations should be both formal and informal. Informal evaluations happen daily, with little if any advance warning. For example, discussing a passage from an assigned reading can serve as an excellent evaluation. If such a discussion is done properly, a student doesn't need to know that evaluation is taking place. These informal evaluations are easier for the teacher (requiring less preparation and grading; see sample 1 at the end of this chapter for informal assessment) and their casual and candid nature will appeal to the students. The formal evaluation requires advance notice, allotted time to complete the assessment, and a rubric. A teacher who employs skits, projects, stories, or essays (all excellent multifaceted formal assessment tools) must develop a rubric (see sample 1) to indicate how the assessment will be graded.

Finally, we need to be conscious that our evaluation challenges the development of our students. The core of education—especially Christian education—should be the children's holistic development, but the types of assessment used in many classrooms do not reflect that goal. In the typical school setting, academic achievement is the primary focus, and our tests are oriented to determine what the students learned, what facts they memorized, and how much they can reproduce. Although achievement is certainly important, we should never lose our focus on the development of a student as a learner (and a "lifelong learner"). In this case, development refers to the progress the student made over time: not simply recalling factual information but comprehending, appreciating, and applying the material.

For instance, in a study of Shakespeare's *Macbeth*, a test that requires the students to place events in the order in which they happened or to match quotations with the characters who spoke them will give the teacher a sound evaluation of what the students have achieved academically. But such a test fails to take advantage of a much greater opportunity for determining and challenging their academic development. A test that asks the students to explain what themes they found in the play, or how the characters relate to each other, or what biblical principles the characters violated will indicate whether or not the students have been able to comprehend universal themes in the play that can be applied to life. Every teacher needs to evaluate his goals: Is it more commendable to fill a student's mind with literary information or help that student learn to appreciate literature? Next, the educator must examine his evaluation techniques to see exactly what is being assessed. If appreciation is the goal, he must keep in mind that it is never necessary to test students over material they can look up. Today, the Internet provides a boundless and ever-available resource for factual information. Forcing students to memorize what they have at their immediate disposal seems a waste of precious class time. However, enabling students to understand and form connections between the curriculum and their lives provides them with an invaluable tool they will use for a lifetime.

Assessment in Practice

To base assessment practices on a philosophy that values students as unique creations of God, the teacher needs to follow several steps:

If the goals and objectives for the course were established in the planning process, the teacher simply needs to make sure that the assessment will show whether those goals and objectives have been met. For example, if the school's mission statement includes "to develop students who are biblical thinkers," our questions should assess whether our students are thinking biblically in the context of their literature studies and whether they are using analysis, synthesis, evaluation, and application.

The practice of assessment is a process. Just as a student learns gradually over time from her accomplishments as well as her mistakes, the classroom teacher should be prepared to try various kinds of assessment. The methods that lead to further development of the student should be noted and repeated, and those that prove unproductive should be modified or abandoned. Thus, for the teacher, assessment involves a learning process that gradually results in improvement. There are, however, certain guidelines that all teachers should follow in order to achieve authentic assessment. What follows is a collection of those guidelines: practical hints and tips to follow (and improve on when possible) in order to develop one's own methods of assessment.

Testing and Grading

For better or worse, testing has become the hallmark of the grading and assessment process. The formal, structured test has typically been viewed as the culmination of the process and is weighted accordingly. However, this should not be the case, for such a test cannot fully measure what students have learned.

Testing Tips

- Use pretests and posttests. The pretest is important in establishing a baseline of the student's prior knowledge and an understanding of what will be taught. Both pretests and posttests can be done in the traditional structured format, using similar tests at the beginning and end of a unit as a part of an ongoing assessment. Progress is seen by comparing the results of the two tests.
- Give students multiple attempts at the same test. Many students will learn more going over a test they have taken than they did in preparing for it. Although the test should appear in a different format, it shouldn't matter if it is retaken as long as the student learns the content.
- Remember that tests indicate not only how much a student has learned but how well we have taught. If a student is failing, the teacher is failing—until he finds out the reason why. Our job as teachers is to be diagnosticians in the assessment process. The teacher who has taught well and assessed in an ongoing, multifaceted way will find each student's areas of weakness and address them before giving a grade.
- Don't test students over what they can look up. Teach them how and where to find information.

- Be creative in your testing. Not only are Scantron tests dull and tedious, but they are rarely capable of testing the upper levels of Bloom's taxonomy. Create application-oriented assessments that challenge students to think. (They may even enjoy such assessments.)
- Taking a test doesn't necessarily mean sitting down at a desk with paper and pencil. Evaluation can be done through problem-solving activities or relevant projects. Think outside the box!

Homework

Many teachers use the evaluation of homework as a major part of a student's overall grade. While this practice isn't necessarily a problem, it is a die-hard tradition in our schools, and explaining why we assign homework can be difficult. Teachers should use homework as an instructional or assessment tool when it is the best means, but they certainly should not feel any need to make daily take-home assignments. Assessment is possible without homework, and teachers are not failing if their students leave the classroom without having a task to complete for the next day's class. When assigning homework, teachers should keep the following in mind:

- Parents can regularly be heavily involved in "helping" their children with homework. Teachers should be sure they're assessing their students instead of the willingness of the parents to become involved.
- The teacher cannot count on the necessary resources being equally available to all students. A student who has resource materials at home, lives near a library, or has a good computer with Internet access enjoys a distinct advantage over one who doesn't.
- Because evaluating homework authentically is nearly impossible (for the reasons noted above), it is wise not to include it in the student's grade. Returning an assignment to the student for correction and resubmission has more potential, both for instruction and for ongoing assessment.
- Many students don't like homework. Not that our classrooms should be run as democracies, but if the same objectives can be met using, for instance, conversation in discussion groups, teachers can take advantage of that fact.

Late Assignments and the Use of Zeros

For the teacher who doesn't rely on homework or out-of-class assignments, late assignments are not a problem. The teacher who depends on homework, however, needs to determine what she accomplishes by lowering the grade of a late assignment. In most cases, late assignments are a result of some character issue, such as irresponsibility. Such character qualities, though they can be appraised, should never be included in the grading of an academic subject. The teacher should grade the student on his academic achievement and deal with character issues through nurturing and training, not grades.

Assigning a zero is one of the most devastating things a teacher can do to a student. A zero is typically given to students who fail to turn in assignments or turn them in late, without names, or defective in some other way. The practice fails to represent the student's true academic accomplishments, discourages the student, and destroys his motivation to learn. If the student makes any attempt to do the assignment, grade it.

Effort

Effort is often included as part of a student's grade even though it is difficult if not impossible to measure. Though we may say that we know what our students are capable of doing, the development of the child has too many variables—intellect, background knowledge, ability, learning style, interest—that prevent us from evaluating effort accurately.

Grading in Class

One of the most detrimental things that can happen to a student is for another student to know his grade. Many teachers have students trade papers and grade each other's work. Some even have students call out their grades so they can be recorded. Though this practice is convenient and time-saving, it is hardly considerate of the individual. For students who struggle or are unprepared, the results are often poor, and those students earn a reputation with the others. For those who consistently do well, the results are good academically, but they too earn a negative image, that of a "nerd" or "brain." When others know what a given student did on an assignment or test, they develop an image of that student, who is soon labeled. If the teacher is trying to nurture students and celebrate their uniqueness, this practice certainly violates that purpose.

The Use of Rubrics

A rubric is a tool used in evaluating each piece of work in an ongoing assessment. Rubrics monitor a student's performance by showing exactly what the teacher expects. They are especially helpful for multifaceted or nontraditional assignments, for which it is imperative that students be provided with the guidelines by which they will be graded.

Rubrics can also be used for students' self-evaluation of what they have learned in accordance with the stated rubric. Peer evaluators can also use rubrics in assessing one another's work. The student may more easily spot errors and weaknesses in her own and others' work with the guidance afforded by a rubric. (See sample 1.)

When developing a rubric, teachers should remember to do the following:

- Give examples of good work and poor work, describing what makes them good and poor.
- List criteria for what is to be included.
- Study other rubric models.
- Use self-assessment and peer assessment to get students' feedback on, and involvement with, the rubric from time to time.
- Revise the rubric, using the performance of the students to evaluate both it and your teaching strategies; be willing to change teaching strategies or the rubric itself in order to better assess student learning.

(Andrade 2002)

Narrative Grading

One of the best ways to communicate the quality of a student's work is to use a narrative form of grading. Essential learning skills are established for each subject at each academic level. The teacher then evaluates the student in a particular area and writes a complete description of the student's growth. (See sample 2.) This process is lengthy and should happen more often than once at the end of each six-week grading period. Some schools have coupled a narrative form of assessment with a checklist of skills, content, and behaviors to be mastered. (See sample 3.)

"Bell Curve" and Grade Averaging

Using a bell-shaped curve to arrive at students' grades is probably the least biblical method of all. The teacher arrives at a grade by comparing each student with the others in the group rather than assessing individual progress. Education isn't a competition, and our students shouldn't be forced to contend with each other for a grade. If every student in the classroom exhibits *A* work, then every student should receive an *A*.

Grade averaging also represents a student's learning inadequately. A student may have done poorly at the beginning of a term, when she was first struggling with a concept, but may show progress once she has learned it. Yet her final grade is affected adversely when the teacher averages in the initial low grades. Similarly, any number of circumstances can cause a student not to do well on a given examination. Although she may know the material, she may not do well on a particular day. Some teachers have tried to improve the system of averaging by weighting certain assessments more heavily than others in order to give a truer picture of what the students know. However, most teachers weigh only major tests more heavily, resulting in an inaccurate report on students' knowledge.

Portfolios

The goal of Christian teachers should be to establish the most authentic methods of assessment possible. Through ongoing and multifaceted assessment, the teacher gains a reasonably accurate picture of what the student has learned, is learning, and still needs to learn. Traditional multiple choice and true-false exams give little information, showing only how many answers the student got right or wrong. One way to provide a more accurate assessment of what the student has actually learned is to use portfolios that include multifaceted assessments—pre- and posttests, journals, creative projects, role plays, and scenario analyses. The portfolio becomes a paper trail that follows the student through the year, showing his strengths and weaknesses with the course content.

Conclusion

Since we all have sinned and live in a world affected by the Fall, there can never be a perfect grading system. And of course there will never be perfect tests or students. The best we can do is use a grading system that edifies the individual student as a child of God. All our students are unique. They all learn differently. Our system must use a variety of means to assess the authentic learning of each one. We need to make sure our assessments help to fulfill our mission of producing biblical thinkers and lifelong learners.

About the Authors

Timothy L. Heaton is an associate professor of education at Cedarville University, Cedarville, Ohio. He has over thirty years' experience in Christian education as a teacher and principal. He has authored numerous articles about education and is a frequent speaker at teacher conventions and school in-services. Dr. Heaton most recently presented nationwide an ACSI Enabler on "Choosing Textbooks for Christian Schools."

Brian Coon is a senior integrated language arts education and theater major at Cedarville University. This chapter on "Christian School Assessment: Philosophy and Practice" is the result of a collaborative project on alternative assessment done in Dr. Heaton's Philosophy of Education class.

Sample 1: Rubric for Assessing Students Informally

Rating Scale

1 poor **2** fair/needs improvement **3** average/satisfactory **4** good **5** high/excellent

Categories evaluated informally Circle the number that best describes the student.

1. Interest in subject area

• Uninterested/poor knowledge base (intervention needed)	1	2	3	4	5
• Interested and does work assigned	1	2	3	4	5
• Very interested, curious, wants to learn more	1	2	3	4	5
• Excited about topic, has knowledge, makes application	1	2	3	4	5
• Bored, critical, has excellent knowledge of topic	1	2	3	4	5

2. Participation in collaborative group

• Prepared with work for the group	1	2	3	4	5
• Shows responsible leadership with role in group	1	2	3	4	5
• Productive talk; good use of time	1	2	3	4	5
• Strives for unity in group; good problem solving	1	2	3	4	5

Other categories that could be developed (vary according to subject area)

Use of language in written work
Use of vocabulary in written work
Application of biblical principles in problem solving
Character development
Creativity

Sample 2: Weekly Narrative Evaluation

Name: *Johnny Smith* Teacher *Mrs. Coon*
Subject *Mathematics* Date *9/30* Grade level *3rd*

Criterion Mastery in reciting from memory the multiplication table to nines.
Johnny has improved in his memory work on the multiplication tables. He has mastered all but the eights and nines tables, which he tends to mix. He has improved in the nines by using a finger system, and he will be practicing it to help him distinguish the answers for the two tables.

Sample 3: Weekly Narrative with Criterion Checklist

Name *Jon Jones* Date 9/15 Teacher *Mrs. M. Harrlman*
Subject *Spelling* Grade Level 1

Jon is having problems in the areas below that are not marked with a check. We have decided to color code all the letters in a word, using green for the first letter and red for the last letter. He has achieved satisfactory mastery in those areas that are marked with a check.

Recognizes and identifies all vowel sounds	✓
Identifies diphthongs in two-syllable words	✓
Identifies digraphs in two-syllable words	
Recognizes and identifies consonants	✓
Does weekly oral spelling correctly	✓
Writes weekly spelling words correctly	

Strengthen Your Foundations

1. In light of God's sovereignty and His plan for our lives, why should we as Christian teachers be concerned about assessing our academic achievement? Will it actually make any difference?

2. In Christian education we talk about the development of the whole child. However, how much time do we really spend on the teaching of character qualities, the development of the children's God-given gifts, and the formation of their sense of morality and biblical thinking skills? If these are truly important, how can we properly assess these items and give an accurate representation of where students are in their growth process?

3. Honestly think about, and discuss with other teachers, how important grades are to the total education of a child and whether there is a better evaluation/assessment method to show us what a student really knows.

4. How does Christ assess us? How can we use His methods of evaluation to assess academic and character qualities in the classroom?

5. The education system as we know it today, with grades, grade levels, classrooms, and tests, is a fairly recent invention. Consider and study how people have been taught and evaluated throughout the ages and try to conceptualize whether a new Christian school model/structure is needed rather than a copy of the secular institutions.

6. How are we assessed in real life? How frequently are grades used? What criteria are used to measure our performance? Are these methods biblical? What implications does this have for our assessment of students in the classroom?

References

Agnew, John E. 1985. The grading policies and practices of high school teachers (March /April). Paper presented at the annual meeting of the American Educational Research Association, Chicago, IL.

Anderson, Rebecca S. 1998. Why talk about different ways to grade? The shift from traditional assessment to alternative assessment. *New Directions for Teaching and Learning* 74: 5–16.

Andrade, Heidi Goodrich. 2002. Understanding rubrics. Retrieved July 2, 2002, from http://learnweb.harvard.edu/alps/thinking/

docs/rubricar.htm; retrieved July 17, 2003, from http://www.middleweb.com/rubricsHG.html.

Austin, Susan, and Richard McCann. 1992. Here's another arbitrary grade for your collection: A statewide study of grading policies (April). Paper presented at the annual meeting of the American Educational Research Association, San Francisco, CA.

Blanchard, John F. 1970. Toward a Christian approach to grading. *Christian Teacher* (November/December).

Brookhart, Susan M. 1994. Teachers' grading: Practice and theory. *Applied Measurement in Education* 7, no. 4: 279–301.

Brown, Diana. n.d. Homework ... help or horror experience? FEA/United. Retrieved June 2, 2002, from http://www.yesiteach.org/homework.htm.

Bursuck, William D., and Dennis D. Munk. 1997. Can grades be helpful and fair? *Educational Leadership* 55, no. 4: 44–47.

Cizek, Gregory J. 1998. The assessment revolution's unfinished business. *Kappa Delta Pi Record* 34: 144–49.

Cizek, Gregory J. et al. 1995. Further investigation of teachers' assessment (April). Paper presented at the annual meeting of the American Educational Research Association, San Francisco, CA.

Cross, Lawrence. 1995. Testing Memo 6: *What kinds of grades should be averaged?* and Testing Memo 11: *Absolute versus relative grading standards: What does a percentage mean?* Blacksburg: Office of Measurement and Research Services, Virginia Polytechnic Institute and State University.

Culbertson, Linda Doutt, and Mary Renck Jalongo. 1999. But what's wrong with letter grades? Responding to parents' questions about alternative assessment. *Childhood Education* 75, no. 3: 130–35.

Curren, Randall R. 1995. Coercion and the ethics of grading and testing. *Educational Theory* 45, no. 4: 425–41.

Failing grades for late assignments: Teaching responsibility or giving permission to fail? Retrieved July 2, 2002, from http://www.middleweb.com/INCASEfailingrades.html.

Frisbie, David A., and Kristie K. Waltman. 1992. Developing a personal grading plan. *Educational Measurement: Issues and Practice* (fall).

Guskey, Thomas R. 1994. Making the grade: What benefits students? *Educational Leadership* 52, no. 2: 14–20.

Kohn, Alfie. 1994. Grading: The issue is not how but why. *Educational Leadership* 52: 38–41.

Kuhlman, Edward. 1986. *The master teacher.* Old Tappan, NJ: Fleming H. Revell.

MacIver, Douglas, and David A. Reuman. 1994. Giving their best: Grading and recognition practices that motivate students to work hard. *American Educator: The Professional Journal of the American Federation of Teachers* 17, no. 4: 24–31.

Maine, Karen, n.d. Let's worry more about assessing students and less about grading them. Retrieved July 2, 2002, from http://www.middleweb.com/INCASEgrades.html.

Marzano, Robert J. 2000. What are grades for? In *Transforming classroom grading.* Retrieved July 17, 2003, from http://ascd.org/publications/books/2000marzano/chapter2.html.

Marzano, Robert J., Debra J. Pickering, and Jay McTighe. 1993. *Assessing student outcomes: Performance assessment using the dimensions of learning model.* Alexandria, VA: Association for Supervision and Curriculum Development.

Mead, James V. 1992. *Teachers' evaluations of student work.* East Lansing, MI: National Center for Research on Teacher Learning.

O'Conner, Ken. 1995. Guidelines for grading that support learning and student success. *NASSP Bulletin* 79, no. 571: 91–101.

Perkins, David N., Heidi Goodrich, Shari Tishman, and Jill M. Owen. 1994. *Thinking connection: Learning to think and thinking to learn.* Reading, PA: Addison-Wesley.

Ray, Susan. n.d. A teacher researches a middle school's grading practices. Retrieved July 2, 2002, from http://www.middleweb.com/INCASEgrdresrch.html.

Reedy, Randy. 1995. Formative and summative assessment: A possible alternative to the grading-reporting dilemma. *NAASP Bulletin* 79, no. 573: 47–51.

Robinson, Glen E., and James M. Craver. 1989. *Assessing and grading student achievement.* ERS Report. Arlington, VA: Educational Research Service.

Schneider, Tom. 2000. Everybody's a winner. Retrieved July 2, 2002, from http://www.connectingwithkids.com.

Terwilliger, James S. 1989. Classroom standard setting and grading practices. *Educational Measurement: Issues and Practice* 8, no. 2: 15–19.

Warren, Jonathan R. 1975. *The continuing controversy over grades.* TM Report 51. Princeton, NJ: ERIC Clearinghouse on Tests, Measurement, and Evaluation.

Wasley, Patricia A. 1991. Stirring the chalkdust: Changing practices in essential schools. *Teachers College Record* 93: 29–58.

Wendel, Fredrick C., and Kenneth E. Anderson. 1994. Grading and marking systems: What are the practices, standards? *NASSP Bulletin* 78, no. 558: 79–84.

CHAPTER THIRTEEN

Moral and Character Development

Milton V. Uecker

A school's philosophy of education is evident through an examination of its mission, core values, and goals or outcomes. Cognitive, affective, and psychomotor standards must be carefully aligned with philosophy. During the "outcomes-based education" debates of the late eighties, education was criticized for the disproportionate number of affective outcomes as compared to cognitive ones. Critics contended that schools were meant to be academic (focused on the cognitive domain) and that affective standards (those related to values and behavior) were the culprit behind the "dumbing down" of curriculum. The contemporary call for school excellence continues to emphasize the need for academic rigor and to cast suspicion on "nonacademic" agendas. Still, a Christian school that does not give prominence to affective goals cannot fulfill the requirements of a Christian philosophy of education.

Commit to the Goal of Spiritual Formation

The Christian worldview is the basis for curriculum in a Christian school. In *Steppingstones to Curriculum* (2002), Harro Van Brummelen writes that a biblical curriculum must focus on four scriptural injunctions: the Creation Mandate, the Great Commission, the Great Commandment, and the Great Community. The Creation or Cultural Mandate is the motivation for cognitive outcomes. Through a study of the arts and sciences, we acquire the knowledge and skills for work and care of the creation. However, the remaining three injunctions require obedience to all that God has commanded and include the other-directed behaviors that characterize a life of love and service to others. Consequently, the goal of Christian school education must be to move the learner beyond salvation to spiritual formation and growth in character. "Sanctification is the lifelong process of bringing every thought, attitude, and action into captivity, allowing the Holy Spirit to convict and transform so that we are changed into the image of Christ, from one degree of glory to the next" (Uecker 2002, i). For the Christian school, moral and character education is inseparable from spiritual formation. The goal of biblical instruction is always a changed learner. Understanding involves seeing what significance the knowledge has for oneself and acting on it—changing to conform to it. Christian school education thus transforms the learner's life. "Both the planned and the hidden curricula develop attitudes, foster the acceptance of certain values, instill dispositions, and encourage certain commitments" (Van Brummelen 2002, 58). Character is a pattern of behavior and is demonstrated in relationships toward one another, and it is the goal of Christian school education that this behavior be characterized by moral excellence and other-directedness as defined by God.

David Krathwohl (as cited in Ornstein and Hunkins 1993) defines five levels within the affective domain ranging from receiving, attending to, and knowing values and beliefs to "characterization," his term for the highest level of internalization. At this level the student's behavior reflects a given set of values and demonstrates a philosophy of life. When moral and character development is the issue, it is imperative that the target be characterization. Too often educators are satisfied with a knowledge of definitions and memorization of biblical texts, or knowing rather than doing. The Bible itself makes clear that we are to move beyond hearing to doing (James 1:22).

The Bible gives us the blueprint for spiritual formation, or moral and character development, in Psalm 78:1–8 (NASB), where God outlines the steps in training a generation that would be unlike previous "stubborn and rebellious" ones, a generation characterized not by forgetting God's works but by *keeping His commandments*. Students are to be surrounded by teachers who proclaim God's "wondrous works" (v. 4). God is the center of the teachers' lives, and they can't seem to get over what He has done in and for them. Students who are seeking the reality of God find it in their teachers, who know and faithfully teach the "appointed law" and testimony found in God's Word (v. 5). The Word of God is the center of their instruction and is integrated into every concept. Critical to the process is the necessity to teach so that "the generation to come might know" (v. 6). It is one thing to teach so that students acquire facts but yet another to teach so that students see for themselves the significance of those facts and are made ready to act upon them. It is this "higher level knowing" and the methods that enable students to reach it that are the key to transforming the character of each learner. Outcomes must focus on behavior that is a fitting response to what has been learned. The first and most important response of students is to "put their confidence in God" (v. 7), and this response is the starting point for spiritual formation. Leading each child into a personal relationship with God through Jesus Christ must be a core value of the Christian school. It is a prerequisite in order that students will "not forget the works of God, but keep His commandments" (v. 7). Disciples of Jesus Christ are taught to "observe," or obey, all that He has commanded (Matthew 28:20).

For the Christian educator, morality is grounded in God's Word. Early-nineteenth-century editions of the dictionary referred to the law of God as the standard against which morality and character were to be determined. Unlike the relativity of the twenty-first century, the Judeo-Christian worldview of that time was evidenced in a revealed, absolute standard for right and wrong. When the Word is the standard, character education is a kind of biblical integration.

Understand Affective Development

Morality and character are formed through a gradual process that parallels cognitive growth and faith development. The environment and accompanying experiences are the dynamic variables related to a child's growth and development. The social dynamic between the learner and individuals of greater competence and maturity is a key to all learning and to character formation as well. Spiritual formation occurs through the interaction of mature models and the mediation of the Holy Spirit in the life of the learner. As the learner sees and experiences the truth within mentoring relationships, the Holy Spirit brings deeper understanding of the truth as well as the internalization and motivation that result in obedience. Paul understood this when he urged his students to imitate him and observe his pattern of behavior in "those who so walk" (Philippians 3:17). The Christian school shapes character not only by individual example but by the way administrators, teachers, and staff live together in community.

The moral development taxonomy, as described by various theorists, outlines stages that reflect Piaget's theory of cognitive growth. Each theorist refers to a growth in moral thinking that is based first in the learner's concrete experiences, including the rewards and punishments that accompany behavioral choices, then in choices motivated by a desire to conform and belong, and finally in the internalization or commitment to a belief or value.

An understanding of James Fowler's taxonomy of faith development (as cited in Astley and Francis 1992) is likewise essential when addressing spiritual formation. During the early childhood and elementary years, children are left with deep impressions of faith through the activities and celebrations of faith. They learn the "story" of their faith, and they slowly gain knowledge of the origins and behaviors of their faith group. By the time they reach preadolescence, their faith has become a set of beliefs and behaviors that identify them with that group—a family, a given denomination, and often a Christian school. The preadolescent has learned what to believe and do in order to belong. This immature view of faith is not in and of itself bad; however, should spiritual growth never move beyond this point, the young person will be vulnerable to putting on those behaviors and values that fit the context in which he or she operates. Moving students from the level of conforming faith to chosen faith is the critical work of adolescence and the Christian high school experience. By examining various beliefs and choosing some, the student makes a personal commitment to Christ and a Christian lifestyle. Christian faith becomes a part of the person's identity.

Although the process and its outcome may seem somewhat obvious, actualizing them in a school is a complex task. What characterizes a school that successfully promotes growth in moral thinking and character, one that graduates students who have chosen to live under the lordship of Christ?

It is in the public school arena that we find research that suggests "best practices" regarding character development in schools, since little comparable research exists for Christian schools. However, these best practices, when supplemented with Christian school philosophy, provide useful guidelines for developing effective Christian school programs. Thomas Lickona and Catherine Lewis (1997) suggest eleven characteristics of successful programs in character education. These characteristics provide the framework for the practices that follow.

Articulate Affective Standards

Christian schools have the distinct philosophical advantage of having an established standard for determining right and wrong behavior. However, even though they do not have to determine what character traits are important, they must define targeted outcomes, assign them developmentally, and then align them with the curriculum. Unless specific outcomes are identified, the scope of biblical character becomes unmanageable. The Ten Commandments, the fruit of the Spirit, the "one-anothers," and countless passages of Scripture (e.g., Romans 12, Colossians 3:12ff, 1 Peter 3:8–11) are the starting point. These biblical behaviors must be written as standards, or curriculum objectives (i.e., *Students will respond to the needs of the poor through acts of service within their community and around the world*). Each standard must then be assigned to an appropriate age group, which is arrived at by considering the developmental nature and needs of the students. For example, young children must learn to honor and submit to those in authority; preadolescents should learn biblical principles for their social growth and for handling relationships of all types; adolescents must learn to discern good and evil as they deal with life choices. In addition to student developmental levels, standards can align with the content of literature selections, social studies units, and the Bible curriculum itself.

Describe Character with Active Verbs

Too often the goals of character education take the form of verbal restatement. Such goals can be mastered by any student with a good memory, and they can be evaluated by means of definitions or verses on paper-and-pencil tests. It is one thing to articulate what God expects, but it requires an entirely different level of affective learning to reach standards that result in observable changes in behavior. Robert Coles says it this way:

> It is one thing to make a list of qualities that in their sum make for a good person or child; it is something else to try to picture oneself enacting this or that virtue, to live it out in daily life ... take those nouns that denote good moral traits and *with the help of students* try to convert them into verbs; tasks to accomplish, plans for action, to be followed by the actual work of doing. An imagined plan or plot is a mere prelude to a life's day-to-day behavior, yet over the long run of things, the sum of imagined plans turned into action becomes one's character. (1998, 16)

The standard "Children will honor their mother and father" must be translated into behaviors that demonstrate honor at the preschool or kindergarten level. In this example the children might help their mother set the table. Teachers would in turn teach them how to set the table so that they will learn what it means to "honor."

Create a Caring Community

A caring community offers students an immersion experience. As students work and interact among people who are other-directed, they experience character firsthand. A caring community provides abundant examples of the translation of *character* from a noun to a verb. What observable behaviors characterize a caring school community? Students experience servant leadership as they observe the administration serving teachers, parents, and students. Teachers observe and listen to students, control their own tongues, and reach out to those who struggle socially and academically. Rather than dismissing students with special needs, teachers embrace them. They help colleagues whose schedules have become overwhelming, and they encourage parents who are down. Students learn in such a school to have a heart for the lonely and to reach out to peers in need of friendship. The entire community is burdened for the lost and provides encouragement for spiritual growth. The school family demonstrates patience, compassion, and forgiveness. Everyone is valued and affirmed as an individual.

A school cannot expect its students to rise above its own character. When tension, cold interactions, self-interest, and barriers among faculty and students characterize a school, a nonbiblical set of affective goals have become the standard.

Provide a Moral Community

A moral community lives under authority and within defined standards of conduct. The school's leaders interpret the standards and provide just and loving discipline when necessary. Teachers view discipline and classroom management as important teaching opportunities, not as distractions from instruction. Discipline *is* instruction toward the goal of righteousness (Hebrews 12:11).

A moral community that leads to character is not militaristic. Rigidity, harshness, and fear are not marks of moral excellence, and the stress they cause prohibits both cognitive and affective learning. Old Testament motivations for godly behavior were primarily external, but New Testament motivations were to come from within. An environment characterized by external behavioral controls provides little or no opportunity for students to grow in self-control and personal responsibility.

A moral community is not legalistic. A legalistic environment elevates personal desires and behavioral expectations to the same level as biblical imperatives. Living according to the school's standards is equated with spirituality. The danger is that students can exhibit the expected behavior and mistakenly believe that such behavior is what it means to be Christian. It is true that a student whose life is yielded to Christ will be motivated to abide by the code, but abiding by the code is not the goal. Within every school there are clear biblical and moral imperatives that are part of the standards of conduct. These standards need to be taught as such. At the same time there are standards that have their origin in the school and are usually included to ensure a safe and orderly learning environment. These standards are followed because the student has voluntarily entered into membership. Rules about not chewing gum, not running in the halls, and dressing appropriately may be important to the functioning of the school, but they are mere preferences and should be justified as such. Not every rule and its appropriateness should be defended biblically. When a biblical defense is inappropriate, the outcome may be a legalistic mindset and lifestyle.

A moral community is authoritative. Love and control are balanced. When love dominates, the environment can become permissive, and when control becomes dominant, the school is legalistic. William Damon identifies characteristics of authoritative parents that can be applied to the school setting. They enforce commands consistently, showing a commitment to their importance. Their commands are direct and honest, not indirect and manipulative. They value obedience and associate good behavior with compliance with legitimate authority, and they confront students explicitly about any action that may harm others. In addition, Damon views induction as the most effective method of transmitting values. He describes induction as a technique for "ensuring the child's compliance through some form of control, but at the same time drawing the child's attention to the reasons behind the standard" (1988, 61). Within an effective moral community the reason behind a standard is viewed as the primary focus as opposed to the punishments and sanctions that result from violating it. Punishment appeals to the lowest level of moral development, while a focus on the rationale for the standard appeals to the highest level of moral reasoning and to an internal, personal commitment to the behavior.

School standards should be kept to a minimum in order to assure consistent follow-up. Any rule that cannot be consistently enforced should be reevaluated. Ownership of the rules by every member of the faculty is imperative. When teachers pick and choose which infractions are worthy of the effort of enforcement, the message is clear—one's choices about whether to obey are based on personal preference. Ownership does not always imply agreement. While the standards are being formulated, there is room for disagreement, but once standards are published, everyone must commit to them.

The published standards must include clear statements of the purpose behind the expected conduct, eliminating the need to ask why. Unless a good rationale can be articulated, the rule should not be included. Published standards should be agreed on annually and made available to the entire school community.

Allow Opportunity for Moral Action

Character, like biology and chemistry, needs a lab experience. While it is true that the school itself provides opportunities for moral action, students need to reach out into the larger community. In recent years schools have taken a renewed interest in community service, and service hours are often a requirement for particular courses or for graduation. Service beyond the school is in keeping with God's heart for one's neighbor, including the poor and dysfunctional members of the community, and as such is essential to building biblical character. As obvious as this may seem, many school boards and the parents themselves view hours off campus as an infringement on the school's academic agenda. If the school's goals were purely cognitive, such a concern would be justified. Time spent in service to others is evidence that the school takes affective standards seriously.

A student's motive for community service must be a sincere desire to "love your neighbor" as opposed to the fulfillment of mandated requirements:

> Service learning may, indeed, become another "should" in the curriculum, imposing by external command rather than appealing to students' emerging compassion and generosity. Community service *should* take students beyond "rules" to empathy, beyond fulfilling mandated "service learning" requirements to finding meaning and purpose through giving. (Kessler 2000, 70)

The school's role can be that of opening doors to community service by announcing opportunities and allowing time for participation. A small number of required hours often serves as a catalyst for the reluctant, but it is when students extend their hours beyond the requirements that they begin to internalize the value of service. The school needs to value and affirm these choices.

Make Learning Meaningful

Schools that build character connect learning to life, making the connection that provides intrinsic motivation for all of learning. This connection is particularly important in the middle and high school years when students are striving for personal identity and meaning. For Christian school educators the connection is particularly important when teaching the Bible. Spiritual formation or changed behavior is possible only when a knowledge of Scripture finds personal application in the life of the learner. Too often the expectations of the teacher are for recall and restatement of biblical truth rather than application and personal response. Larry Richards, in *Creative Bible Teaching,* points out that:

> Faith is that which expresses itself as a fitting response in each contact with God. Because response is essential, the teacher must focus the thoughts of his students on response. The teaching must not just communicate a particular truth, but guide students to discover how God wants them to respond to that truth. (1970, 62)

The teacher's role is to expect change and observe students' lives to determine whether the goals of Bible instruction are being realized.

Facilitate Critical Thinking

Critical thinking should characterize student thought across all grade levels. However, adolescents by reason of their more formal or abstract thinking ability can and must move their understanding of faith beyond what "significant others" have believed to what *they* believe. For this to happen, students must examine and evaluate their values. Too often teachers and parents view the questioning of beliefs as rebellion and as inappropriate for a Christian. Thus, through their negative reactions, they shut down the process both directly and indirectly. Rather than discourage this "grappling," however, teachers must be prepared to articulate the reasons for their beliefs and values along with the arguments that caused them to believe as they do. Perhaps the most fundamental questions include the following: *Is the Bible really the authentic and authoritative Word of God? Why should this book be accepted as Truth when other religions accept their book as the benchmark for truth?* Unless adolescents understand and personally affirm the answers to these questions, they see biblical morality and principles for living not as The Standard but merely as one possible standard, and moral relativity guides their behavior. Critical thinking skills include the formation of a standard for judging beliefs, an understanding of the thinking behind other worldviews, behavior in harmony with beliefs, listening and reading with discernment, and an apologetic for one's values. Students who have not examined their beliefs critically are unable to take a stand and live a life of intellectual integrity.

Academic Challenge Accompanied by Time for Personal Growth

Schools that develop character provide an academically challenging curriculum. Christian schools have consistently done this in that education's private sector usually follows a college prep model. Concern in this area may therefore rest in whether or not the curriculum has become too challenging. More of a good thing is not always better. Character and spiritual formation takes time. Students need time to grapple with beliefs and values. They need time for relationships with mentors and time for involvement in the lives of others. When they are preoccupied with their own achievement, they have little time to learn about or care for the needs of others. Too much stress on academic achievement and on getting into the right colleges, as well as too many extracurricular activities, has its cost. In addition to robbing students of time for the work of adopting values, such a focus delivers a materialistic value system as a by-product. Other-directedness is difficult to achieve when the focus is on personal gain. Effort must be expended to educate school boards and parents on the risks of a "more is better" mentality.

Evaluate Character Education

To realize educational outcomes at all levels, a school must use an effective evaluation system. Once clearly defined outcomes are in place, a school must determine and implement the means of measuring them. *What should graduates of the school know? What skills should they have? What should their behavior be like?* An emphasis on measuring achievement through standardized tests diminishes or even eliminates the need for character education, since paper-and-pencil tests cannot measure growth in character. Educators who shun the idea of alternative or more authentic means of assessment (i.e., behavioral checklists, student interviews, demonstrations of learning) will find it difficult to evaluate affective outcomes. When character education emphasizes the active verbs, then much of the work of evaluation has already been done. Through teacher observation and other feedback on student behavior, schools can measure their success. When the results of character education are less than satisfying, it is time for the school to revise its strategies. In turn, success needs to be acknowledged, and students need to be recognized and praised for who they are becoming.

Sanctification is a lifelong process, and therefore schools do not graduate finished products. However, schools can graduate students who evidence growth in Christ and have a desire to increase in righteousness. The struggle to train Christian school students for righteousness must be viewed as warfare. Change is a product of victory over the attempts of the enemy to hold each student captive to the values and ways of the world. The work of character and spiritual formation is therefore the work of prayer. Parents and teachers must pray on behalf of each student for the empowering work of the Holy Spirit in each classroom and throughout the school community. A teacher known for the spiritual growth of her students was asked about the key to her success. Upon reflection she humbly responded by describing how she began each day. She prayed while walking the perimeter of her classroom, claimed the space for God's glory, and asked that the students experience the work of the Holy Spirit in their lives. She claimed victory over Satan's strategies to hold her students captive. That prayer, combined with memorizing as many as 300 "fighter verses" (keyed to standing against temptation), transformed her students and their families.

Without clearly defined educational outcomes, along with specific strategies to attain them, desired goals are seldom realized. The affective dimension cannot be left to chance. A "Bible-added" curriculum is not enough. Spiritual formation must be emphasized and carefully sought after if a Christian school philosophy is to be actualized in the lives of the students.

About the Author

Milton V. Uecker earned his doctorate from the University of Virginia, with emphasis in early childhood education, social foundations, and evaluation. Dr. Uecker, who has served in Christian schools for 35 years, is currently dean of the graduate school at Columbia International University in Columbia, South Carolina.

Strengthen Your Foundations

1. Using Romans 12, write three affective standards that are appropriate to middle school or high school students.

2. Given the affective standards you listed for question 1, create a list of verbs that would accompany each standard, or describe the behavior of a student who has actualized each one. Then list behaviors that would characterize a student who does not evidence that standard.

3. Consider the learning community of your college, university, or Christian school. Would you characterize it as a caring community? If so, what attributes or practices characterize the community? What could be done to move toward greater caring?

4. Evaluate the standards by which your school operates. Explain why each rule is important. Are all rules being upheld in a consistent manner? If not, why not?

5. What avenues for moral action currently exist within your educational setting? What ones could be created? What evidence is there that these contribute to character formation among the students?

6. Use a recent lesson plan. Is there evidence of critical thinking in the lesson? How might you "remodel" the lesson to provide for worldview thinking and moral "grappling"?

7. Reflect on your own adolescence. To what extent were you given opportunities for personal growth and spiritual formation? What can a high school do to provide the right balance between academic challenge and personal growth?

8. Suggest and discuss some kinds of evaluation that would provide an authentic assessment of affective outcomes.

References

Astley, Jeff, and Leslie J. Francis, eds. 1992. *Christian perspectives on faith development: A reader.* Grand Rapids, MI: Eerdmans.

Coles, Robert. 1998. *The moral intelligence of children.* New York: Putnam.

Damon, William. 1988. *The moral child: Nurturing children's natural moral growth.* New York: Free Press.

Kessler, Rachael. 2000. *The soul of education.* Alexandria, VA: Association for Supervision and Curriculum Development.

Lickona, Thomas, and Catherine Lewis. 1997. *Eleven principles of effective character education* (video). Port Chester, NY: National Professional Resources, Inc.

Ornstein, Allan C., and Francis P. Hunkins. 1993. *Curriculum foundations, principles and issues.* Boston, MA: Allyn & Bacon.

Richards, Larry. 1970. *Creative Bible teaching.* Chicago: Moody Press.

Uecker, Milton V. 2002. *Biblical foundation for curriculum: Study guide.* Columbia, SC: Columbia International University.

Van Brummelen, Harro. 2002. *Steppingstones to curriculum: A biblical path.* 2d ed. Colorado Springs, CO: Purposeful Design Publications.

CHAPTER FOURTEEN

Discipline: Philosophy and Practice

Jerry L. Haddock

Few times are more exciting than the first day of a new school year. Students are eager to end the boredom of their long summer break, and veteran teachers return with renewed strength, hope, and enthusiasm. New books, new supplies, and new rosters of students give faculty and students alike a sense of new beginnings ... an opportunity to start afresh. The excitement of both groups pales, however, in comparison to that of another group—the new teachers, who nervously but enthusiastically are beginning that first teaching assignment. All goes well until that great educational menace appears—classroom disruption!

For most classroom teachers, techniques for dealing with disruption have scarcely been addressed in their formal training. Typical teacher education programs provide knowledge of content and teaching methods, but training in classroom management is rare. While the lack of such training is a problem, an even greater one is the omission of a clearly defined philosophy of discipline. An individual teacher's approach to classroom management depends heavily on that underlying philosophy.

Studies in child development reveal major philosophical differences. If we read the available materials on the topic, all the way from John Dewey, America's most influential educational theorist, through Alfie Kohn, author of the recently touted book *Beyond Discipline: From Compliance to Community*, we recognize major differences between constructivist and biblical perspectives. Constructivism renounces discipline in any form, viewing it as archaic, controlling, and harmful. Conversely, the Bible teaches that discipline is natural and necessary.

Constructivists reject the concept that children are affected by the *Fall* and their nature distorted by *original sin.* They oppose the idea that children are capable of genuine wrongdoing and require training and moral boundaries.* Their view of human nature, advanced clearly by Jean-Jacques Rousseau in the eighteenth century, is that humans are born in a natural state of innocence and are made evil only by the world that surrounds them (Colson and Pearcey 1999, 333). Today, the view throughout secular education is that humans are inherently good and the job of educators is to draw out their goodness and creativity. According to such thinking, the idea that humans are born with a proclivity for sin and wickedness is ignorant and passé. Those who reject the biblical view of human nature negate the reality of the *Fall, sin,* and *redemption,* and they are blind to a child's need for moral direction (334).

Mentioned earlier, *Beyond Discipline* offers a thorough presentation of the above theories and more. Upon its publication in 1996, it was mass-distributed by the Association of Supervision and Curriculum Development (ASCD), which has a membership of 150,000 educators. The title reflects the book's philosophy, which is radically different from a biblical Christian philosophy of discipline. The following excerpt illustrates how the book's philosophy translates into today's classroom:

> Children, like adults, are not passive receptacles into which knowledge is poured. They are not clay to be molded, or computers to be programmed, or animals to be trained. Rather, they are active meaning makers, testing out theories and trying to make sense of themselves and the world around them....
>
> When children are instead required to accept or memorize a ready-made truth, they do not really "learn" in any meaningful sense of the word. This is what we witness when students have to do problem sets in math, multiplying rows of naked numbers; or make their way through worksheets until they can identify vowels or verbs; or slough through textbook lessons about scientific laws or historical events. This may be the way to prepare children to take standardized tests (though it doesn't appear very successful); it is not the way to help students to become learners.... At best, they learned how to spit out someone else's right answers....
>
> Exactly the same is true if those right answers concern how one is supposed to *act.* (66)

The irony, of course, is that the very theorists who lament the imparting of truth from one to another become the most serious violators of their own theory. If this is not the case, for what purpose do they write books? Is it not to impart what they view as truth? Furthermore, why the disdain for any approach differing from their own? Consider the following quotation from Kohn that disputes everything he espoused in *Beyond Discipline:*

> The only way to help students become ethical people, as opposed to people who merely do what they are told, is to have them construct

> moral meaning. It is to help them figure out—for themselves and with each other—how one ought to act. That's why dropping the tools of traditional discipline, like rewards and consequences, is only the beginning. It's even more crucial that we overcome a preoccupation with getting compliance and instead bring students in on the process of devising and justifying ethical principles. (67)

Modern society goes one step further from the truth by suggesting that wicked acts of humans are not of their own evil nature but are the result of a society that causes them to do wrong. This philosophy regards student misbehavior as a problem with the school. Correction is unnecessary; educators simply need to figure out what culprit is causing the student to misbehave. To do otherwise demonstrates a dim view of children. A likely culprit could be the curriculum, as illustrated in the following statement:

> If we reject an unduly pessimistic view of children's basic motives, if we recognize that the quality of the curriculum has a lot to do with students' enthusiasm (or its absence), then we will be less likely to revert to the simplistic opposition of control versus chaos, in which teachers think they "must choose between putting up with behavior problems and being the big boss and stamping them out." (63)

Certainly we all agree that an excellent curriculum is appealing, age appropriate, and interesting, all of which are important to quality instruction and meaningful learning. However, what happens when a child decides she isn't interested in math, or science, or English? If the child dislikes the curriculum being taught and decides to misbehave, do we change the curriculum rather than dealing with the rebellion or defiance? Kohn's philosophy teaches that our goal must be to create in students a sense of autonomy rather than a desire to learn the content and skills necessary to function in life. Traditionally, schools, at least in the United States, have been influenced by biblical principles. Today, that system is regarded as tired and worn.

The philosophies and practices mentioned above are widespread in schools nowadays. Their exposure in this work illustrates the diversity of ideas about the right way to train children, and it accentuates the necessity for Christian school educators to define a biblical approach clearly. In this brief overview of the Christian philosophy and practice regarding discipline, three critical approaches are presented—a biblical approach, a relational approach, and a management approach.

Designing the Discipline Framework—A Biblical Approach

A Christian philosophy of discipline begins with the premise that children are *not* beyond discipline. Discipline is biblical, and thus it is an important matter for Christians involved in the development and training of children. A Christian teacher's biblical framework of discipline is foundational to everything that happens in the classroom. For this reason a Christian philosophy of discipline must be defined prayerfully and carefully.

A biblical approach to discipline encompasses two foundational distinctives: (1) recognition of the sinful nature of humans and (2) acceptance of parents as the child's primary authority figures.

Realizing the Sinful Nature of Humans

In our culture, sin has largely been written out of existence. "Even Christians who should understand the basic truth that *all* are heirs of Adam's Fall and thus *all* are sinners are influenced, often blinded, by humanist values" (Colson 1987, 96). King David cried, "Surely I was sinful at birth, sinful from the time my mother conceived me" (Psalm 51:5, NIV). This is a very different view of human nature from the prevailing theory that we are born with a heart inclined to be good.

Many factors influence a child's decision making, including an ungodly home environment, the media, and peer pressure. These influences are not root problems however, for even without them, the human heart is basically rebellious and sinful. Jeremiah warned that "the heart is deceitful above all things" (Jeremiah 17:9). The goal of the Christian school teacher should be to guide students from a rebellious mindset to a proper relationship with God, self, and others. The teacher who fails to discipline (disciple students in the Lord's way) will cause the school to fail in its mission.

Accepting Parents as Authorities

The Christian school exists to assist parents in carrying out their God-given responsibility of educating children in a Christ-centered environment. This task becomes difficult in an era when the role of the institution increases as the role of the family is diminished. The Christian school plays an important role in preserving parental authority as mandated in Scripture (Deuteronomy 6:4–9).

In the passage cited above, Moses makes clear that parents are responsible for the biblical values instilled in children. This training should not be delegated to anyone not under the watchful eye of a parent, and parents are not to deny or avoid the responsibility. Placing children under the care of others and failing to fully assume the God-given responsibility of parenting is clearly a violation of God's Word. Because of the biblical mandate, Christian school educators expect parental participation in their children's education. When parents neglect that responsibility, the school oversteps the bounds of its authority, assuming responsibilities that belong to parents. John Whitehead, founder of the Rutherford Institute, concurs: "In the area of education, the Bible lists several options for education, but none of them replace or overrule the parents. The *parents* are the first and main teachers. They also are responsible to supervise any outside instruction the children may receive" (1985, 60). Education without parental input is less than God's perfect design for children.

Another vivid biblical illustration of parental responsibility is the story of Eli. Samuel tells of God's anger toward Eli for allowing disobedience in his sons (1 Samuel 3:12–13). God held Eli accountable for his sons' sinful and adulterous lifestyles. Although Eli heavily rebuked their sinful behavior, the Bible says they "did not listen to their father's rebuke" (1 Samuel 2:25, NIV).

God expects no less of Christian parents today. Parents who assume biblical responsibility for training their children and working in harmony with a church and a Christian school that support their values will develop "a cord of three strands," which "is not quickly broken" (Ecclesiastes 4:12, NIV).

Partnering for Results: A Relational Approach

Not only does Scripture reveal the role of parents in the discipline and training processes; it establishes the necessity for proper relationships. The Bible places great importance on honor, respect, trust, and love for one another. Paul the Apostle writes, "Do nothing out of selfish ambition or vain conceit, but in humility consider others better than yourselves. Each of you should look not only to your own interests, but also to the interests of others" (Philippians 2:3–4, NIV). Affirming this principle, one management consultant warns, "Failure to give consideration to the interests of others is the major cause of problems in all forms of personal relationships.... If you want to build strong relationships, avoid overemphasizing yourself" (Rush 1983, 15).

To establish a relational approach that produces positive results, consider the following strategies: (1) winning through respect and trust, and (2) strengthening relationships through effective communication.

Winning Through Respect and Trust

We are commanded to "show proper respect to everyone" (1 Peter 2:17, NIV). A nationwide survey of Christian school teachers reveals students are greatly concerned that they be treated with respect by their parents, teachers, and peers (Gibbs and Haddock 1995, 8–9). Everyone from the youngest child to the most hardened criminal wants respect. Foundational to biblical self-discipline is respect for God, self, and others. Respect demonstrates honor or consideration of someone else. When others are honored, trusting relationships develop.

A teacher's manner of classroom discipline provides opportunity to develop a relationship of trust not only with students but with parents as well. The concern is to meet student needs. The teacher's first priority in building relationships is to demonstrate personal interest in the lives of students and their families. When relating to parents, teachers should make every effort to identify and focus on the parents' perception of their children's needs. The attitude should always be, *How can we work together in the development of your child?*

Teachers determine needs by analyzing students' work, their social interactions and private conversations, and parental feedback. Healthy relationships develop through a constant process of affirmation and involvement. Goethe once said, "Treat a man as he appears to be, and you make him worse. But treat a man as if he already were what he potentially could be, and you make him what he should be" (Wilkinson 1992, 56).

Young people are fragile and easily scarred by careless or critical remarks. Such comments destroy trust. A pastor shares this personal story about something he experienced as a young child:

> Watermelon season was one of my favorite times of year [when I was a boy]. Rather than buy our melons at the market where they were sold by the pound, we usually bought ours right off a farmer's truck. One summer day as our family was taking a walk, we saw a farmer selling his truckload of watermelons. They were the first ones of the season.
>
> Dad picked a nice ripe one. "Can I carry it?" I asked.
>
> "I'll carry it," said my father in his normal, abrupt manner. My father,

a product of the work ethic, did not express himself well verbally. To him, what one did spoke louder than anything said. I didn't understand this as a boy.

I was very conscious of my skinniness and knew I wasn't physically as well built as most boys my age. Dad's rebuff was painful to my ego. Again I asked, "Please, Dad, let me carry the watermelon."

"You're not big enough," he said.

My ego was shattered. I began to whimper. "Why don't you let him try?" my mother suggested.

"All right," he said, and he plunked the melon in my arms. I had no idea that watermelons were so heavy, and I wasn't prepared for the sudden weight. It slid right through my arms and cracked open on the pavement below.

"See, I knew you couldn't do it," said my father as he bent over to retrieve the pieces. Inwardly I felt as crushed as the broken watermelon on the pavement.

Sounds like an innocent comment, doesn't it? I'm sure my dad forgot it within the hour. But so many years later I still remember the pain of that moment, though I fully realize my father in no way meant to hurt me. (Bubna 1988, 73–74)

Such stories are far too common. Unfortunately, most of us can recall similar hurtful stories from our own childhood. Christian educators should pray for sensitivity and wisdom in dealing with such situations. Rather than shattering a child's confidence and sense of self-worth, the effective Christian school teacher seeks opportunities to build up by praising and affirming. The following story illustrates the contrast between negative and positive input and the influence of each on a child:

My high school typing teacher didn't like me. I'm glad I don't remember her name. "You'll never pass this course," she said to me one day. "You're behind! I don't care if you were sick. You're not going to make it."

Frustrated by her words, I mentioned my problem to the school counselor. "She's not going to give you a chance," the counselor said, when we were alone. "Drop the course and come here each day at that period and help me with a major project. I could use your skills." She developed a sense of confidence in me as I worked with her in the school office for the rest of the semester. Her affirmation put me far ahead of where I would have been had I continued to struggle in that typing class. Later I made up the typing course with another teacher.

> That counselor was one of the reasons I even attended college. "You have the potential and can do college work," she said. She wasn't concerned about the fact that no one else on either side of my family had ever completed college. She believed in me, and that was enough to encourage me to make much better grades in college than I had in high school. (Bubna 1988, 77)

This story illustrates how one person can make a difference in the life of a student. Correcting the negative isn't enough. One must follow up with affirmation. Harvard psychologist Robert Rosenthal summarized a technique that gives personal attention by concluding, "Tone of voice, facial expressions, touch, and posture may be the means by which—often unwittingly—teachers communicate their expectations to their pupils. Such communication may help a child by changing his perceptions of himself" (Wilkinson 1992, 57).

Strengthening Relationships Through Effective Communication

Finally, in partnering with parents for results, the teacher develops an effective plan for communicating with them. Although often neglected, communication is a highly beneficial tool for building trusting relationships. The parent survey referred to above revealed that the number one frustration parents felt toward teachers was a teacher's failure to notify them of problems at school (Gibbs and Haddock 1995, 36). This study confirms that adequate and timely communication before problems arise increases parental support and minimizes classroom disruption.

It would be naive, however, to think that all parents are eager to deal with problems their youngster experiences at school. Educators sometimes hear, "I pay tuition to have you handle the problems!" This view that refuses to acknowledge parental responsibility violates the biblical design for parenting and must be addressed lovingly but firmly.

Close contact and communication with parents before problems arise goes a long way toward preventing rage in a volatile moment. Teachers should contact the parent when there is good news to report. This is the first level of communication. Taking only a few minutes each day to call one or two parents with positive reports may save hours spent in unpleasant parent-teacher conferences. Although a conference is sometimes required, parents who are informed and are convinced of the teacher's love and concern for their child are unlikely to retaliate with anger and hostility.

Planning for Success: A Management Approach

Once one has defined the biblical and relational approaches to one's philosophy of discipline, it is time to develop a management plan that implements that philosophy. Those biblical and relational principles become the foundation for the plan.

Rules and procedures (management) are required to incorporate the values of the Christian school (biblical, relational). The Christian school teacher, for example, seeks the active involvement of parents in the management plan. Parental involvement is essential because it has a biblical basis and is effective in building strong, supportive relationships.

This final section presents three practical steps to discipline planning: (1) avoiding disruption through management and planning, (2) identifying the schoolwide and classroom plans, and (3) recognizing and relating to individuality.

Avoiding Disruption Through Management and Planning

The first step is to identify the desired plan for management and discipline. Selecting an effective plan is difficult. Many books have been written describing numerous classroom discipline theories. In Gibbs and Haddock's *Classroom Discipline: A Management Guide for Christian School Teachers,* 1995, Appendix D is an "Overview of Nine Classroom Models" (159–69). The same book refers to ACSI's Master Teacher Questionnaire (Appendix E), which revealed that the choice of a particular discipline program had "minimal influence on [teachers'] success in the classroom" and that "the majority of teachers tailor-made their own discipline program" by modifying and adapting a variety of plans (75). Whatever technique they use, Christian school teachers are responsible for implementing a biblically based approach to discipline.

Regardless of the label, student discipline is a system for producing desired behavior through an effective implementation of rewards (encouragement, praise, positive reinforcement) and consequences (correction, punishment, negative reinforcement). The particular system or program used to accomplish this goal is not nearly as important as consistency in implementing it. In other words, it doesn't matter whether the system involves a checkmark on the chalkboard, a traffic light at the desk, or some kind of reward as an incentive. What matters is that teachers develop a system and implement it consistently day after day.

Like everything else, the discipline program must be well planned before it is implemented. Many discipline plans fail, not because they are based on unsound principles but because they simply are not well planned and executed. One insightful administrator concludes:

> Developing a school discipline plan—whether it's for a single classroom or an entire school district—can be compared to building a house: If you don't consider the result you want before you begin, the project will end up costing far more than you planned and the finished product (if you achieve it) might be unrecognizable.
>
> The comparison isn't exact, though: The costs of correcting an ill-conceived building plan are primarily financial. Correcting mistakes in a discipline plan likewise is expensive in staff time and money. But an ill-conceived discipline plan is even more costly in terms of the personal development of students and relationships among their peers, teachers, administrators, and parents. (Williams 1993, 27)

Identifying Schoolwide and Classroom Plans

As mentioned earlier, it is of paramount importance to gather input during the design stage of the plan. Decisions need to be made concerning appropriate standards, rewards, and negative consequences, and parents and students often provide useful feedback that not only enhances the plan but provides group ownership, which is invaluable during implementation. Parental support of the standards, for example, strengthens the teacher's ability to fully implement them. On the other hand, the most effective reward and consequence systems are often designed by the students under the guidance of a teacher. This process provides the teacher with beneficial information for determining appropriate rewards and negative consequences.

Appropriate implementation is critical in defining the classroom plan. When dealing with standards and the consequences for their infraction, educators should not emphasize or accentuate the negative. Encouragement, support, and praise are the expected focal points of all classroom discipline. Pray that you will not "pocket the praise we should pass on to others [students] or sidestep the practical help we could offer to open the way for another to succeed" (Dunn 1985, 29).

Recognizing and Relating to Individuality

Every child is different, and the differences must be taken into account when one is rewarding and disciplining students. Not all students appreciate twenty minutes of free reading as a reward. Conversely, some will consider detention after school to be a retreat, more pleasant than returning home to the chores that await them. When a reward or negative consequence fails to work for a child, the teacher must try something different. The important thing to remember is that standards are fixed for every child, but rewards and consequences are flexible. It is flexibility that many commercial discipline programs lack, and rigidity is less than desirable when one is working with children of diverse backgrounds, personalities, maturity levels, and abilities. Teachers must know the students before any approach can be implemented successfully.

Conclusion

The role of spiritual leader is an important one for the Christian school teacher, so it is appropriate to conclude this chapter with a few words of encouragement on developing this side of the teacher's life. The Christian teacher spends time and exercises self-discipline in developing her personal spiritual life. She makes time for daily devotions in which she prays diligently for the students who have been entrusted to her. She also demonstrates sincerity. Christian school students will detect whether their teacher's Christianity is genuine.

Above all, the teacher must be the example. Many teachers can't discipline effectively because they aren't disciplined. A teacher's well-disciplined personal life speaks louder than words. As students see personal adherence to high standards, they will be inclined to hold fast to them. The example set by the teacher may be remembered for a lifetime.

About the Author

Jerry L. Haddock holds an Ed.D. in educational administration from the University of Arkansas. He currently serves in LaHabra, California, as the director of ACSI's Southern California Region.

Strengthen Your Foundations

1. Refer to Gibbs and Haddock's *Classroom Discipline: A Management Guide for Christian School Teachers* (available from ACSI) for a comprehensive review of the philosophy and practice of Christian school discipline.

2. Compare and contrast models of classroom discipline. Prepare a written report of your findings. (See *Classroom Discipline: A Management Guide for Christian School Teachers,* pages 159–69, for an overview of nine classroom discipline models.)

3. Design a biblically based discipline plan that includes teachers' expectations of parents and students, classroom standards, rewards, and consequences. Utilize ideas from various discipline models.

4. Develop a program that provides strong school/home relationships through parental involvement.

References

Bubna, Donald. 1988. *Encouraging people.* Wheaton, IL: Tyndale House.

Colson, Charles. 1987. *Loving God.* Grand Rapids, MI: Zondervan.

Colson, Charles, and Nancy Pearcey. 1999. *How now shall we live?* Wheaton, IL: Tyndale House.

Dunn, Janet. 1985. Inspiring others. *Discipleship Journal* 5, no. 4 (July).

Gibbs, Ollie, and Jerry Haddock. 1995. *Classroom discipline: A management guide for Christian school teachers.* Colorado Springs, CO: Association of Christian Schools International.

Kohn, Alfie. 1996. *Beyond discipline: From compliance to community.* Alexandria, VA: Association of Supervision and Curriculum Development.

Rush, Myron D. 1983. *Richer relationships.* Wheaton, IL: Scripture Press Publications.

Whitehead, John. 1985. *Parents' rights.* Wheaton, IL: Crossway Books.

Wilkinson, Bruce H. 1992. *Almost every answer for practically any teacher!* Portland, OR: Multnomah.

Williams, Joseph E. 1993. Principles of discipline. *American School Board Journal* (February).

SECTION FOUR

Cultural and Sociological Foundations

Jesus said, "Let the little children come to me, and do not hinder them, for the kingdom of God belongs to such as these" (Mark 10:14, NIV). Jesus spoke of children many times and often blessed them as they came to Him. Christian educators are called on to do the same—love their students and be a blessing in their lives.

God made parents responsible for educating their children, and the Christian school seeks to assist parents in that process. He made each person unique. Our students represent many modes of learning, and our schools need to provide a quality education for all kinds of children. This section begins by highlighting the need to understand various cultures as Christian schools everywhere become more and more culturally diverse. Next, Christian educators are challenged to develop programs for exceptional children, those with special needs. Serving such children reflects Jesus' heart as He reached out to the children around Him, blessing them and warning people not to neglect any of them. Another challenge Christian educators face is to reach out to the students in urban areas, where training is usually inadequate and the needs are many and varied. Creative new kinds of ministry are required in those areas that have been too long neglected by most Christian educators. A fourth challenge is to reach the children of missionaries and nationals in other lands. Gifted teachers and administrators are needed so that our Christian schools can provide a quality education for God's children wherever they are. The section concludes by offering some practical ways for our schools to train children and young people to reach out to others. Included are age-specific suggestions for service that begins in the home and moves outward, with the goal of teaching students how to practice the Great Commission.

Section 4 asks, *How can we reach the world's children for Christ?* May our answer provide the catalyst for a growing ministry to children who may have been neglected in the past. The important question is, *How will you respond to the challenge?*

C H A P T E R   F I F T E E N

Understanding Cultural Context

Daniel J. Egeler

Teresa* had just come to a saving knowledge of Jesus Christ while attending a Christian middle school. The child of recent immigrants, she was sincere in her desire to have an authentic walk with God. Her Bible class was studying the book of Daniel, and she was particularly receptive to its portrayal of uncompromising obedience to God's commands. In particular, she was deeply moved by the examples of Shadrach, Meshach, and Abednego, who refused to bow down to the image of gold that King Nebuchadnezzar had set up (Daniel 3). Teresa's parents expected their children to honor the memory of their ancestors by bowing down before images. This ritual was a part of the heritage and culture of their homeland that they wanted to instill in their children. They were willing to have their children adopt certain aspects of a new culture, but they also wanted them to have a sense of history, understanding, and empathy for their place of origin.

Teresa wanted to honor her parents by giving homage to her ancestors, but she also wanted to be obedient to God's standards. She approached her Bible teacher with her dilemma. Her questions were, "If I bow down before an image of my ancestors, am I compromising my faith in Jesus Christ? Or do I follow the example of Shadrach, Meshach, and Abednego, and refuse to bow down and thereby dishonor my parents by turning my back on our culture and heritage?" These were difficult questions to answer as the teacher was charged with the task of discerning the intent behind the custom *and* the transcendent biblical truth that applied to it. Was this ancestor *worship,* or was it simply honoring the memory of those who had gone on before? To provide wise counsel, this teacher needed to understand the student's culture and then apply the relevant biblical principles to that particular practice.

Understanding the various cultures in our classrooms can be a challenge as our Christian classrooms become more and more culturally diverse. The world is becoming smaller because of globalization,

* Name has been changed.

a phenomenon that will only increase in the foreseeable future. When faced with challenges of cultural diversity, as illustrated by Teresa's story, you as a teacher can be tempted to throw your hands up and take the position that, as a Christian educator, you should simply teach out of your own cultural understanding. After all, by trying to "be all things to all people," you'll end up sinking to the lowest common denominator, a way that can only lead to mediocrity. By teaching only from the vantage point of your own culture, you would make it the responsibility of your students to adapt to your perspective.

Richard Edlin, in *The Cause of Christian Education*, calls it "cultural idolatry" for an educator to measure the rightness or wrongness of a response or behavior in terms of his own cultural perspective. He goes on to advise the following:

> Teachers in a multi-ethnic school (and most schools are multi-ethnic to some degree these days) must get to know their students and families very well. They must learn where their students come from culturally and what expectations they bring with them. They must find ways of making the classroom lessons relevant to their students' geographical and cultural settings so that learning is concrete and not abstract wherever possible. They must learn about the ethnic composition of the local area in which the school is located in order to give a local context to content and skills and thus help students appreciate and relate to the culture where God has called them and their parents to live. Then, the teachers must find out the geographical, academic, social, and vocational destinations of their students and structure the students' courses to prepare them for these. Effective teachers will be able to view the classroom and the curriculum from the perspective of the learner. (1999, 155)

What do the Scriptures say about understanding the cultural context of our students?* Is teaching from a single cultural perspective in a multicultural classroom "cultural idolatry"? It appears that the apostle Paul would argue that mature Christians should adjust their teaching methods to suit the cultural context. The foundation for adjusting one's teaching methods is an understanding of the cultural context of the learner. The apostle Paul says, "I have become all things to all men so that by all possible means I might save some. I do all this for the sake of the gospel, that I may share in its blessings" (1 Corinthians 9:22–23, NIV). He then demonstrates the application of this principle in Acts 17 when he teaches to two different audiences. He instructs the Jews in a synagogue in Berea and the Greeks in a

* The next two paragraphs are adapted from a TCK-PFO seminar, Classroom Implications of Cultural Differences, presented in 2000 in Denver, Colorado, by David Wilcox, Director of International School Services for Asia and Latin America, ACSI.

marketplace in Athens. He attempts to bring these two very different audiences to the same learning outcome—to know that Jesus was raised from the dead. He understands the culture of both the Jews and the Greeks, and he is able to connect with each. For the Jews, he teaches in the synagogue out of the Old Testament. For the Greeks, he teaches in the marketplace, using their concept of the "unknown god." In other words, Paul seeks to understand the cultural context of the learners, and he adjusts his content and methods in order to be as effective as possible in getting his message across.

Revelation 7:9 (NIV)speaks of a great multitude standing before the throne from "every nation, tribe, people and language." Clearly, it is God's purpose to attract people from every nation, tribe, people, and language; and this diversity is celebrated before the throne and in front of the Lamb. We will all celebrate our cultural diversity in the presence of Jesus when we stand before the throne. This is a call to cultural understanding and the kind of sensitivity that values people's differences instead of ignoring or minimizing them.

Thus we see that effective teachers view the classroom and the curriculum from a learner's perspective and that they have an attitude of cultural sensitivity that the Scriptures support. But realistically, how can they live out these attitudes in a multicultural classroom? The foundation for cultural sensitivity should be authentic love expressed by genuinely seeking to understand and accept each student. Josh McDowell (2002), the well-known Christian apologist, stresses the importance of making a "relational connection" when instructing the next generation. Jesus Christ pointed out the importance of loving relationships as a mark of discipleship when He said, "By this all men will know that you are my disciples, if you love one another" (John 13:35, NIV). In my experience, an authentic expression of love transcends culture and speaks a language that everyone understands. Young people from every cultural background crave connection and authenticity, so they will respond to a genuine demonstration of the love that Jesus emphasized.

Simply loving the learner, however, is not enough to make you an effective Christian educator in a multicultural context. You must go beyond and seek to understand the cultural context of each student. Duane Elmer, a professor at Trinity International University, tells an allegory of a monkey and a fish that powerfully illustrates the need for understanding a cultural context when seeking to demonstrate concern and compassion (2002).

As the story goes, a typhoon temporarily stranded a monkey on an island. While feeling secure and waiting for the waters to recede, the monkey spotted a fish struggling against the current. It seemed quite obvious to the monkey that the fish was in need of assistance. Being kind and compassionate, the monkey resolved to help the fish. A tree dangled precariously over the very spot where the fish was struggling. At considerable risk to himself, the monkey moved far out on the limb, reached down, and snatched the fish from the threatening waters. Immediately scurrying back to the safety of his shelter, he carefully laid the fish on dry ground. For a few minutes, the fish demonstrated its gratitude for being rescued by vigorously flapping its tail and excitedly wriggling on the ground. After several minutes, the fish settled into a peaceful and contented state of rest. Joy and satisfaction swelled inside the monkey. He had helped another creature and had done it successfully.

There are many things that we can say about the monkey. We can point out his good intentions, obvious love and compassion for another creature, courage, bravery, altruistic motivation for service, and willingness to risk and take action when a need arose. Most of us, however, would have to conclude that, despite his good intentions, the monkey did significant harm to the fish. The lesson is that love and compassion without an understanding of the cultural context can cause significant harm. The monkey demonstrated love from his own frame of reference, but in the final analysis his expression of love resembled oppression more than compassion. He assumed that what was good for him was good for the fish. As Christian educators, we will have many students who come from a cultural background different from any we know and understand. Thus we need to heed the lesson of the monkey and the fish by seeking to understand our students' cultural contexts in order to express our love effectively. We cannot assume that what is good for us is good for them.

Geert Hofstede (1997), who wrote *Culture and Organizations: Software of the Mind*, provides a helpful conceptual model for understanding cultural context in a multicultural classroom. Hofstede's theory describes several dimensions that are found in empirical research. These dimensions compare and contrast the cultural contexts of more than fifty countries. This chapter will adapt one of these dimensions to the educational setting to illustrate how this theory can facilitate an understanding of cultural context within family relationships and the classroom.

Hofstede's first dimension is called *power distance* and is defined as "the extent to which the less powerful members of institutions and organizations within a country expect and accept the fact that power is distributed unequally" (1997, 28). Inequality exists in all cultures, but the degree to which it is tolerated varies. *Small power distance* cultures are more egalitarian. People value personal initiative, independence, and spontaneity and emphasize respect for all people regardless of age, authority, or status. The United States and most Western European nations are small power distance societies. *Large power distance* cultures stress absolute authority and tradition, value conformity and harmony, and respect people on the basis of age, authority, and status. Most of the nations in Latin America and Asia are large power distance cultures.

Hofstede's concept of power distance provides insight into the cultural context in family relationships, which is helpful for Christian educators working with students and parents from other cultures. In small power distance cultures, people value independent behavior by the child. The goal of parental education is to let children take control of their own affairs as soon as they can. Parents encourage active experimentation, and children have the right to express their feelings openly—including the right to say no. When children reach adulthood, they are expected to be emotionally and financially independent, and they are rarely expected to solicit their parents' advice or permission when making decisions. It is left up to the adult child to decide whether to solicit parental permission or advice.

The Influence of Power Distance on Family Relationships

Small Power Distance *United States and Western Europe*	**Large Power Distance** *Latin America and Asia*
Independent behavior on the part of the child is highly valued, and active experimentation by the child is encouraged.	Independent behavior on the part of the child is not encouraged.
Children are permitted to contradict their parents and to say no at an early age. Formal respect and deference are seldom shown.	Respect for parents and other elders is seen as a basic virtue with children rarely if ever contradicting their parents or other elders. Formal respect and deference are always shown.
The goal of parental education is to let children take control of their own affairs as soon as possible. When children reach adulthood, there is no expectation that they will ask their parents for advice or permission concerning major decisions; whether to do so is left up to the children.	Respect for parents and other elders lasts through adulthood. When children reach adulthood, there is an expectation that they will continue to ask their parents for advice or permission when they need to make major decisions.

In large power distance cultures, children are expected to be obedient to their parents, honoring their opinions and desires. Even as adults, they show deference and respect to their parents and elders. As young people they are not encouraged to behave independently, and they continue under some parental authority as long as their parents are alive. The chart above summarizes Hofstede's ideas as applied to family relationships.

Understanding the influence of power distance in family relationships was invaluable when I served as a high school principal in Latin America. Coming from a small power distance culture (the United States), I had to develop an understanding of the cultural context of students who came from large power distance cultures.

Jimmy* was a bright, energetic, personable student who came from a large power distance culture. His parents had immigrated from Asia to Latin America and had opened a successful business. Jimmy enrolled in our school to learn English and to prepare to attend a selective university in North America. By the time Jimmy was a senior, he was fluent in English and was a well-rounded student who was extremely popular with his teachers and classmates. Just one month into the first semester of his senior year, Jimmy came into my office quite distraught. I asked what was wrong, and he could barely choke out a reply. When I finally coaxed an answer out of him, he told me that his father had made the decision to emigrate to Canada by the end of December—halfway through his senior year. Jimmy had genuinely bonded with many of his classmates and teachers, and he couldn't bear the thought of missing out on his last year of high school with these friendships. I then asked him the pivotal question: "Jimmy, have you told your father how you feel?" Jimmy looked at me with a quizzical expression and responded, "Of course not. I have to honor his wishes, and to express any desire to remain here would not honor his authority. It would shame him and cause a big problem in the family." I could feel his pain, but I knew how critical it was to support Jimmy's cultural value of deference to parental authority.

The next day I met with Jimmy and proposed a solution. I asked him whether it would be appropriate for me to speak with his father. Since I was highly respected by his father (educators are highly respected in large power distance cultures), I wondered if it would be offensive for me to share my opinion about what would be best for his son and, in that context, my knowledge about Jimmy's true desires. Jimmy embraced the idea, and we met with his father the next week. His father was a delightful man, and when I proposed several educational options for his son upon their departure, he immediately asked for my opinion. I then gently shared that his son's desire was to finish out the entire school year where he was, living with relatives after his parents left. His father immediately looked over at his son with tears in his eyes and asked him directly if this was what he wanted. Jimmy nodded his head in affirmation, and his father granted his wish. When they stood up to

* Name has been changed.

leave, they warmly embraced each other. In this situation, it was appropriate for me to convey Jimmy's heart's desire as it did not directly challenge his father's decision. In addition, I was in a position of high esteem so that my opinion was valued.

The concept of power distance has some implications for the classroom as well. In small power distance cultures, emphasis is placed on pursuing knowledge from sources other than the teacher. Student initiative is rewarded—particularly when it manifests itself in the independent pursuit of truth. To a considerable extent, then, the quality of learning is determined by the excellence of the student. Teachers expect students to initiate communication, and students are encouraged to participate in class discussion and ask questions if they don't understand something. It's not uncommon for a student to challenge or question a teacher's statements or ideas. Also, it's considered appropriate and desirable for teachers and students to maintain a friendship outside of class, and younger teachers are often quite popular as they can readily relate to their students (Hofstede 1997).

In large power distance cultures, there is much more emphasis on the teacher's imparting knowledge and wisdom rather than encouraging a student's independent pursuit of knowledge and wisdom. With this approach, the quality of learning is largely dependent on the excellence of the teachers, who maintain strict order in the classroom and initiate all communication. Students will not speak in class unless the teacher invites them to do so. They never contradict or question a teacher publicly, and they treat their teachers with deference even outside the classroom. Older teachers are given more respect than

The Influence of Power Distance in the Classroom

Small Power Distance *United States and Western Europe*	**Large Power Distance** *Latin America and Asia*
An emphasis is placed on pursuing knowledge from any reliable source. Quality of education depends on the excellence of the student.	An emphasis is placed on personal "wisdom" that is transferred in the relationship with a teacher. Quality of education depends on the excellence of the teacher.
An emphasis on student-centered education with a premium on student initiative.	An emphasis on teacher-centered education with a premium on maintaining order.
A teacher expects a student to initiate communication.	A student expects a teacher to initiate communication.
Students will speak up in class in response to a general invitation by the teacher.	Students will speak up in class only when they are personally called on by a teacher.
Students are allowed to contradict or criticize the teacher.	Students never contradict or publicly criticize a teacher.
Learning is facilitated by two-way communication in class (class discussion, questioning).	Learning is facilitated by one-way communication (lecturing by the teacher).
Teachers are treated as friends outside class.	Deference for teachers is maintained outside class.
Younger teachers are often more popular than older teachers.	Older teachers are more respected than younger teachers.

younger teachers by virtue of their greater wisdom and experience. The chart at the right summarizes Hofstede's ideas as applied to school.

Understanding the influence of power distance in the classroom was particularly helpful to me in my experience as an educator in Latin America. Joe* was an outstanding Korean student who learned English in our school and went on to graduate second in his class—quite an accomplishment in our competitive academic environment. Joe, however, was really upset one day when he came into my office. He had earned his first *B,* and it was in health class. I was surprised, as health was not the most rigorous class Joe was taking. During our conversation, I finally realized what was happening. Health *was* the most difficult class for Joe because he came from a large power distance culture. It was hard for him to function when there was often no single "right" answer for a particular problem. Furthermore, rather than imparting knowledge and providing the right answer, the teacher expected the students to come up with solutions to dilemmas. The situation was extremely frustrating for Joe, who expected the teacher to impart knowledge that would include the right answer for every situation. I was able to explain the cultural differences to Joe. Once he understood them, his level of frustration greatly diminished, and he went on to finish the year well.

In another situation, I noticed a lot of discipline referrals coming from our Spanish department. We had made a philosophical decision to have Spanish taught by native speakers who were host country nationals. We anticipated that our students would not only learn the Spanish language but at the same time would come to appreciate the culture and history of the host country. The discipline referrals, however, were symptomatic of an educational cross-cultural divide that was growing between our small power distance students (mainly from North America) and our large power distance teachers (from Latin America). Our Latin American Spanish teachers exhibited all the attitudes and behaviors associated with their cultural perspective—emphasis on maintaining order, teacher-initiated communication, no contradicting or questioning of teachers. Our North American students, on the other hand, were eager to pursue knowledge but were doing so from their cultural perspective! They would initiate communication and class discussions, would readily contradict a teacher if they felt the teacher was imparting incorrect information, and considered a

About the Author

Daniel J. Egeler is the ACSI Director of International School Services for Europe and Africa. Dr. Egeler has served as a teacher, coach, and administrator of Christian schools in Tuscaloosa, Alabama, and Quito, Ecuador.

* Name has been changed.

teacher-centered approach boring with its heavy emphasis on lecturing. Needless to say, the teachers perceived the students' behavior as disrespectful—hence the heavy volume of discipline referrals. We had to work first on having both parties understand each other's cultural context before we could begin improving the classroom climate.

In *What's So Amazing About Grace*, Philip Yancey develops the concept of grace. Grace is a prerequisite for any Christian educator facing the challenge of understanding cultural context as it is a significant component of authentic love—the kind of love that transcends cultures. Yancey develops a wonderful word picture of grace:

> A phrase used by both Peter and Paul has become one of my favorite images from the New Testament. We are to administer, or "dispense," God's grace, say the two apostles. The image brings to mind one of the old-fashioned "atomizers" women used before the perfection of spray technology. Squeeze a rubber bulb, droplets of perfume come shooting out of the fine holes at the other end. A few drops suffice for a whole body; a few pumps change the atmosphere in a room. That is how grace should work, I think. It does not convert the entire world or an entire society, but it does enrich the atmosphere.
>
> Now I worry that the prevailing image of Christians has changed from that of a perfume atomizer to a different spray apparatus: the kind used by insect exterminators. *There's a roach!* Pump, spray, pump, spray. *There's a spot of evil!* Pump, spray, pump, spray. Some Christians I know have taken on the task of "moral exterminator" for the evil-infested society around them. (1997, 146)

A Christian educator who does not make an attempt to understand cultural context risks being perceived as arrogant, and that arrogance can come across as "bug spray" to the students. On the other hand, a Christian educator who humbly seeks to understand the students' cultural context will be about the business of dispensing the "perfume of Christ." As Christian educators, we would do well to heed the apostles' exhortation to dispense God's grace as we seek to understand the cultural context of our students.

Strengthen Your Foundations

1. What counsel would you give Teresa as her Bible teacher? What aspect of biblical truth would you include in your counsel? What understanding of and sensitivity to her cultural heritage would you demonstrate in your counsel?

2. Can you provide any examples of how assuming what was culturally right for you as a teacher may have caused hurt or harm to a student?

3. Have you experienced the effects of Hofstede's *power distance* dimension in your classroom? If so, how?

4. What concrete teaching strategies can be implemented to address the effects of differing perceptions of *power distance?* Describe how these teaching strategies would enhance learning in a multicultural classroom.

References

Edlin, Richard J. 1999. *The cause of Christian education.* Colorado Springs, CO: Association of Christian Schools International.

Elmer, Duane. 2002. A pilgrimage to servanthood (January). Keynote address delivered at the International Christian Educator's Conference, Quito, Ecuador.

Hofstede, Geert. 1997. *Culture and organizations: Software of the mind.* New York: McGraw-Hill.

McDowell, Josh. 2002. *The disconnected generation.* Dallas, TX: Josh McDowell Ministries.

Yancey, Philip. 1997. *What's so amazing about grace?* Grand Rapids, MI: Zondervan.

CHAPTER SIXTEEN

Exceptional Students in Christian Schools

Sharon R. Berry

Serving students with special needs is a challenge to education in general and to Christian schools in particular. This chapter establishes a biblical foundation for such service and suggests issues to be resolved and potential strategies to employ. Christian schools are encouraged to extend their programs to a broader range of students, and counsel is given about who should be served and how.

Recognizing a Responsibility

Christian schools have historically served families who desired a uniquely Christian education for their children. Programs were developed that responded to the needs of average and above-average students in traditional classrooms with traditional curricula. Often the students who could not participate successfully in the regular classroom routines and curricular experiences were excluded. Thus, the exceptional students were denied an opportunity for a Christian education because the schools lacked professional and financial resources.

As Christian schools mature, most are expressing a desire to partner with Christian families in the education of *all* the children under the umbrella of their ministry. Therefore, schools are exploring programs appropriate for exceptional, or atypical, students.

Jesus told a parable that challenges our tendency to serve only the more proficient students, the leaders of tomorrow. "When you give a dinner or a supper, do not ask your friends, your brothers, your relatives, nor your rich neighbors,... But when you give a feast, invite the poor, the maimed, the lame, the blind. And you will be blessed, because they cannot repay you; for you shall be repaid at the resurrection of the just" (Luke 14:12–14).

Christian educators would agree that our schools are offering the feast of educational excellence. The challenge is to evaluate ourselves and, in accordance with the biblical command, invite exceptional students to the banquet—because of both the blessing we can be to them and the blessing they can be to our student body.

Defining the Population

Christian schools have a unique opportunity to meet the educational needs of exceptional students from Christian families. These students need educational programs and related services beyond those normally provided. These services range from simply being sure a student receives daily medication to providing an extensive array of special education personnel.

Exceptional students may be disabled by various physical, emotional, or sensory disabilities, or they may be gifted academically, artistically, or athletically. It is estimated that up to one-third of the students in a given class will need some modification of their educational program at some time during their school years. The interventions can range from preferential seating to short-term home-based instruction that is not technically identified as special education. Approximately ten percent of students will need a number of accommodations, sometimes extensive ones, to meet their special needs. These students display a variety of learning problems and may require broad and intensive services.

Some students are considered mildly disabled and function at or near grade level. In fact, most students with special needs can be served in regular classes by teachers who are sensitive to their needs. Others can receive small-group instruction in a resource room, or the one-on-one attention of an educational therapist. For those who are blind, physically disabled, or hearing impaired, schools can make low-intensity accommodations by addressing issues of access and emergency procedures.

A second and moderate level of service intensity involves students who may be as much as two years below grade level or may need supportive services to maintain their grade level. Depending on the students' particular needs, the range of services offered can include personal assistance in the classroom, itinerant teachers, individual therapy, or attendance in a resource room for parts of the day.

The third level of service intensity involves students who are functioning three or more years below grade level and for whom instruction must be greatly modified. Typically, these students are served in a resource room and are mainstreamed for nonacademic subjects, or they attend special classes full-time. The number of students at this level (only about one per thousand) is so low that it is unlikely many Christian schools will have a sufficient population at compatible age levels to offer appropriate programs.

Developing Services

The following pages will describe plausible approaches for schools that desire to provide special services across various categories of exceptionality, degrees of need, and age levels. The purpose is to explore the possibilities of providing appropriate services to exceptional students in Christian schools.

Speech Impairments

Speech-impaired students are those who have disorders of vocal production that distract attention from the message they are trying to communicate. The disorder usually involves defects of articulation, phonation, fluency, and/or language delays. Following are some options for providing services to these students:

1. Full- or part-time speech therapists, as members of the staff, provide individual or small-group speech-therapy sessions. The average caseload for a full-time speech therapist is 60 to 75 students. A caseload would have to be identified, a therapist secured, and financial arrangements made to cover the extra costs.
2. The students and their parents can be encouraged to seek therapy services from other sources, including local universities, private therapists, clinics, or public schools. Under current legislation, parents can obtain free therapy through their public school system, but they are normally responsible for providing transportation to and from the public agency. If a sufficient number of speech-impaired students attend a given Christian school, current legislation allows for cooperative arrangements, usually highly restrictive. Therapists in the public school system would bring therapy services to the Christian school premises on an itinerant basis.

Visual Impairments

Visually impaired students may have defects of visual acuity or a limited field of vision. If they are without other handicaps, they are good candidates for inclusion in regular classrooms. The

Commissions for the Visually Handicapped offer a wide range of ancillary services that are available regardless of a student's educational placement. These include the supply of low-vision aids, talking books, special recording equipment, instruction in Braille, basic concepts, and orientation and mobility training on an itinerant basis. As with physically-disabled students, the schools must attend to issues of building access and emergency procedures.

A visually impaired student can be served in the regular programs of Christian schools in cooperation with personnel from community resources. The students' teachers should be prepared to make the necessary modifications for class intervention and participation. Volunteers can be used as necessary to translate materials into Braille or to read to and tutor students. Current computer technology greatly enhances the opportunities for blind students to participate in regular programs.

Physical Disabilities

Physically disabled or other health-impaired students represent a wide variety of needs. Physical disabilities may include impaired limbs, cerebral palsy, muscular dystrophy, spina bifida, or such medical conditions as heart defects, seizures, or asthma. When unaccompanied by other disorders, these disabilities may require only some modifications in the physical environment, a reduction of time spent in school, the provision of limited medical services, a generous absentee policy, and emergency procedures that assure the students' safety. Building adaptations include ramps, appropriate washroom facilities, and sometimes extra space to ensure classroom accessibility.

The enrollment of physically disabled children in regular classes must be considered on a case-by-case basis. Teachers may need to meet unique needs by modifying their instructional programs slightly through the use of special materials, methods, and volunteers. The parents of such children are usually very knowledgeable and can assist the school staff in handling both daily needs and emergency situations.

Two additional considerations should be noted. Physically disabled students are usually receiving ongoing medical treatment and are enrolled in programs of physical and occupational therapy. The parents usually assume responsibility for obtaining these services, but coordination with instructional personnel is a necessity for developing adaptive physical education and assuring the carryover of special techniques or exercises. Thus all staff must be alert to continuing health needs and ready to respond to emergencies. Also, for a homebound student, special computer and telephone systems or video-conferencing can allow participation in instructional programs that are based in a Christian school.

Hearing Impairments

Hearing-impaired students have defects in hearing that limit their ability to process normal sounds in the environment. The disability is related to a limited level of language understanding and production, which in turn affects performance in all academic subjects. Hearing-impaired students will typically function at three or more years below the normal academic level, even when they have normal or above-normal intelligence. Therefore, programming in regular classrooms for students with severe to profound hearing impairments is difficult. The following options are suggested:

1. When optimally aided, hard-of-hearing students with slight to moderate losses who are near grade level and have adequate language skills can generally function in an oral environment and do not need to learn sign language. They can be integrated into regular classes, but they need auxiliary speech therapy and tutoring. They will also require minor accommodations in their instructional program, including preferential seating.
2. Deaf and hard-of-hearing students who have adequate language and academic skills can be integrated into regular classes (mostly at upper grade levels) with the services of an interpreter who translates the class proceedings into sign language at the direction of the instructor. A few students have been successfully included in regular classrooms by using a voice-translation computer system.
3. A special or resource classroom for deaf and hard-of-hearing students can be established when as many as six students are identified and a teacher with appropriate certification is hired. Instructional aides and volunteers can provide additional support. Such students can be integrated into regular classrooms and activities for lunch, chapel, physical education, and other subjects in which their instructional needs are similar to those of the other students. Because deaf and severely hard-of-hearing students will not develop language and communication skills without intense instruction, methodology usually includes the use of sign language in addition to emphasis on developing speech and understanding the speech of others.

Ideas That Work

Ask parents or fellow students to read aloud and tape chapters so that the special student can read and listen simultaneously. If possible, structure the listening process so that the student is listening for specific information. (A recording service is available free of charge for visually impaired and learning-disabled students.)

Use several avenues of information in order to capitalize on strengths in visual or auditory channels. These students often benefit greatly from diagrams, charts, and other visual information.

When grading, consider giving both a content grade and a form grade—or at least a limited penalty for misspellings and similar errors.

When a student has really tried, consider providing extra credit for projects or special reports, or consider allowing optional assignments.

Emotional Conflicts

All students experience adjustment problems at some time in their lives. These conflicts can be of such an intensity and duration that they disrupt students' educational progress and interpersonal relationships. By the nature of a Christian environment, students with problems will find warm, supportive relationships and good biblical counsel in a Christian school. However, sometimes parents see the school as a panacea for long-standing emotional problems that grow out of dysfunctional family situations. Christian schools should be wise about enrolling such students.

A student who is experiencing severe conflict seldom makes academic progress. The frustrations encountered in an academically oriented environment may add to the conflict. Certainly, Christian schools are open to ministering to students with emotional conflicts, but they must consider two questions: *Can the school provide an appropriate educational environment for the student?* and *Can the school do so without major disruption to the educational process for other students?* If the answer to both questions is yes, the school should work closely with the family and require a commitment to professional counseling as a condition for enrollment.

Growing numbers of students are being diagnosed with autism, which is marked by disordered bonding relationships and poor social interactions. These students can be served in special classes or resource rooms. Students with Asperger's syndrome may be at grade level but still have problems relating to peers and learning within the classroom environment. However, they can participate in a regular classroom when supportive assistance is available to them.

Attention Deficit Hyperactivity Disorders

Attention deficits have recently become a defined diagnosis for students whose difficulty in sustaining attention has a negative effect on their academic progress. The attention deficit syndrome may exist with or without hyperactivity. These students may or may not have other disabilities that would make them eligible for special services. The origin of the syndrome is neurological and developmental, and the resulting behavior is not completely under the child's control. In general, the observable behaviors that alert parents and teachers are as follows:

1. The student will often lose his place and appears to be daydreaming or engrossed in something other than the task at hand.
2. The student is very easily distracted. His attention will shift to the traffic outside, or he will be picking up pieces of paper from

the floor while everyone else is on page 98 of the textbook.

3. The student does not follow directions well, especially if they consist of several steps. She will often act as if she has not heard the directions.
4. The student is poorly organized, never seems to know where her papers are, knows she did the homework but now can't find it. Typically, her work space is messy.
5. The student's class work is sloppy and partly unfinished. The student can miss large areas completely and often makes careless errors.
6. The student is impulsive, talks out, has difficulty waiting her turn, doesn't think before acting. She can be restless and fidgety. She will repeat the same wrongdoing or error, not because she does not understand right and wrong but simply because she lacks self-control.
7. The student has poor social skills. He can be very immature, oblivious of the needs and feelings of others, and often in trouble. These qualities can lead to a low self-concept and anger at what he feels is people's dislike or misunderstanding of him.

Extensive research into the six types of ADHD may greatly improve our ability to make good diagnoses and offer appropriate medical intervention. Until then, parents and educators are faced with limited treatment options that extend in two directions.

1. A lifestyle approach that establishes a high level of direction over proper nutrition, exercise, sleep patterns, organization of personal space, reduction of stressful schedules, focus on organizational and study skills, along with behavior-management techniques and parent counseling.
2. Medical intervention using Ritalin, Adderol, Tofranil, or other medications. Even though many Christian professionals and parents resist using drugs to treat what they see as a behavior problem, medications can have significant positive effects and may be the optimal course of treatment when other interventions have proven ineffective.

If the attention deficit is accompanied by delayed academic development, placement in an environment with high standards may be frustrating for everyone involved. Treatments must be in place to address the full range of a student's needs, especially if other areas of need are present such as emotional conflicts or learning disabilities. If not, the regular classroom teacher will be the person to implement accommodations (usually called a 504 plan) recommended by a child psychologist or medical professional.

Whether medicated or not, students with ADHD are generally well served in Christian schools, where there are typically fewer distractions, more structure, closer parent contact, and a planned progression through the curriculum. The lower student-teacher ratio allows for the personal attention and spiritual nurturing that encourage students to be responsible for their own behavior.

Learning Disabilities

The category of exceptionality called *learning disabilities* was identified in federal legislation in 1975. At that time it was thought to include only a small part of the anticipated 12 percent of the school population expected to need special education services. Currently, however, it is the largest category of exceptionality, as about 50 percent of all students receiving special services are diagnosed as learning-disabled. These are students who have average and above average intelligence but perceive, process, store, retrieve, and express information differently than normal. To be considered learning disabilities, these neurological differences must be unrelated to any other disability or environmental disadvantage, and they must have a negative effect on academic progress, generally seen in the inability to learn to read, write, spell, or do math calculations. The population is extremely heterogeneous, with one student having little in common with another.

The population generally served in public schools is functioning two or more years below grade level in the major academic areas. Thus they are different from those attending Christian schools, who may not have fallen behind but still demonstrate the underlying learning differences. These differences cause great frustration for the students, who must exert enormous energy to get passing grades even though they may, in fact, be capable of high achievement. Christian schools have recognized the need to initiate special programs for such students in order to prevent academic delays, recognizing that two years of failure as a prerequisite for help only compounds the problems of emotional and social adjustment.

Programs to assist students with learning disabilities have followed two general patterns. The first model is basically tutorial with a focus on repetition in the context of the regular classroom. The service is provided by a visiting teacher or in a resource room where a variety of students come and go throughout the school day. The teacher uses various materials and teaching strategies to assist students to achieve and maintain grade-level competencies.

The second service model is therapeutic intervention, which has its roots in the cognitive therapy used with stroke victims and others

Ideas That Work

Reduce the length of assignments, but be sure that the essential material is covered. Circle the priority questions, or assign problems from each section.

Provide lots of structure for assignments, especially long-term ones. Break them into several parts with checkpoints along the way.

Insist that the student keep a daily assignment notebook. Use a buddy system to make sure the assignments are written correctly. Ask parents to initial the completed assignments.

Keep the room as free of distracters as possible. Noises from fans or vacuuming, for example, can be disastrous. Visually, the room should be well organized, with items having a specific place and pictures arranged neatly, not haphazardly.

with minimal brain injuries. Its goal is to change the way a student's brain perceives and processes information. The techniques have been used widely in hospitals and in private practice, but Norfolk Christian Schools implemented the first school-based program. Using some 21 different techniques that involve educational materials, teachers see students individually approximately three hours a week, working intensively to strengthen their areas of weakness. The result is students who function independently at grade level with minimal frustration. Because of the success of students in the program, the National Institute for Learning Disabilities (NILD) was established to provide teacher training and special materials to organizations wanting to develop services for those with learning disabilities.

Mental Challenges

Students with mild to moderate mental challenges can be successfully served in Christian schools. These schools must be willing to make considerable modifications in their curriculum expectations, since the students may reach only half to two-thirds of the objectives established for students in the normal range of intelligence. Appropriate services include classes with personal assistants, resource rooms, and special classes with mainstreaming options. These students can provide a school with great opportunities for service and for expressing love in a Christian community—opportunities that could be obtained in no other way. As the discrepancy in academic competence grows wider, the school's challenge is to provide creative instruction in daily living skills and vocational training.

Giftedness

Exceptional students are often defined as those with significant problems, and the special needs of gifted students are overlooked. Because their students score on average two or more years above grade level, Christian schools serve as ideal environments for gifted students. However, every school faces the question of how best to serve students with superior intelligence. The initial changes must occur in the regular classroom environment, where students can be allowed to pursue their own research interests after having demonstrated competence in the basic curriculum requirements. Controlled structure and repetition are not in their best interest. They must be directed to expand and enrich their learning through challenging individualized projects, some acceleration of content, computer-assisted instruction, and contracting for grades. Other options are resource rooms and independent study.

Issues to Address

Most Christian school administrators express a desire to broaden their arena of service, especially when school families have a long-term commitment to Christian education. Their questions as to whom and how to serve should not be interpreted as resistance but rather as an honest seeking of God's direction when they must respond to competing priorities with the limited resources available. Schools that are considering how to serve students with special needs must address several issues.

Financial Resources. Many Christian schools and the parents they serve are hard pressed to pay for the basic services provided. A student with special needs can require costs up to four times those of a student in the regular program. Thus schools struggle with how to make special services affordable for families without having a negative impact on the general budget, and they approach the challenge in various ways. A few charge a single tuition rate regardless of any special services a student might need. Others provide special services, with parents paying any costs that are additional to the basic tuition. Most schools choose some combination of those two options—for example, charging the excess personnel and materials costs to parents but covering operations and capital expenditures in the general budget.

Personnel Resources. Teachers and therapists for students with special needs require advanced training and skills. Such trained professionals who share the school's philosophy are often difficult to locate. A program formed under the tutelage of such an individual may have to be abandoned when the person leaves. Thus, selecting and maintaining quality teachers for exceptional students may be the most difficult challenge.

Because the teacher-student ratio is much lower than it is in the public schools, Christian schools must employ more teachers in order to offer the services of speech therapists, physical and occupational therapists, nurses, aides, or psychologists. If a school cannot provide these services, it must obtain them through relationships with local professionals.

Space and Management of Resources. While the number of students with special needs may be small, their space needs are greater. Their parents often require support. Policies and procedures related to their special programs must extend beyond those required for regular classes. Thus schools are faced with a central dilemma—the desire to extend services but the reality of limited resources. Jesus taught the wisdom of counting the cost prior to building a tower (Luke 14:28–29). Administrators must make wise decisions about the allocation of resources if they hope to assure the longevity of their ministry.

Public School Relationships. Under federal and state laws, parents have extensive rights to services for children with special needs regardless of their placement in a private school setting. These rights include diagnostic testing and limited direct services that can be obtained through a local public school. In a few states the collaboration between public and private educators is extensive, providing for special teachers, therapists, materials, and transportation at public expense. Administrators need to know what services are available locally and how to access them.

Enrollment Policies. Defining the needs of your current enrollment and assessing how to extend the necessary services will help your school consider what opportunities God has placed under the umbrella of your ministry. Then your school can gradually and wisely add the services needed. A school cannot be all things to all people. Pressures may build to accept more special-needs students than can reasonably be handled. It is unwise to accept more than eight to ten percent at each grade level, or to overload a given classroom with more than two to three special-needs students. Your first duty is to protect the integrity of the corporate whole so that all students have a normal classroom in which to learn. If all Christian schools served their share of special-needs students, all of them could be invited to the banquet table.

Extensive Accommodations. The word "accommodation" denotes changes made in the physical environment, teaching strategies, and testing procedures to ensure that a student has optimal conditions for learning and for demonstrating competence. While a diagnostic evaluation should be required to certify the need for accommodations, thus keeping the teacher from having to justify why one student is treated differently from another, the necessary accommodations should be granted generously. They include strategies and materials such as copies of the teacher's notes or color-coded text, additional time for writing assignments and tests, reduced homework focused on essential content rather than repetition, books on tape or in large print, and the use of computers—anything that helps a student learn. Some students and their parents may make the matter an issue of fairness. Yet fairness is defined as providing what each student needs. If the other students needed the accommodation, it would be offered to them just as readily.

Ideas That Work

Post the rules for classroom behavior. They should be few in number but consistently enforced. Draw the students' attention back to the rules when problems occur. Provide positive instruction as needed on the reasons for the rules.

Help the student organize her space—a shoe box for small items, folders of different colors for different subjects, maybe color coordinated with textbooks, for example.

Use an overhead projector rather than a board so that you can maintain eye contact. Also, the contrast is better and the print type is similar to that used in testing. If you must use the board, write the information ahead of time, and do not talk with your back to the students.

Place your notes or book upside down (facing the student) and lecture from his desk. He then has an immediate copy for reference, and you can easily indicate the correct place in the lesson.

Limited Modifications. The word "modification" implies a change in the content to be learned, such as a fourth grader working in a second-grade reader, or a tenth-grade biology student taking a seventh-grade life science course. These modifications may be appropriate in meeting the needs of a given student, but they create additional issues that must be addressed, such as accuracy in reporting student progress and the kind of diplomas to be received. Content modification may be necessary in order to serve the needs of high school students. A teacher can make limited modifications by focusing on the core curriculum and modifying certain expectations for a given student. Or for courses in the basic curriculum, a grading base can be established that allows a teacher to add points to keep within a passing range a student who has made a good effort and maintains a positive attitude. The primary effort is to help a student obtain a quality education while developing spiritual maturity. Limited modifications can assist in achieving this goal.

Summary

Jesus' parable in Luke 14:12–14 contains both a command and a promise. The command is to invite those with special needs to the feast. Therefore, Christian schools have a mandate. Whether it relates to accepting a student with special needs into a regular class or developing an array of special programs, God has a plan for His people. His is a ministry of restoration. Since Christian education is right for all children in the body of Christ, it is certainly right for children with special needs.

When your school is given the opportunity to serve such children, first seek the Lord in prayer. How does God want your school to respond? Perhaps you can meet the need—perhaps you cannot. Either way, you will have conscientiously determined His will. When the direction is clear, you will also have assurance that He will resolve the challenges you face in inviting these children to the banquet.

The promise in the parable is also straightforward and simple: You will be blessed. Your students with special needs will learn as much as, or more than, the regular students. They will bring a unique character to your school that will bless your students. We tend to respond more to the needs of starving children in foreign countries than we do to the special needs of those already in our circle of influence. Why not invite these special children to the banquet and enjoy the blessings?

About the Author

Sharon R. Berry, Ph.D., served several years in public education before joining the Christian school movement in 1982. She is the editor, developer, or author of almost 200 publications, including ACSI's preschool and kindergarten programs, spelling series, Bible series, and the initial stages of the math series.

Strengthen Your Foundations

1. Interview the Christian parent of a special-needs student. Determine what needs the parent feels the student has and whether the parent believes that a Christian school can meet them.

2. Observe a classroom containing two or more special-needs students, especially those with attention deficit hyperactivity disorder. Note the challenges faced by the special-needs students, the regular students, and the teacher.

3. Research some media articles related to medicines used in treating ADHD. Determine the validity of arguments both for and against using medication.

4. Choose an area of exceptionality and suggest teaching strategies that would allow the student to be successful in the regular classroom.

5. Study Exodus 4, Psalm 139, John 9, Romans 9, Romans 12, 1 Corinthians 1, and 1 Corinthians 12. Determine biblically why God allows disabilities and what the Christian response should be.

6. Develop a list of potential modifications you could make to accommodate the needs of gifted students in your classroom.

References

Akers, John. 2000. *This we believe: The good news of Jesus Christ for the world.* Grand Rapids, MI: Zondervan.

The Baptist faith and message: A statement adopted by the Southern Baptist Convention. 1998, revised. Nashville: LifeWay Christian Resources.

Berkhof, Louis. 1939. *Manual of Christian doctrine.* Grand Rapids, MI: Eerdmans.

Bewes, R., P. Blackman, and R. Hicks. 1999. *The essential Bible truth treasury and journal.* Bath, Avon, England: Gospel Gifts.

Boice, James Montgomery. 1986. *Foundations of the Christian faith.* Downers Grove, IL: InterVarsity Press.

Bounds, E. M. 1966. *Heaven: A place, a city, a home.* Grand Rapids, MI: Baker Book House.

Brown, L. D. 1980. *Truths that make a difference.* Nashville: Convention Press.

Chafer, Lewis Sperry, and John F. Walvoord, eds. 1974. *Major Bible themes.* Grand Rapids, MI: Zondervan.

Christian Learning Center, associated with the Christian Reformed Church and Schools, 2520 Eastern Avenue Southeast, Grand Rapids, MI 49507.

Criswell, W. A. 1966. *The Holy Spirit in today's world.* Grand Rapids, MI: Zondervan.

Dollar, T., J. Falwell, A. V. Henderson, and J. Hyles, eds. 1977. *Building blocks of the faith: Foundational Bible doctrines.* Nashville: Fundamentalist Church Publications.

Evans, William. 1974. *The great doctrines of the Bible.* Chicago: Moody Press.

Heatherley, E. X. 1997. *The parables of Christ.* Austin, TX: Balcony Publishing.

——. 2000. *Our heavenly home.* Austin, TX: Balcony Publishing.

Hobbs, Herschel H. 1960. *Fundamentals of our faith.* Nashville: Broadman Press.

JAF Ministries (Joni Eareckson Tada). PO Box 9333, Agoura Hills, CA 91376.

Kennedy, D. James. 1980. *Why I believe.* Nashville: Word Publishing.

Kirk, S. A., J. J. Gallagher, and N. J. Anastasiow. 2000. *Educating exceptional children.* Boston: Houghton Mifflin.

Little, Paul. 2000, revised and updated. *Know why you believe.* Downers Grove, IL: InterVarsity Press.

McDowell, Josh. 1999. *The new evidence that demands a verdict.* Nashville: Thomas Nelson.

McGrath, Alister E. 1991. *I believe: Exploring the Apostles' Creed.* Downers Grove, IL: InterVarsity Press.

Morris, Henry, and Henry Morris III. 1974. *Many infallible proofs.* Green Forest, AR: Master Books.

National Institute for Learning Disabilities, 107 Seekel Street, Norfolk, VA 23505.

Pentecost, J. Dwight. 1965. *Things which become sound doctrine.* Grand Rapids, MI: Zondervan.

Pippert, Rebecca M. 1989. *Hope has its reasons: Surprised by faith in a broken world.* New York: HarperCollins.

Ryrie, Charles C. 1972. *A survey of Bible doctrine.* Chicago: Moody Press.

Sisson, Richard. 1983. *Answering Christianity's most puzzling questions,* vol. 2. Chicago: Moody Press.

Stringfellow, Alan B. 1981. *Through the Bible in one year,* vol. 3. Tulsa, OK: Hensley Publishing.

Sutton, Joe P., ed. 1993. *Special education: A biblical approach.* Greenville, SC: Hidden Treasures Ministries.

Thiessen, Henry. 1979, revised. *Lectures in systematic theology.* Grand Rapids, MI: Eerdmans.

Torrey, R. A. 1998. *What the Bible teaches.* Peabody, MA: Hendrickson Publishers.

Turnbull, Ralph G., ed. 1967. *Baker's dictionary of practical theology.* Grand Rapids, MI: Baker Book House.

Wayside Language Center, 12721 Northeast 101st Place, Kirkland, WA 98033.

Weis, Nita. 1995. *Raising achievers: A parent's plan for motivating children to excel.* Nashville: Broadman & Holman.

Willmington, Harold. 1981. *Willmington's guide to the Bible.* Wheaton, IL: Tyndale House.

CHAPTER SEVENTEEN

Urban Schools: A Christian Philosophy That Impacts Culture

Vernard T. Gant

The urban centers in America and throughout the world are facing crises of unparalleled proportion. Normally, the greatest threats to a nation or a people have come from enemies and potential enemies from outside. In our central cities, however, there is an enemy within that is not subject to legislative action, government policy, the size of the military, or even a strong economy. Pathological social and cultural lifestyles are eroding the nation's interior like a cancerous tumor, leaving only the question of how long before its total demise. While this phenomenon threatens the whole nation, it is most calamitous in its urban centers. What we are witnessing and experiencing is analogous to a virus that infects an entire family by initially striking its weakest and most vulnerable member. The social, cultural, and moral decay spreading through America is most pronounced in the central cities and most evident in the lives of urban youth. The verdict appears to be in—children living in the inner cities of this nation are in imminent danger of falling prey to some of the most virulent ills of our society. The consensus is that in America's urban centers, one generation of youth is all but "lost," while another waits at the threshold of impending disaster. These urban youths are prime targets, prime candidates, and prime victims of drugs, crime, and teen pregnancy. And they are generally characterized by poor academic performance.

To compound matters, an effective education (historically a way out for at-risk youths) has all but eluded them, though such an education represents the only hope of breaking the cycles of deprivation and decadence that have been perpetuating themselves from one generation to the next. The nation, however, appears at a loss to know how to educate urban youth effectively. According to published reports, of the nearly 600 urban school districts in the nation serving approximately one-fourth of all school-age children, not a single one is considered academically successful (*Education Week on the Web* 1998).

The Rise and Fall of Urban America

To understand the modern urban phenomenon and address the problems effectively, particularly in the area of education, one needs to trace the history of urban America, identifying its components and contributing factors. The timeline below chronicles the rise and fall of urban America (Lemann 1986). The urbanization of America's central cities is largely related to the Northern ghettoes prominent during the middle part of the last century. The ghettoes were born of and fueled by two societal movements: the great northern migration of African Americans from Southern farms to the cities and the great exodus of the middle class from the cities to the suburbs. Left behind in the cities was a socially and politically disenfranchised underclass that retained the cultural values and practices of tenant farm life in the South.

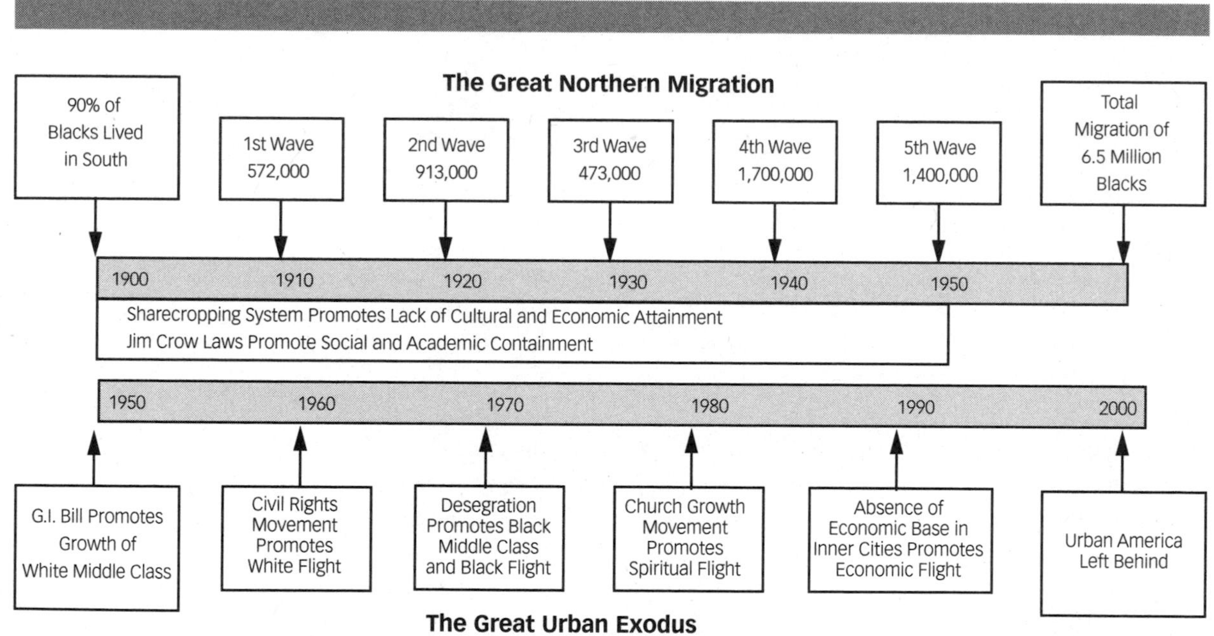

Those living in America's ghettoes (or even near them) who could get out, did so. The urban dwellers left behind continued in the lifestyles and values inherited from the rural South. In essence, the culture was one of poverty and family disorganization including crime, low educational aspirations, teenage pregnancies, and dependency. These indexes of social pathology were neither born of nor fueled by the Great Society welfare system. Rather, they became a way of life long before the welfare system was introduced. Black historian E. Franklin Frazier noted more than a half century ago:

> As a result of family disorganization a large proportion of [inner city] children and youth have not undergone the socialization that only the family can provide. The disorganized families have failed to provide for their emotional needs and have not provided the discipline and habits which are necessary for personality development. Because the disorganized family has failed in its functions as a socializing agency, it has handicapped the children in their relations to the institutions in the community. Moreover, family disorganization has been partially responsible for a large amount of juvenile delinquency and adult crime ... (Moynihan 1987, 25).

The disorganized family is often a broken family, and the leading factor in that disorganization is the incidence of female heads-of-household. According to published reports, children from single-parent homes are four to five times more likely to live in poverty than children living with both their birth parents. Moreover, they are more likely to:

- be born with a low birth weight
- have an undereducated parent
- have an underparented parent
- lack proper nutrition
- grow up in a poor neighborhood
- attend a low-achieving school
- become a victim of crime
- commit a crime
- drop out of high school

And poverty means there are few if any resources (financial or relational) to alleviate the situation.

With the middle class exodus, the characteristics of family disorganization listed above became increasingly apparent and prevalent in the low-income urban centers of America. These characteristics would in time be identified as family risk factors because the children who were subject to them would have a high incidence of practicing the same behaviors and thereby perpetuating the downward spiral. The following graph indicates that children living in central cities have a far greater probability of experiencing family risk factors than their suburban or rural peers:

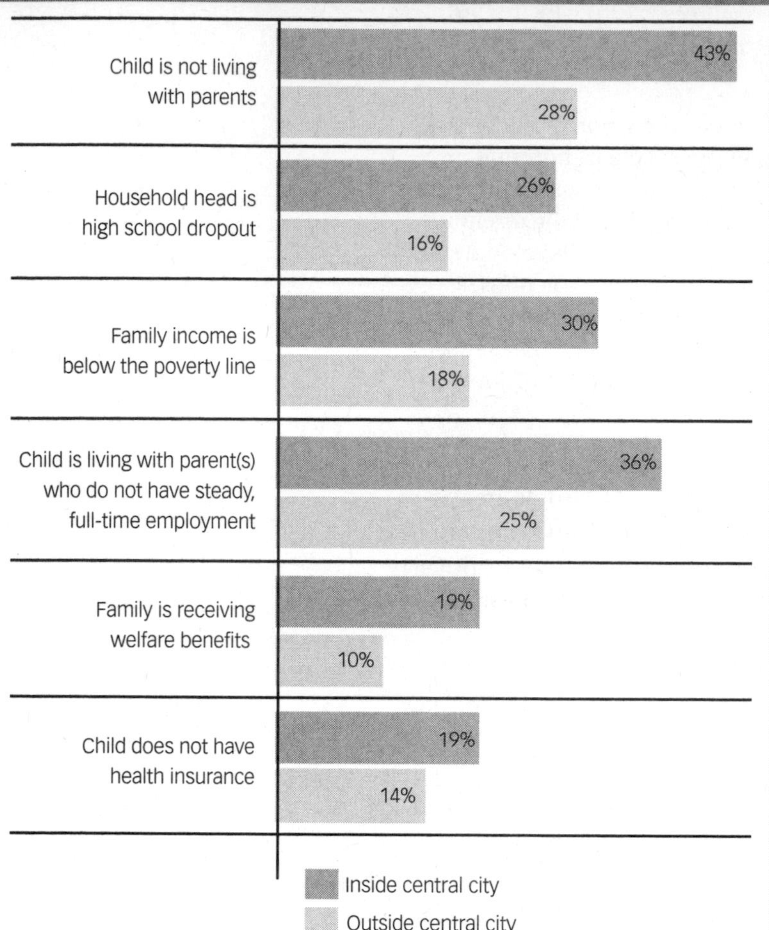

The Educational System's Contribution to the Problem

To compound matters, this disorganized class of urban dwellers, who lack a strong family structure and a solid economic base, have not received and are not receiving the academic foundation that could offer the hope or promise of relief. This problem too is rooted in American history.

Not long after the establishment of chattel slavery as an economic institution, an educational "system" was put in place to ensure the institution's success. Under this system, education would be used as an instrument for the nonintellectual development of the slaves for the sole purpose of the economic development of the South and the prosperity of white landowners. The aftermath is still with us today. Instead of being a means for the personal attainment of African American youth, the American education system is an instrument of their social containment. The most vulnerable ones are the most affected by the system. This deleterious system unfolded in three phases.

The first stage was the *forbidden education* of the slaves. Because of the economic and social threat that formal education represented to the white power establishment, laws were passed making it a crime to teach a slave to read. An eyewitness writing from personal experience, Frederick Douglass (1845) describes it best:

> Very soon after I went to live with Mr. and Mrs. Auld, she very kindly commenced to teach me the A, B, C. After I had learned this, she assisted me in learning to spell words of three or four letters. Just at

> this point of my progress, Mr. Auld found out what was going on, and at once forbade Mrs. Auld to instruct me further, telling her, among other things, that it was unlawful, as well as unsafe, to teach a slave to read.

Carter G. Woodson adds:

> After these laws had been passed, American slavery extended not as that of the ancients, only to the body, but also to the mind. Education was thereafter regarded as positively inconsistent with the institution. The precaution taken to prevent the dissemination of information was declared indispensable to the system. The situation in many parts of the South was just as Berry portrayed it in the Virginia House of Delegates in 1832. He said: "We have as far as possible closed every avenue by which light may enter [the slaves'] minds. If we could extinguish the capacity to see the light, our work would be completed; they would then be on a level with the beasts of the field, and we should be safe! (1999, 170)

Phase two was an elaborate strategy of *miseducation*. This strategy involved a two-part approach. Part one was to educate the blacks that they were racially, intellectually, socially, culturally, and spiritually inferior in every way to whites. The goal was simply to shackle the minds of the slaves, thereby reinforcing the physical shackles that already bound their bodies. Part two, equally important, was to convince the whites that, no matter their social or economic status, they were superior to blacks in every way simply because of the color of their skin. Finally, to seal the matter, both teachings were given the weight of Scripture so as to leave no room for doubt or refutation.

The third phase was naturally born of the first two—the *undereducation* of African American children. Initially, African American children were undereducated in the South to limit their occupational options (Anderson 1988). To guarantee a supply of cheap labor to replace the former slave labor, the Southern landowners, businessmen, and politicians established a school system that would, for all practical purposes, promote a slave mentality, one that would be just as effective as physical slavery. One of the principal figures in the Southern education movement, which started in 1898, Northern philanthropist William H. Baldwin, Jr., advised black Southerners, "Avoid social questions; leave politics alone; continue to be patient; live moral lives; live simply; learn to work … know that it is a crime for any teacher, white or black, to educate the negro for positions which are not open to him" (Anderson 1988, 84). Serving with Baldwin at the Conference for Education in the

South, Charles W. Dabney, then president of the University of Tennessee, asserted, "We must use common sense in the education of the negro.... We must recognize in all its relations that momentous fact that the negro is a child race, at least two thousand years behind the Anglo-Saxon in its development." He then concluded, "Nothing is more ridiculous than the programme of the good religious people from the North who insist upon teaching Latin, Greek, and philosophy to the negro boys who come to their schools" (85).

As a result, the progeny of slaves, although born free, did not fare much better than their slave ancestors. They were bound to work as sharecroppers and laborers in order to advance the farming economy of the South. Basically, the system dictated an inferior education to ensure inferior status. Today, several generations later, the *system* is now self-sustaining largely because of widely held beliefs about the intellectual inadequacy of African Americans.

Fully 90 percent of African Americans lived in the South at the turn of the last century and were victims of a faulty system of education. This fact, along with the culture, beliefs, rules, and practices of tenant farm life, basically guaranteed a life of poverty along with all the indexes that accompany it. Now, the modern education establishment finds itself in a quandary. How can public education successfully teach children who are not being trained effectively at home and whom the school was not historically designed to teach successfully? These children are basically inheriting the lifestyles of their parents, who inherited them from their parents.

For example, renowned African American sociologist Kenneth B. Clark wrote in 1965:

> Unless firm and immediate steps are taken to reverse the present trend, the public school system in ... America will become predominantly a segregated system, serving primarily Negroes. It will, in addition, become a school system of low academic standards, providing a second-class education for underclassed children and thereby a contributor to the perpetuation of the "social dynamite" which is the cumulative pathology of the ghetto....
>
> It is an ironic and tragic inversion of the purpose of education that ... as [Negro children] proceed through school [they] fall further and further behind the standard for their grade level in academic performance. The schools are presently damaging the children they exist to help....
>
> The fact [is] that these children, by and large, do not learn because they are not being taught effectively and they are not being taught because those who are charged with the responsibility of teaching

them do not believe that they can learn, do not expect that they can learn, and do not act toward them in ways which help them to learn.

The progeny of the children Clark referred to now populate our urban schools. And, as was the case forty years ago, the urban schools are failing to educate a large percentage of the children assigned to them. According to one published report (*Education Week on the Web* 1998):

- There are nearly 600 urban school districts in this nation. (An *urban* district is defined as one in which 75 percent or more of the households served are in the central city of a metropolitan area.)
- Over 12 million children attend schools in urban districts.
- Some 43 percent of minority children attend urban schools. (Most urban schools are predominantly, often completely, minority.)
- In most urban schools more than half the students are poor, qualifying for free or reduced-price lunches.
- Two-thirds or more of urban school children fail to reach even the "basic" level on national tests. Urban students perform far worse, on average, than children who live outside central cities on virtually every measure of academic performance. The longer they stay in school, the wider that gap grows.

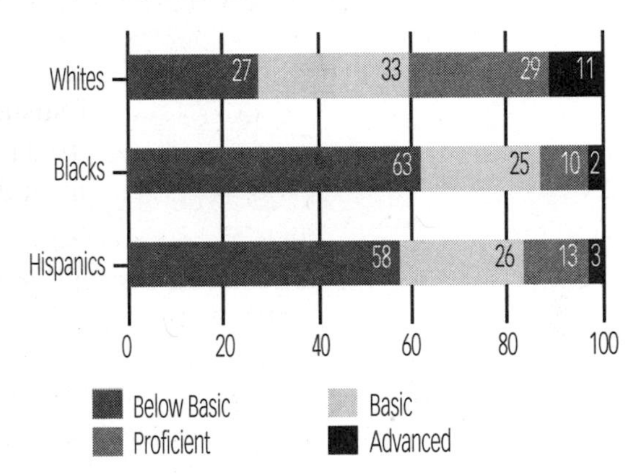

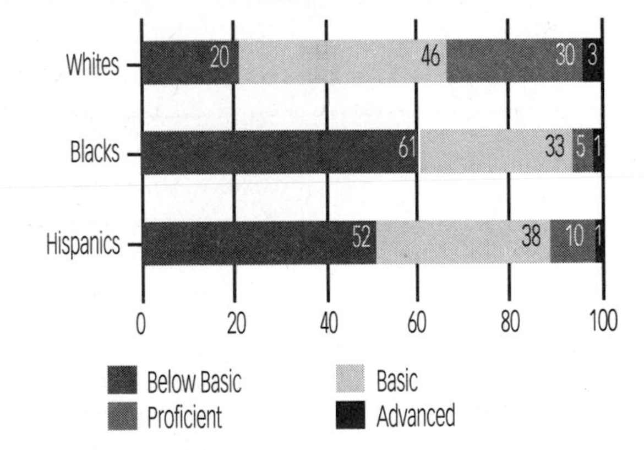

The charts at the right compare fourth-grade achievement levels in reading (Donahue et al. 2001) and math (Braswell et al. 2001) for the year 2000. A glance at the percentages of children who are below basic and basic will suggest the enormity of the problem.

What is most alarming is the stakes involved. For those who have little hope of an academic future, the chances of a successful social future are equally dim. Add poverty to the equation, and the numbers reach calamitous proportions. Eighty-six percent of poor African American children read below the basic level. Given the fact that their current level of education offers few positive options for their future endeavors, the chances are great that negative options will prevail. Perhaps this explains why two-thirds of the prisoners in state correctional institutions do not have a high school diploma.

Poverty's Contribution to the Problem

To effectively address the educational plight of the urban poor, one must understand the nature and extent of the poverty and what it means to be impoverished. While the term usually refers to financial status and income level, finances represent only one kind of resource needed for productivity. A broader definition of *poverty* is "the extent to which an individual has a deficiency of the capital needed to be productive." Here, *capital* refers to the "assets available for use in the production of other assets." Consequently, the more capital one has, the more capital one is able to produce. Many urban children grow up to be unproductive or underproductive citizens because they never amass the capital necessary for becoming productive. The ability to amass capital is largely determined by societal factors that work either for or against an individual. In many central city communities, children start out with a deficiency of these growth-determining factors. They start out behind, and often remain behind, their more capital-rich peers.

Just as there are family lifestyle factors that put children at risk, there are also capital assets that determine the presence of, the nature of, and the ability to escape poverty:

1. *Financial capital:* Those material goods that are developed by acquisition and that can be used productively. Conditioned by:
   a. the family income
   b. the employment status and employability of the parents
   c. the spending habits of the family (reflecting their priorities and values)
2. *Cultural capital:* Knowledge of the beliefs, customs, practices, and rules of a social group that can be used productively. Conditioned by:
   a. the marital status of the parents

b. the neighborhood where the child starts out and grows up
c. the family support structure in place for the child

3. *Intellectual capital:* Those human capacities (mental and physical) developed by education that can be used productively. Conditioned by:
   a. the educational level of the parents
   b. the amount and degree of early language experience (ELE) and informal pre-education (IPE) the child receives
   c. the academic climate of the child's first school
4. *Social capital:* Those relationships and contacts that develop naturally and can be used productively. Conditioned by:
   a. the child's race
   b. the racial climate of the child's primary communities and the racial attitudes of the child's caregivers (including teachers and administrators)
   c. the social networks available to the child
5. *Emotional capital:* Those feelings of sufficiency and determination that can be used productively. Conditioned by:
   a. the emotional maturity of the primary caregivers
   b. the stressors being brought to bear on the child and the household
   c. the emotional buffers and options available to the family
6. *Spiritual capital:* those belief structures that provide the bases for purpose, morals, values, discipline, and self-worth that can be used productively. Conditioned by:
   a. the spiritual life of the primary caregiver
   b. the church environment
   c. the practice of biblical values in the home

Again, the formula is simple—the more capital available to the child, the more assets the child has for productivity. Urban children, as portrayed above, have few of the capital assets for being productive. As a result, these variables become limiting factors in the child's development. The failure of attempts to educate these children is by and large a failure to recognize and address all these factors. This is particularly a dilemma for public school systems because schools were neither designed nor equipped to provide the kind of holistic undergirding necessary to address the multifaceted dimensions of poverty. Schools exist to dispense information and to impart knowledge. This is usually done in a group setting and is best done when children come with the discipline, values, respect, and academic orientation that are most conducive to learning. Children from homes with anemic family structures and little or no emphasis on education lack the training that provides the best conditions for academically group-processing children. Again, the moral quandary of modern education is, How do we effectively teach children at school who have not been effectively trained at home? In other words, how do we teach children when they have so many socio-environmental factors working against them? How do educators overcome the child's environment?

Christ-centered urban schools can address these socio-environmental factors because they can do more than educate children; they can help rear them. For some children, this simply means reinforcing the values and principles instilled at home, whether by two parents or a single parent. For other children, it means introducing and instilling alternative values and practices. The procedure can be as mild as gently correcting the child who says, "My momma said if somebody hits me, I can hit them back." Or it can be as firm as conveying to a child whose mother has had multiple children out of wedlock that such behavior is morally wrong.

These children must be shown "a more excellent way" (1 Corinthians 12:31). It must be a part of the curriculum, the school environment, and the children's total educational experience. It won't just happen through a period of character education offered in the course of the school day or during Bible class. It must be fully integrated into the school's program. To be effective, these factors must be seen as determining variables in the children's development. If they are in short supply and are not addressed, the child's ability to develop the life skills necessary for productive behavior and relationships will be greatly hampered.

The Solution—Kingdom Schools

Therefore, the Christ-centered urban school must function as a kingdom school. Kingdom schools target and serve children who are academically and socially broken. In urban centers throughout this nation, urban children are suffering from societal ills that threaten their lives and their futures. These children can be compared to the sheep of Ezekiel 34 about which God reproves the shepherds for failing to nurture them: *The weak you have not strengthened, nor have you healed those who were sick, nor bound up the broken, nor brought back what was driven away, nor sought what was lost* (Ezekiel 34:4).

As a result, He promised through the prophet Jeremiah that He would raise up shepherds according to His own heart who would feed His people with knowledge and understanding (Jeremiah 3:15). In like manner, urban children can be categorized as academically weak, emotionally sick, economically broken, socially driven away, and spiritually lost. They are the lost sheep that God has on His heart. And in response, He desires to raise up, and is doing so, a generation of Christian schools to facilitate His own heart for these children—schools that feed them with "knowledge and understanding." These schools can succeed and are succeeding because they understand the dimensions of poverty and what is needed to address them.

Children with a deficiency of *financial capital* must be given a quality education in a place where tuition is not a barrier. The school must set its tuition policy according the families' ability to pay. While every family should pay enough to have made a material investment in their child's education, that education must not be priced beyond what the family can afford.

Children with a deficiency of *cultural capital* must be given an education that includes training in and development of cultural skills (Dowd and Tierney 1992). The skill training falls into three basic categories:

1. *interacting skills* such as:
   a. greeting others
   b. talking with others
   c. getting attention
   d. making requests
2. *giving skills* such as:
   a. giving an apology
   b. giving criticism
   c. giving a compliment
3. *accepting skills* such as:
   a. accepting instructions
   b. accepting criticism
   c. accepting disagreement

Children with a deficiency of *intellectual capital* must be given an education that:

1. assumes that nothing is fundamentally wrong with them and that they have a God-given ability to learn
2. assesses where they are academically so as to take the guesswork out of teaching them
3. assigns instructional materials according to what will best fit

their learning styles, and takes their home environment into consideration

Children with a deficiency of *social capital* must be given an education:

1. by teachers culturally, racially, and socially sensitive to them
2. that recognizes their limited social network and seeks to compensate for it, usually with the help of volunteers
3. that exposes them to the broader community outside their urban districts

Children with a deficiency of *emotional capital* must be given an education that:

1. is more relational than institutional
2. works with the parents so that the home and school form a partnership in their development
3. provides teachers who are aware of the children's situation and are able to distinguish between pity and mercy*

Children with a deficiency of *spiritual capital* must be given an education that:

1. is biblically integrated
2. seeks to disciple them in a relationship with Christ
3. speaks to their heart as well as their head

Such a holistic approach to educating urban children (or any children) results in a quality education. To put it more succinctly, a quality education is as simple as ABC:

- **A**cademically excellent, as children are taught the ***mental*** 3Rs of **r**eading, '**r**iting, and '**r**ithmetic
- **B**ible-based, as children are taught the ***spiritual*** 3Rs of **r**epentance, **r**egeneration, and **r**econciliation
- **C**haracter-shaping, as children are taught the ***social*** 3Rs of **r**espect, **r**esponsibility, and **r**esourcefulness

With such an education Christ-centered schools are able to:

- **Instruct** children in **a**cademics, or what they should know in their **heads**
- **Instill** in children **b**iblical principles, or what they should believe in their **hearts**
- **Influence** children's **c**haracter, or what they should do with their **hands**

* Pity focuses on the giver and is designed to make the giver feel better. Mercy, on the other hand, focuses on the recipient and is designed to enable the recipient to do better. Usually, pity leaves the recipient in the condition that prompted the gift, while mercy enables the recipient to do for himself and thus reach the point where the gift is no longer needed.

A prevailing mentality has been that low-income urban parents either don't care enough or don't know enough to seek out quality education for their children. Thus these children are being written off as lacking the wherewithal to perform and succeed academically. This myth has been largely dispelled by the responses to the privately funded voucher programs sweeping the nation. These programs provide tuition assistance that gives the children of economically disadvantaged families access to the schools of their choice. The responses have been overwhelming, and the numbers most compelling. Poor families, on average, have been willing to pay $1,000 a year to find an alternative way to educate their children. This willingness reveals that for many urban parents the level of their income is not a measure of the degree of their caring for their children. When quality education is made accessible, available, and affordable to economically disadvantaged families, many are as willing as families of means to make sacrifices for their children.

Furthermore, with the results pouring in, the indications are that low-income minority children benefit greatly from school choice in general and Christian schooling in particular. Independent studies on the effects of vouchers were conducted by the Manhattan Institute for Policy Research and the Program on Education Policy and Governance of Harvard University (Greene 2000). The studies indicate that African American students who received privately funded vouchers (such as the one outlined above), enabling them to attend the schools of their choice, posted considerable academic gains over their public school peers who applied for the vouchers but were not chosen.

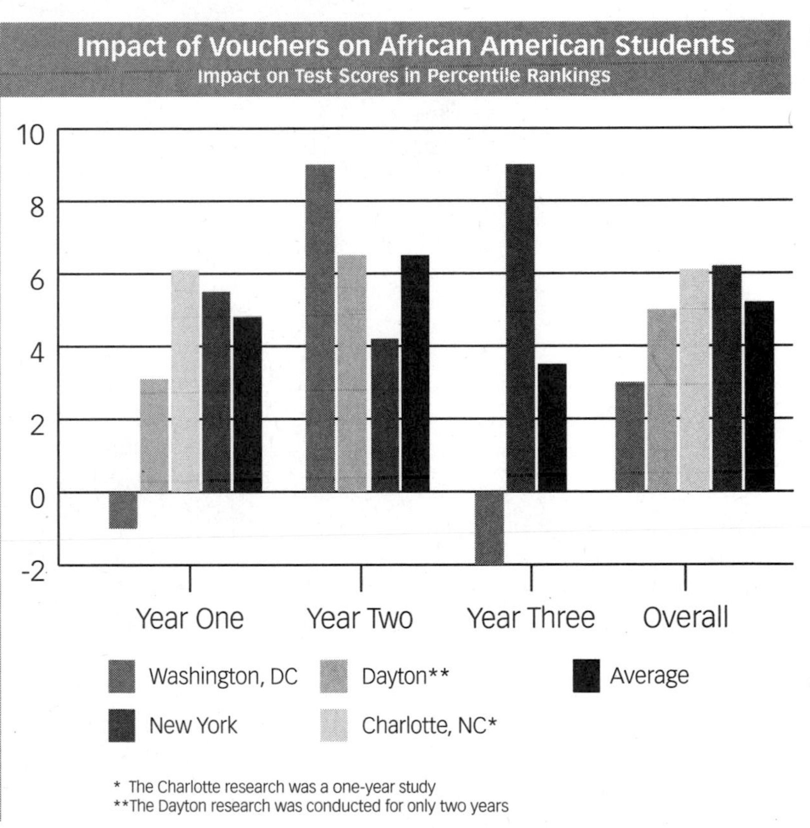

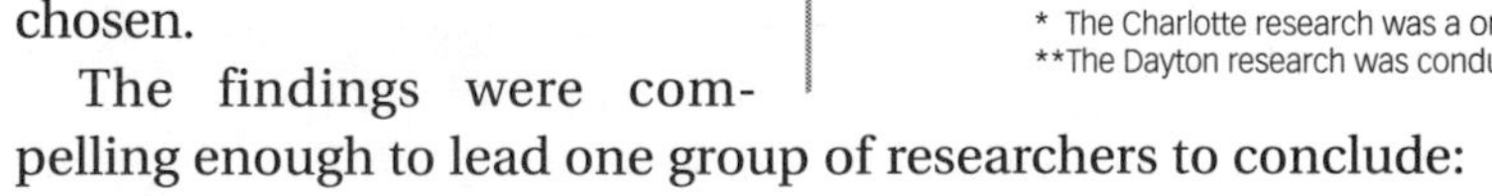

The findings were compelling enough to lead one group of researchers to conclude:

> If the trend line observed over the first two years continues in subsequent years, the black-white test gap could be eliminated ... for black students who use a voucher to switch from public to private school. (Howell, Wolf, and Peterson 2000)

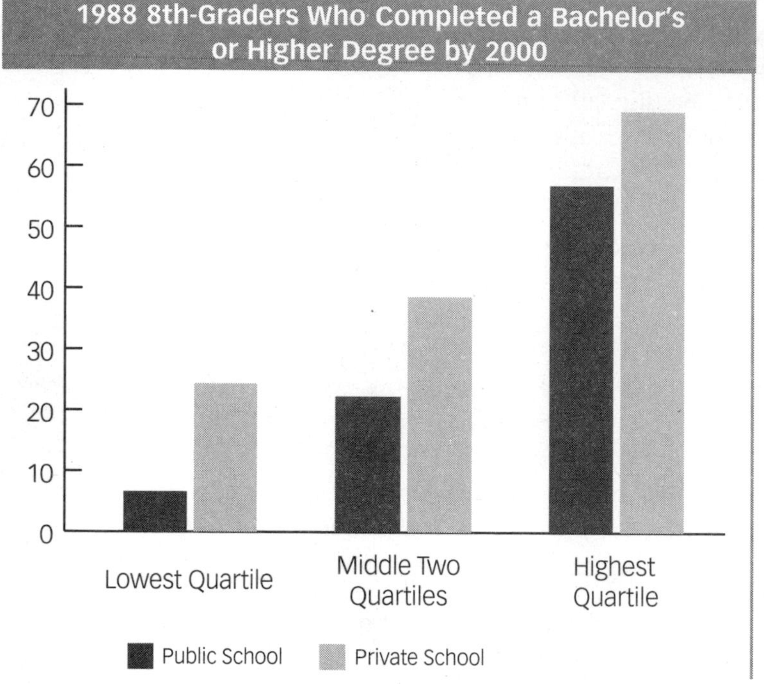

Moreover, according to a follow-up study by the National Center for Education Statistics (NCES) on the National Education Longitudinal Study of 1988, low-income children who attend private schools are nearly four times more likely to complete college than their public school peers (U.S. Department of Education 2002). The vast majority of children in private schools attend religious or faith-based schools. This is especially true for low-income families because the normal cost of attending a Christian school is considerably less than the price of private school tuition. According to the NCES, 85 percent of private school students attend faith-based schools. What these schools are demonstrating and what the research shows is that there is nothing fundamentally wrong with the children. The same children who have been basically written off as uneducable, under-educable, learning challenged, and learning disabled in public schools are achieving and excelling academically in the private school setting. They are behaving, they are going to college, they are graduating, and they are becoming productive citizens.

And this is to be expected. Two fundamental principles should characterize the approach of God's people to children. First, no educational institution in the world should be able to out-educate God's people. As Frederick Douglass said so succinctly in 1894, our education represents "truth and light," making it the greatest education in existence No one should be able to outdo the children of God, who are instruments of His love, in caring. For there is no greater love than the love of God. Therefore, with a Christian education, not only can we educate children by equipping them with the tools necessary to function effectively and successfully in this life; we can also prepare them for life eternal.

About the Author

Vernard T. Gant came to ACSI from the Children's Scholarship Fund of Birmingham, Alabama, to serve as Director of Urban School Services. Dr. Gant believes that the most effective way to help reverse the multi-generational breakdown of urban center families is the Christ-centered school.

Strengthen Your Foundations

1. How do the urban centers of today compare with the ghettoes of the '50s and '60s? How are they alike? How are they different?

2. Catholic schools have had a long, rich history of educating urban/ghetto children. Nearly a generation ago, one author observed: "The only institutions with a record of consistently getting people out of the underclass are the parochial schools" (Lemann 1986, 21). Why do you think that was so? Do some research to determine what practices and principles made those schools succeed where others did not.

3. Do some research to ascertain the role that education has played historically in lifting individuals and families from one socioeconomic status to another.

4. "Christian schools do not exist to evangelize!" Do you agree with this statement? Why or why not? Cite Scripture passages as a biblical basis for your explanation.

5. A cultural gulf exists between the urban student and the middle class teacher. What kinds of training and preparation would best equip a teacher to serve effectively in such a cross-cultural setting?

References

Anderson, James D. 1988. *The education of blacks in the South, 1860–1935.* Chapel Hill: University of North Carolina Press.

Braswell, J. S., A. D. Lutkus, W. S. Grigg, S. L. Santapau, B. Tay-Lim, and M. Johnson. 2001. *The nation's report card: Mathematics 2000,* NCES. Office of Educational Research and Improvement. National Center for Education Statistics. Washington, DC: U.S. Department of Education.

Clark, Kenneth B. 1965. *Dark ghetto.* New York: Harper & Row.

Donahue, P. L., R. J. Finnegan, A. D. Lutkus, N. L. Allen, and J. R. Campbell. 2001. *The nation's report card: Fourth-grade reading 2000,* NCES 2001–499. Office of Educational Research and Improvement. National Center for Education Statistics. Washington, DC: U.S. Department of Education.

Douglass, Frederick. 1845. *Narrative of the life of Frederick Douglass.* Mineola, NY: Dover Publications.

——. 1894. The blessings of liberty and education. An address delivered in Manassas, Virginia (3 September). In *The Frederick Douglass papers* 623. Edited by J. Blassingame and J. McKivigan, 1992.

Dowd, Tom, and Jeff Tierney. *Teaching social skills to youth.* Boys Town, NE: Boys Town Press.

Education Week on the Web. 1998. Quality counts '98: The urban challenge. Retrieved April 10, 2002, from http:/www.edweek.org/sreports/qc98/intros/in-n.htm.

Greene, Jay P. 2000. *The effect of school choice: An evaluation of the Charlotte Children's Scholarship Fund Program.* Civic Report No. 12 (August).

Howell, William G., Patrick J. Wolf, and Paul E. Peterson. 2000. Test-score effects of school vouchers in Dayton, Ohio, New York City, and Washington, DC: Evidence from randomized field trials (August). Retrieved July 23, 2002, from http://data.fas.harvard.edu/pepg/.

Lemann, Nicholas. 1986. The origins of the underclass. *Atlantic Monthly* (June). http://www.theatlantic.com/politics/poverty/origin2.htm (accessed August 7, 2003).

Moynihan, Daniel Patrick. 1987. *Family and nation.* San Diego: Harcourt Brace Jovanovich.

U.S. Department of Education National Center for Education Statistics. 2002. *The condition of education.* NCES 2002–025. Washington, DC: U.S. Government Printing Office.

Woodson, Carter G. 1999. *The education of the Negro.* Brooklyn, NY: A&B Book Publishers.

CHAPTER EIGHTEEN

International Christian Schools

Philip M. Renicks

The year was 1975. Our family was experiencing the feelings all families have when they are getting ready to make a cross-cultural move—feelings of anticipation and excitement; feelings of anxiety and fear of the unknown; feelings of sadness and withdrawal, knowing we would soon be saying good-bye to family and friends. Yet in our hearts we knew we could step into this new chapter of our lives with confidence and obedience because of Jesus' call to "go therefore and make disciples of all the nations,... teaching them to observe all things that I have commanded you" (Matthew 28:19–20).

Since its founding in 1978, the Association of Christian Schools International (ACSI) has recognized the importance of Christian schools in the global context. In 1985 ACSI deepened its commitment by creating an International Ministries Department within the association and naming a vice president to oversee the implementation of the mission, goals, and services of ACSI as appropriate (with cultural and national sensitivity) in the global context. Today ACSI serves Christian schools in 106 countries with international offices in Guatemala City, Guatemala; Asunción, Paraguay; São Paulo, Brazil; Budapest, Hungary; Cluj, Romania; Guebwiller, France; Kiev, Ukraine; Manila, Philippines; and Johannesburg, South Africa. ACSI serves more than 1,000 schools and 250,000 students outside of North America.

Yes, we would be missionaries, but missionaries of a different kind. We were trained teachers, and God had directed us to use our gifts and experience in a school for the children of missionaries. We were about to become involved in a remarkable opportunity involving education and missions. Those nine years of experience brought me to the realization that Christian schools, regardless of their cultural context, are one of the greatest tools for evangelism and discipleship known to the church of Jesus Christ today.

Throughout the world God is using Christian schools to accomplish His purpose. Jesus commanded us as His followers to go into all the world and "make disciples." Christian teachers in countries from Russia to Rwanda, from Uzbekistan to Uganda, and from India to Indonesia recognize that Christian schools are the answer to many of the social, political, and spiritual ills of society. Thus their desire for their students is that they will, in the words of ACSI's vision statement, "acquire wisdom, knowledge, and a biblical worldview as evidenced by a lifestyle of character, leadership, service, stewardship, and worship." They recognize the importance of raising up a generation of young people who "will mature to loving God with all their heart, mind, and soul (Matthew 22:37)—growing in wisdom and stature (Luke 2:52), being willing to stand apart from the world as salt and light (Matthew 5:13–14), and giving sacrificially of themselves and their resources, thus reflecting the essence and love of the Christ who lives and dwells within them (Romans 12:1)."

The National Christian School

Christian schools, whatever their size or location, demand dedication, commitment, and an unwavering obedience to the call of God. One such school is located in a country in West Africa where the students who attend are part of a large Liberian refugee camp. The students, many of them separated from their parents because of the civil war in Liberia, ended up on the wrong side of the conflict. They were forced to flee across the border to Côte d'Ivoire or lose their lives along with thousands of others. Some of their parents were among those countless thousands who didn't make it. Many of the students had their education interrupted for two or three years during the war, and now as orphans they have recognized the need to fill in the gaps in their schooling. In traditional Africa, parents open the way for their oldest son to find meaning and a livelihood to care for his family. For these orphaned students, education has become their mother and father.

The founder and director of Christ the King School was among those who fled Liberia. His wife had just delivered their second child the day before the rebels came to burn their village. Looking over his shoulder and watching his home go up in flames, he carried his wife on his back and his new child in his arms while their other child, a toddler, held tightly to his pant leg. They walked and hid in the bush for several days before they found refuge across the border.*

Despite the fact that they had become aliens and strangers in a new land and had lost all their earthly possessions, once they were established as much as refugees can be, their next step was to begin

* Since this chapter was written, civil war has caused widespread devastation in Côte d' Ivoire (Ivory Coast). Christ the King School is now closed, and many of the teachers and students (refugees from the Liberia civil war) have fled once again out onto the "refugee highway." The school director and his family have fled to safety in Ghana, but many of the teachers and students have traveled back across the border into Liberia, where they face rampant starvation and gross insecurity. Because of that insecurity, aid agencies have been unable to reach the refugees and the internally displaced people, who number in the tens of thousands.

a Christian school to continue the education of the children and young people who had been displaced. There were no fancy buildings or textbooks; in fact there were not even classrooms with walls. The school began meeting under a large tree in the center of the village. However, it was evident that there was a deep commitment to that central command of Scripture, to "make disciples of all the nations ... teaching them to observe all things that I have commanded" (Matthew 28:19–20).

Christian schools outside North America have existed for more than a hundred years. Just prior to the turn of the twentieth century, missionaries began "mission schools" as they established their work across the continents of Africa, South America, and Asia. These schools focused on literacy as a tool of evangelism. National children learned to read and write, and many of them became believers and leaders in their communities and in their countries.

During a visit to Nigeria a few years back, I was introduced to a gray-haired elder whom I'll call Frank. Frank was in his early nineties, his eyes were getting dim, and he was stooped. He had been the chief of his clan for more than forty years. As I sat with Frank in the long shadows of the afternoon, he began telling me how proud he was that his town now had a Christian school. I learned that Frank had grown up in a remote village in eastern Nigeria. He shared how British missionaries had come to his village and started a mission school, and it was in the mission school that he heard about Jesus for the first time. Frank told how Jesus had been a vital part of his life since that time and how he had used the principles of God's word to govern his people. Because of a missionary teacher's commitment, dedication, and obedience to the will of God, Frank's life and the lives of many of his classmates were changed. The impact of these early mission schools may never be known until we gather around the throne of God in eternity.

While some of these mission schools still exist, over the years many have lost their spiritual mission. In some instances trained Christian teachers could not be found, and the schools gradually became secular through the worldview of the teachers who were hired. Others invited non-Christian board members to serve in their governance, and gradually their Christian values were compromised. There are schools scattered around the world that still bear the name of the founding denomination, but they have been reduced to nothing more than secular schools. In still other situations mission schools were annexed by governments, particularly in Africa, as countries threw off the chains of colonialism and nationalized everything. As a result they have become government schools espousing a secular philosophy of education. They have lost their spiritual mission.

Today, there is a new breed of Christian schools that exist in more than a hundred countries. As those churches have matured that were founded through missionary activity before the turn of the twentieth century, they have established Christian schools out of a concern for training the next generation of Christian leaders. The schools vary in size, shape, and degree of sophistication. Some have modern facilities and are well equipped with science and computer labs. Others are functioning in modified space in high-rise apartment buildings, in mud-brick and thatch-roofed buildings, in borrowed facilities, in modified metal shipping containers, or just under trees. Some have few students, while others have several thousand. However, the basic philosophy is the same. It is based on the atoning work of Christ in the lives of students and the difference it makes for both now and eternity. Most national Christian schools have as their central mission a focus on the evangelism and discipleship of their students.

Grace Christian School in Quezon City, Manila, Philippines, opened in 1950 with 185 students. Today the student body numbers more than 5,000. The PK–12 school is housed in a modern four-story building with computer labs at every level beginning at kindergarten. Grace Christian High School is widely recognized for its academic excellence. An untold number of students, parents, and friends of the school have come to know the Lord, and Grace Christian has helped start three churches in the Philippines. The school was started by Mrs. Julia Tan, a widow with five young children.

On the other side of the world, in a bush area outside Lusaka, Zambia, two Christian schools have been established to provide an education for children who have no other access to schooling. One school, which was built through a grant from the European Union, is a cement building with three classrooms. The other is a mud-brick building that was constructed by parents and is located eleven kilometers off the main road. The classrooms are dark, and students sit on hand-hewn wooden benches that rest on a dirt floor. The thatched roof is badly in need of repair, and there is no water or toilet facility.

To arrive at the mud-brick school, our vehicle followed a footpath in the tall grass through the bush until we reached the site. A group of parents and students were there to meet us. The parents are subsistence farmers living on government-owned land. Dressed in his tattered work clothing, a very articulate gentleman stood and addressed us regarding the importance of the school to their community. He began by telling us that this was not an ordinary school. With great pride he explained that the school was a place where their children learned not only the basics of education—reading, writing, and computation skills—but also the Word of God, which would guide them for life.

These schools reflect the cultures of the countries where they are located. They provide an education that in some ways is superior to the educational program mandated by their government. In fact, in most developing countries Christian schools exist in areas where the government does not provide schooling. In some countries, embracing the educational philosophy of the central government can cause conflict for a Christian school. For example a philosophical conflict is brewing in South Africa over a new project entitled "Curriculum 2005." The government has introduced a new curriculum structure, and some basic life skills it teaches are very much in conflict with Christian values and biblical principles.

Educational standards are declining in many countries, especially where a government has embraced educational objectives that are designed to promote a certain social and/or political agenda. In most cases that agenda is anti-Christian. Churches, Christian parents, and Christian educators are combining their talents and expertise to establish new schools that address these issues by providing their children with an education from a Christian worldview.

The MK (Missionary Kid) School

Another group of schools in the international context are those often referred to as MK schools, or schools for the children of missionaries. These schools have been established by mission organizations with the primary purpose of serving the missionary family. MK schools have a rich history, having been in existence for more than 150 years. (The Woodstock school in India was established in 1854. With continuous operation through the present, it serves as an educational alternative for missionary families.)

Before MK schools were established, children stayed in the homeland or were sent back there for their education. J. Hudson Taylor, founder of the China Inland Mission (now Overseas Missionary Fellowship), believed that the children of missionaries should be educated overseas near the location of their parents' ministry. As a result of his strong commitment to the missionary family, he opened a school in Chefoo, China, in 1881. The significance of

Taylor's vision for keeping missionaries' children on the field cannot be overemphasized. His thinking in this area was as revolutionary as many of his other ideas. Once the Chefoo School opened, missionaries around the world were assured that such a thing could be done. MKs could remain on the field rather than be returned to the home country for their education (Danielson 1982, 29).

E. E. Danielson (1982) considered the Chefoo School to be the forerunner of all other schools for missionary children. According to statistics in *Overseas Schools Profiles*, published by the Association of Christian Schools International in 2001, ninety schools for missionary children, both day schools and boarding schools, are functioning in seventy countries, with more than 9,500 students. Approximately twenty-one of the ninety schools offer boarding facilities for 1,520 students. These schools support the mandate of Matthew 28:19–20 and the families that God has called to carry the Good News of Jesus Christ around the world.

C. E. Orr established the importance of the MK school and the close relationship that should exist between its goals and those of the mission. "The operation of a school for missionary children is an integral part of the missionary program. The responsibility of giving their children a well-rounded social, spiritual, and academic education accompanies missionary parents as they respond to Christ's command to preach the gospel. In fact, it is an obligation that cannot be divorced from missions" (1959, 2). This statement embodies the heart of the philosophy behind the establishing of MK schools.

It is important to note the significance of the MK school as an integral part of the missionary program. Missionary teachers who are specifically involved in MK education talk of their commitment to the MK students and their parents, to the mission sending agency, and to the God-given task of worldwide evangelization. Without the teachers' commitment to missionary families, the gospel would be greatly hindered.

Over the years the MK school, while still focusing on missionary children as its primary mission, has broadened its base of operation to include the children of international business executives, the diplomatic corps, and in some cases national pastors and other Christian workers. The Dalat School in Penang, Malaysia, recently redefined its mission as *to prepare young people to live fully for God in a rapidly changing world by enabling them to understand, evaluate, and reconcile that world with the foundation of God's unchanging values.* While these goals are not unique to MK education, they are contextualized within the framework of an educational program that calls students who are growing up in a culturally diverse world to discipleship in a Christ-centered learning community.

The context of the MK school is a culturally diverse world. It is not uncommon to have 15 or 20 different nationalities in an MK school. Many students who make up such culturally diverse schools come from new missionary-sending countries like Korea, the Philippines, and Latin American countries. Missionary families no longer go out exclusively from the traditional sending countries of the West. Other students come from the diverse world of international business and the diplomatic missions of countless embassies.

A missionary kid named Teri Lynn was born in Ecuador of parents who were serving in a small jungle mission station. In order to penetrate the remote tribal groups with the gospel, her father started mission schools at outposts along the Misahualli River in the Ecuadorian jungle. When Teri Lynn was eight years old, her father died and was buried next to one of the churches and mission schools that he had founded. She had three younger siblings. One by one the children left home to attend an MK boarding school in the capital city of Quito. Teri Lynn graduated from the school in Ecuador and attended college in the United States to prepare to return to Ecuador to teach other MKs in the same school from which she had graduated. Shortly after Teri Lynn returned to begin her teaching, her mother, who was still serving as a missionary in Ecuador, died in an accident. Today, in the land where their parents are buried, Teri Lynn and a younger sister continue to support the work of missionary families through MK school education.

Every year in MK schools, hundreds of students encounter Christian teachers, Christian peers, and the Christian faith for the first time. Dozens make a life-changing commitment to Jesus Christ. And because they are part of a highly mobile community, they become ambassadors for Christ in communities that the traditional missionary could never reach.

The International Christian School

Over the past twenty years yet another type of Christian school has emerged in the international context. It is a school whose primary focus is on serving the international community, often with the goal of evangelism. The international Christian school is often found in major cities that have a large concentration of international families. Because of globalization and international development, many expatriate families are living outside their passport country. Parents usually desire an English-language school for their children to attend.

The Network of International Christian Schools (NICS) operates eighteen such schools in fourteen countries. On the NICS website one may find the following expression of vision: *In our schools we are finding great opportunities for sharing Christ with children who come from all over the world. These children are representative of their nations, as well as the major religions of the world. Many of them have never heard a clear presentation of the gospel of Jesus Christ.*

Teachers in the international Christian school use their teaching skills to win the lost for Christ. They answer God's call, and the school becomes their mission field. The nations have actually come to the school's doorstep. They represent a group of people who are virtually unreached by traditional methods of evangelism. Some of them come from countries that are closed to the gospel or that have limited access to missionaries.

Students and their families are attracted to the international school because they can get an education in the English language that will provide them with greater opportunities for success. Many of them desire to attend a university in the United States. While most of these students come from non-Christian religious backgrounds like Buddhism, Hinduism, and even Islam, and most do not embrace a Christian worldview, they will tolerate the teachings about Jesus Christ in order to obtain a quality education in a safe and orderly environment.

In contrast to the MK school, the international Christian school doesn't exist to support an established Christian community (i.e., missionaries) but seeks to grow a new international Christian community among its constituents. In many cases the ministry of the school results in the establishment of a new international evangelical church. While the primary purpose of the international school is to reach out to the diverse international non-Christian community, it also supports the established local community of faith.

The international Christian school faces some interesting challenges. While parents of non-Christian backgrounds give permission for their children to be taught the Word of God, their children's decision to embrace the Christian faith can easily cause conflict in the family.

Chen Wei is a Taiwanese boy who attended an international Christian school in Malaysia because it was the only school in his area that could prepare him to follow his dream of attending a university in the United States. Chen Wei's father, who worked in

Malaysia, was an executive in a large international company. The boy entered school as an eighth grader barely able to speak English. He learned quickly. Because of the consistent testimony of his teachers and classmates, Chen Wei became a Christian in his sophomore year. In the next two years he won his brother and sister to Christ, but his parents remained Buddhists.

Chen Wei was elected president of the student body his senior year. He attended a Bible study on the importance of baptism as a step of obedient faith and a declaration of his relationship with Christ. Chen Wei knew that he had to have his parents' permission before he could be baptized. He knew his parents would see baptism as a point of no return to the family religion. It was difficult for him to ask. Finally he did ask, and on the morning of the baptismal service, Chen Wei's mother came to the school campus to tell him that he did not have his father's permission to be baptized. She also said that if he went ahead with the baptism, his father would take him out of the school and send him back to Taiwan to live with relatives. When he was eighteen, he would be denied all further help from the family. His teachers, recognizing the need for cultural sensitivity, encouraged him to honor his father and mother by waiting until he was an adult to be baptized.

As the other fifteen students were baptized that morning, Chen Wei could be seen sitting off to the side crying because he couldn't publicly identify with the Lord Jesus Christ. Chen Wei recently graduated from Purdue University, where he was the leader of InterVarsity Christian Fellowship. He has been baptized and is following the Lord Jesus Christ. Every year this story is repeated over and over again in international Christian schools around the world.

The expressed mission of the international Christian schools sponsored by the NICS organization is this: *We believe that we can reach people from every country of the world through the influence of international Christian schools. The goal is to reach children and their families, lead them to Christ, and see them return to their home countries as a witness for Jesus Christ.*

Summary

Faith-based education has become an effective tool for reaching other cultures for Christ. In developing countries, Christian schools have impacted the lives of countless millions of children and their families with the gospel of Christ for more than a hundred years. These schools have not only shaped the lives of their students but in some cases have changed the direction of a nation. Graduates of these schools have become leaders of their country, community, and church.

As a Christian school service organization, ACSI has come alongside these schools in support of their ministry through training and consultation. ACSI encourages both educational quality and spiritual depth. Since the worldview of the teacher will gradually condition the worldview of the student, one of the greatest challenges is the retraining of teachers who espouse a non-Christian philosophy they acquired through their training in secular universities.

Growing tension exists in many places today between the Christian world and the non-Christian world. In many countries across sub-Saharan Africa, the Christian school and the Christian faith are confronting the growing threat of Islam and the opening of well-funded (by Saudi Arabia's oil money) Islamic elementary and secondary schools whose goal is "evangelistic"—to bring students and ultimately their families under the domination of the Islamic faith and "Sharia law." The same pattern is emerging in predominately Christian regions of Indonesia.

This trend is cause for great concern and should sound the alarm for Christians to be diligent in making a sacrificial investment in support of Christian schools worldwide. The Lord requires an investment not only of our financial resources but of our lives. Christian teachers are needed in MK schools, international Christian schools, and national Christian schools. Teachers are needed who sense God's call and are willing to invest their lives in obedience by going, making disciples, and teaching the world's children to observe all that He has commanded.

About the Author

Philip M. Renicks, Ed.D., is the Vice President of International Ministries with the Association of Christian Schools International. Dr. Renicks, formerly the high school principal of Alliance Academy in Quito, Ecuador, has a passion for Christian schools. He has traveled extensively with ACSI in the international context, enabling Christian schools and Christian school leaders in more than 70 countries.

Strengthen Your Foundations

1. Explore teaching opportunities in Christian schools around the world by visiting the ACSI website at www.acsi.org. From the home page click on Overseas Teaching Opportunities in the QuickLinks section.

2. Explore the world of ACSI by checking out the International Ministries home page on the ACSI website at www.acsi.org. Explore the work of ACSI in Asia, the CIS, Europe, Latin America, and South Africa.

References

Danielson, E. E. 1982. *Missionary kid (MK)*. Manila: Faith Academy.

Orr, C. E. 1959. The education of missionaries' children. *Occasional Bulletin of the Missionary Research Library* 10, no. 9: 1–11.

Overseas Schools Profiles. 2001. Colorado Springs, CO: Association of Christian Schools International.

Renicks, Philip M. 1986. *Perceptions of administrators in a worldwide study of orientation and induction practices of member schools in the Association of Christian Schools International in overseas locations.* Tuscaloosa: University of Alabama.

CHAPTER NINETEEN

Training World Christians

James W. Braley

This book has considered four important foundations for Christian school education—philosophical, psychological, instructional, and cultural/sociological—all built on the foundation of Jesus Christ and God's truth. Our hope is that as education in the Christian school setting continues to develop, teachers will build their educational programs on these foundations.

Now comes the crucial test! What will students become, and what will they do for Christ with an education built on these foundations? The mark of success for the Christian school educator is what the school's students, and its graduates, are actually doing. Students should learn that God has given each believer a mandate to reach the world for Christ. We know that Jesus did not give us the Great Invitation, but the Great Commission (Matthew 28:18–20). We are to go into *all the world* and *make disciples of all nations*. The learning experience of every Christian school student should include reaching out to family, friends, community, and even cross-cultural groups.

Many Christians are tempted to isolate themselves, building walls of separation from the world and retreating into Christian fellowship. They often equate separation from sinful activity with isolation from sinners, but nothing could be further from the truth of Jesus' teachings. He said, "Go into all the world." The Christian is to be in the world but not of the world, relating to people as Christ related to them in His daily ministry.

Worldly Christians vs. World Christians

Sadly, it is possible for students to attend Christian schools for twelve or thirteen years and still not understand the message of Scripture regarding their relationship to the world around them. In contrast, believers should be world Christians, focused on others' needs rather than just their own. World Christians are committed to being salt and light in their world. They are not ashamed to announce to the world the unsearchable riches of Christ and to actively demonstrate biblical compassion for those in need. Finally, they recognize that God loves all people, and thus they are committed to missions and evangelism around the globe.

Unfortunately, Christian schools can develop self-centered believers who do not understand the scriptural mandates that Christ gave, which call us to reach out into the world around us. In *A Mind for Missions,* Paul Borthwick defined what he called a "worldly Christian":

> A worldly Christian is one who accepts the basic message of salvation, but whose lifestyle, priorities, and concerns are molded by self-centered preoccupation. The selfish spirit of our age leads the worldly Christian to look to God and the Bible primarily for personal fulfillment. The worldly Christian looks to Scripture for personal blessing; prays mostly for immediate personal needs; and sees the Christian faith as a way to "get God on his or her side."(1987, 13–14)

A number of scriptural principles that define our relationship to the world should be carefully presented in the Christian school:

1. Christ has freed us from the bondage of sin (John 8:32, Romans 6:18, Revelation 1:5).
2. Those who have been freed from sin are now children of God (Romans 8:16, 1 John 3:1).
3. Believers are aliens and strangers in the world (John 17:16, 1 Peter 2:11).
4. Believers are ambassadors for Christ in the world (2 Corinthians 5:20).
5. Believers are to live in the world as salt to spread the truth everywhere as salt permeates food (Matthew 5:13), and as light to shine in the dark world reflecting the "Light of the World" (Matthew 5:16).
6. Believers are to be witnesses to the world around them (Acts 1:8, 1 Peter 2:12).
7. Believers are to pray for more workers to be sent into the harvest (Matthew 9:37–38) as well for those who are doing God's work around the world.

Students should learn these principles, recognizing that they are to live a life that attracts people to Christ and the Bible (Titus 2:10). Christians have a responsibility to witness to, and help, the people in their community as well as in the whole world. The Christian school's directive is to separate students from the world so that they can be effectively trained and prepared to live in the world without being conformed to it.

Some view the Christian school as a fortress built to protect those within from the negative influences of the world. However, for the Christian school to be truly Christian, it must teach and practice the Savior's mandates, which are given clearly in Scripture. Christians are to be "incarnational," taking Christ into the world, sharing His message, and following His example by helping those in need.

As a young Christian school teacher, I was often frustrated by the accusation that the Christian school was a hothouse or fortress isolating students from the "real world." After struggling with this frustration for a time, I recalled an incident from my childhood. A stranger moved to our small town in Arizona and built what the locals called a "glass barn." As it grew in size and shape, members of the local "Rock Throwing Club," of which I was one, showed a great deal of interest. We often visited the site, finding the owner always present to meet us, happy to explain what he was doing. Of course with such close supervision we had no opportunity to practice our "art."

As the visits continued, we learned that the stranger was doing something interesting. As a grower, he had experienced great difficulty in the Midwest with all kinds of disease and blight in his corn crops. To solve the problem, he built a hothouse in the middle of Arizona and was raising Iowa seed corn there. In that isolated setting, the grower was developing a hardy strain of corn that could withstand whatever attacked it when it was replanted in Iowa fields.

That grower's project can provide an analogy for the mission of Christian school education. The Christian school is not a hothouse for isolation, raising weak people unable to survive in the real world, but rather a controlled environment in which students can grow in strength and character so that later they will withstand anything the world throws at them.

If we can nurture strong, healthy Christian students, we should not be concerned when they go out into the world with all its challenges and sin. Step by step, through controlled experiences, they will learn how to minister and witness to the world. Proper training is vital, and experiences must be carefully planned so as never to put young children in any danger. With such an education, our students will learn how to live their faith, ministering and witnessing to the world, growing strong enough to be positive forces in their society.

General Principles

The Christian school that desires to prepare world Christians must recognize that students need more than cognitive knowledge of the Bible. The Christian school (its administrators and teachers) must become the bridge for students, helping them apply what they have learned to the real world. In partnership with the home and church, Christian schools should encourage students to be involved in community and missions projects. When students begin to see the world as Christ sees it, their head knowledge and heart knowledge will connect, and they will have compassion for those around them. To reach this goal, the Christian school must be actively involved in programs that strengthen students in their faith and provide ways for them to see how they can make a difference. The programs that work best are those that give students opportunities for hands-on experience in ministry.

Figure 1: The Bridge to Understanding and Ministry

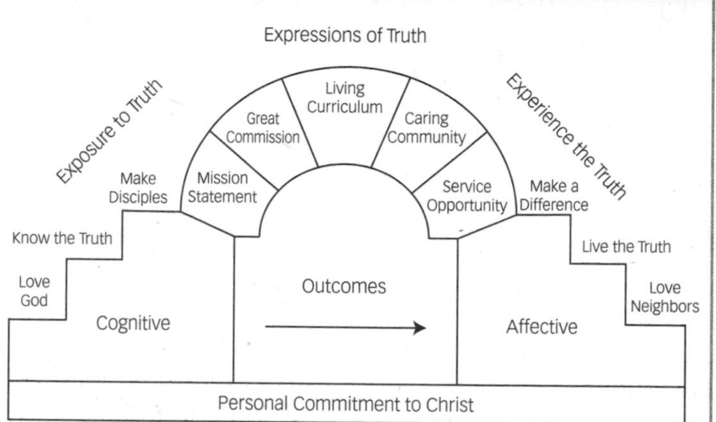

The Christian school should become the bridge that leads to effective ministry. (See figure 1.) Training begins with cognitive input, helping the student know the truth, become a believer, and love God. Recognizing that its purpose is to make disciples, the school develops a mission statement that clearly articulates its purpose of responding to the Great Commission.

All Christian school students should be given the opportunity to pray. Students can be involved in missions around the world through prayer. In their book *Operation World,* Patrick Johnstone and Jason Mandryk provide a day-to-day prayer guide by reporting needs and ministries in many parts of the world. This valuable resource can easily be adapted for use in the Christian school, not only in Bible courses but in history, geography, and missions training as well.

At the apex of the bridge is the *living curriculum,* the teacher whose life is an example of a maturing, ministering believer. The living curriculum in the Christian school is the key to effective training. Jesus taught His disciples, "A student is not above his teacher, but everyone who is fully trained will be like his teacher" (Luke 6:40, NIV). If the bridge is carefully planned, it will lead to caring and serving as students learn to make a difference in their world through living the truth and loving their neighbors.

An example will demonstrate the active role the board and administration can take in becoming the bridge for their high school's students. As the high school program was being planned for a Christian school in Phoenix, Arizona, it was determined that both involvement in prayer and practical experience in reaching out to others were imperative for students who would one day make choices regarding their personal commitment to and involvement in missions. Therefore, all junior and senior students were required to participate in a missions project. There was a balance between home missions and foreign missions, since one objective was to help students recognize that missions and missionaries were as close as their next-door neighbor and as far away as another country and culture. Students were involved in projects in Mexico, rescue missions of inner-city Phoenix, remote towns of Arizona, and Indian reservations.

Many Christian schools have implemented such programs for their students. They are designed to allow both younger and older students to participate in ministry. These experiences must take into account the developmental level of various students and must be structured so as to provide opportunity for direct experiences suitable to each one's age. The challenge is to enable students at all levels to develop a worldview that honestly focuses on the needs of people around them.

Figure 2: Age-Appropriate Ministry Opportunities

Jerusalem	Judea	Samaria	The Ends of the Earth	The Ends of the Earth
Ages 3–6	Ages 7–9	Ages 10–12	Ages 13–16	Ages 17–19
Home and Family	Local Community	Broader Community	Nation	The World

Although Acts 1:8 was not written with the development of children in mind, the sequence Jesus gave His disciples in the Great Commission can be used to suggest the sequence of hands-on involvement that a Christian school can provide for its students. Children and young people can learn about a broader ministry by praying, giving, and being informed by missionaries, films, and stories. The above chart suggests areas in which activities seem most appropriate for the maturing child. Schools can select age-appropriate activities that will challenge students to impact their world.

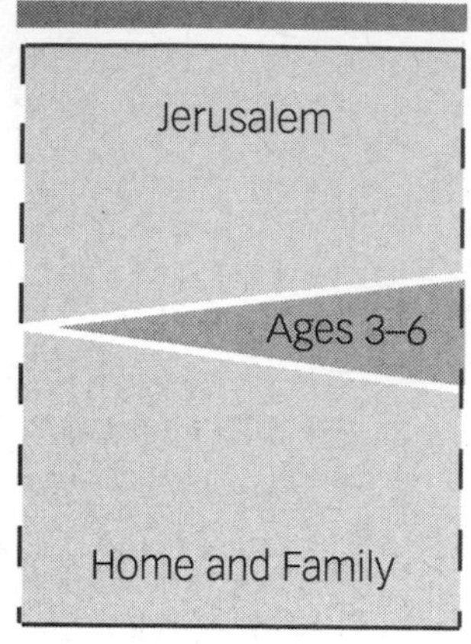

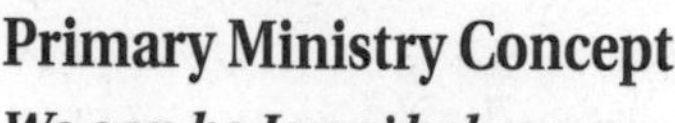

Primary Ministry Concept

We can be Jesus' helpers.

Young students are taught that they can be helpers to each other, their family, and their classmates and teachers in school. The children's primary society is the home, where they come to understand that they are part of their family and have a responsibility to it. When children come to school, this concept extends to include their classmates and teachers. Learning the basic concept of helping begins to prepare the child for ministry.

Secondary Ministry Concept:

We can help share the truth with the world.

Young children can begin to learn about missions and missionaries. Through letters, pictures, chapel speakers, and stories, they can learn what missionaries do. They can even become a part of a missionary's ministry by praying and giving. Being involved in special missions projects can whet their interest in helping people in their own area and around the world. We need to show them that even as young students they can participate, and they can make a contribution right now, not "someday."

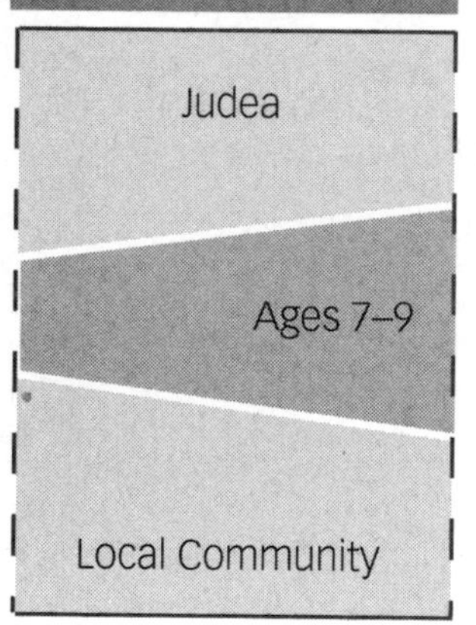

Primary Ministry Concept

Jesus asks us to minister to our community.

Students seven through nine years old are becoming aware of the world nearest to them, their community, and they are beginning to learn about community helpers. We can provide ministries for this age group that allow them to reach out to people around them—their family, church, school, and community. Ministry activities can include preparing gifts of food for families in need, helping to gather clothing and other supplies for the homeless, visiting orphanages or retirement homes, and sponsoring a student in a national Christian school located in a third-world country. We need to develop projects for this age group that offer firsthand experience in serving others.

Secondary Ministry Concept

We can share Jesus' teachings with our friends.

Children can be encouraged to share with their neighborhood what they have learned about the gospel message. Of course, this will be limited, and they must not be pressured to "witness." But often children in this age group are less self-conscious than they will be later, so they can be open and direct with their friends. They can also become involved in sharing the Good News around the world by helping to support missionaries in different fields of ministry and by communicating with them. Prayer becomes important at this age as students learn how to pray for specific needs in other parts of the world as well as in their local community.

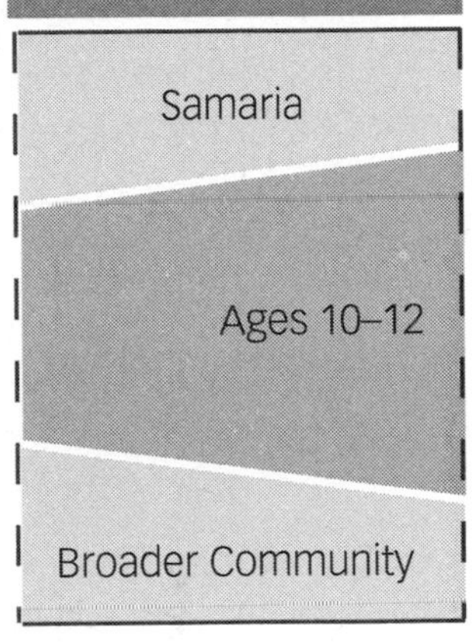

Primary Ministry Concept

God can use my talents and gifts to minister to others.

Students ten through twelve years old can be very active in their ministry opportunities. They are able to do harder physical work than they could before, and they have a better understanding of the Scriptures and of God's call on their lives. A large percentage of missionaries report that they were this age when they first sensed God's call. The Christian school can prepare students for service as well as organize activities and service projects that involve them in ministry.

Students can be involved in many ways—helping the homeless; ministering to shut-ins; completing special projects for missionaries; providing music, drama, readings, and other services for retirement homes and orphanages; raising funds for special missions projects and support of missions work; traveling on short missions trips; and praying regularly for local and world needs. This is a good time for students to begin corresponding with others their age who attend mission schools around the world. Many children of missionaries enjoy having a U.S. penpal.

Secondary Ministry Concept

Jesus wants me to dedicate my heart and life to Him. I can become a servant ministering for the Lord.

We can emphasize personal commitment at this level, but we must take care not to apply undue pressure. Children of this age are often very open to the claims of Christ, and their emotions can carry them away. It is far more important that they be given opportunities to make a genuine commitment to the Lord than be pressured into a response that later may seem uncertain or even unimportant.

It is helpful to provide inspirational missionary stories and tapes as a way of giving students healthy exposure to possibilities for personal ministry. Good missionary speakers in chapel can also provide interesting and challenging input. Children at this age level often have a great interest in knowing what really happens in a missionary's life. It is extremely important not to limit ministry (or missions) to "foreign" missions. Students must become aware that God wants them to be a "missionary" wherever they are for the rest of their lives. The point is not to detract from foreign missions but to emphasize the importance of personal commitment to Christ and willingness to serve anywhere at any time.

Media providing up-to-date information on worldwide missions can be extremely helpful in planning a curriculum for students this age and older. Teachers can enhance lessons in history, geography, and mathematics by using up-to-date information related to the countries studied and their unreached people. (See the book *Operation World* (Johnstone and Mandryk 1993) for examples.)

The middle school and early high school years are often turbulent. Young people of this age are shedding the imposed structures of their childhood and building personal lifestyles and life concepts. If they have had honest and constructive input to this point, they will usually adopt the principles and mores in which they have been trained in earlier years. However, this personal development takes time. Adults need to be wise in how they handle the young teen.

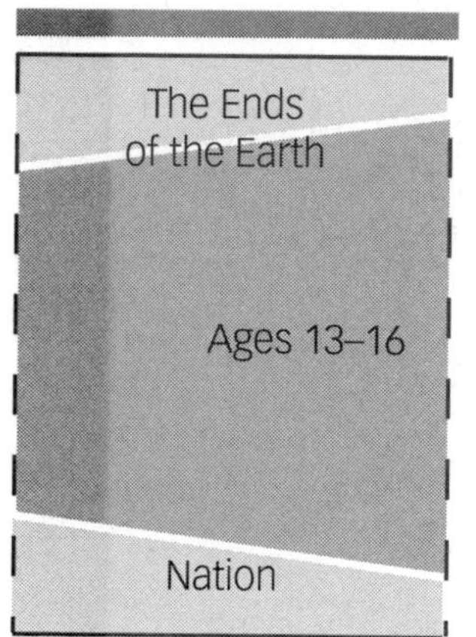

Primary Ministry Concept

God holds me responsible for what I do and say. He wants me to have a servant's heart and a willingness to serve Him and others.

We need to emphasize young people's personal spiritual growth as well as their spiritual responsibilities to the church and the world. God wants them to relate to those around them but not to participate in their sinful activities—to love the sinner and not the sin. This is a difficult concept for teens to understand, especially in Western culture with its emphasis on personal rights and the importance of "me."

Secondary Ministry Concept

God created me to bring glory to Himself. I can trust Him to take care of me and to provide opportunities for ministry and service.

Because young teens tend to be very active, they can become involved in active ministries such as traveling to other areas or countries to do special missions projects; collecting food, clothing, and blankets for the homeless and nearby missions organizations; carrying out special projects for missionaries; working in soup kitchens or shelters; giving testimonies and presenting musical and dramatic productions to groups of shut-ins, the infirm, the elderly, or others; assisting in vacation Bible schools locally or in other states or countries.

In Alabama, junior and senior high school students with little or no prior exposure to poverty were taken to serve a meal in a homeless shelter in a nearby city. What began as fear became real concern for the homeless women there as the students served a meal and then ate with them. They spent several hours in the shelter, and after initially being afraid to go, the students didn't want to leave.

The next day the students returned to clean the facility. Most were eager to do difficult work to provide some kind of service for the women they had come to care for. In the weeks that followed, many students expressed a desire to continue working with the shelter. Their hearts were changed through having the opportunity to practice Christian love and to see that the poor and homeless were people like them who had hopes and dreams just like theirs.

Older teens can be very actively involved in ministry. These young adults can be creative, constructive, and helpful. If they have truly internalized Christian mores and principles, they will be eager to live them out in their own lives and share them with others.

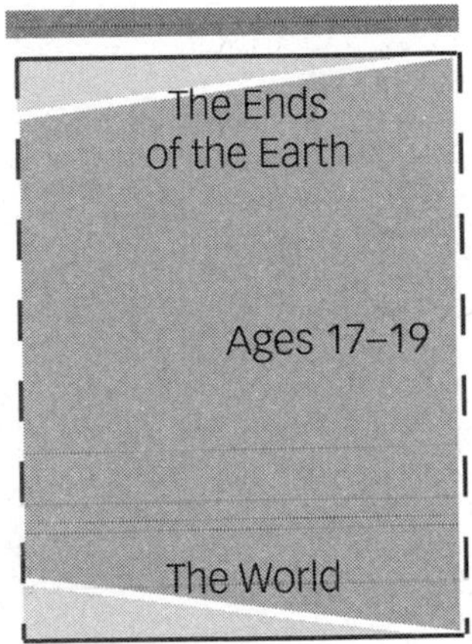

Primary Ministry Concept

God has given me life, and I can give Him my life. The Scriptures teach me that I should be a servant, willing to serve my Savior by reaching out to the community around me, and concerned about ministry around the world.

Much larger ministry projects can be developed for older teens. It is important to challenge them to reach out to the society around them, to overcome the selfish "me first" attitudes of the worldly society they live in and see daily on television and in other media. The influence of such an environment makes it almost impossible to see the world as God sees it and reach out to serve others. The task of the Christian school is to move the students' focus from *possession* to *mission.*

Secondary Ministry Concept

I need to be open to God's call on my life. I am called to full-time service for Christ no matter what my occupation. However, God may also be calling me into full-time ministry, and I need to be willing to seek and accept His direction in my life.

Students are becoming very career conscious at this stage in life. Often the focus is directed toward education beyond high school, marriage and family, a good job that pays well, and enough income to live comfortably. The Christian school needs to present the concept of lifelong ministry and to instruct teens in the importance of following God's call on their lives.

It is important that the school not present these concepts as a matter of *either-or*. Students can go on to higher education, receive quality training, and seek a profession, but they also need to be open to God's call on their lives. Christ's ministry around the world needs well-trained, dedicated persons who will give their all for the Lord. Encourage students to brainstorm and to write papers beginning something like this: "I will use my chosen career to serve Christ in the following ways." The pitfall teens must learn to avoid is thinking that possessions, a good income, a fine home, and a good position will bring happiness and fulfillment. Quality involvement in meeting the needs of others, reaching out to do ministry in different ways, can open teens' eyes to the need and opportunity for ministry and service. The school cannot change the will of the student, but it can present the alternatives and even give experience in some of the possibilities, allowing the Holy Spirit to work in each teen's will, heart, and mind.

Making the Commitment

The important issue for the Christian school is to present the Scriptures in such a way as to make them interesting, contemporary, and vital. Teens respond to honesty and commitment, and they look to significant adults in their lives to see these qualities. Many teens have their hearts opened to ministry because of role models they have observed for many years in the home and classroom (their parents and their Christian school teachers).

Ministry efforts are an important part of the overall training and experience that the school should provide. As students become involved in ministry, they internalize the scriptural call of Christ on their lives. The school is presenting the truth, providing experiences in ministering that truth, and asking the Holy Spirit to work in the lives of the students.

To carry out the mandate of training students to be world Christians, looking beyond themselves and being salt and light in their world, Christian schools need to do the following:

1. Provide quality biblical training, giving students the opportunity to love God and know the truth, making certain that they understand the clear message of God from Genesis 1 to Revelation 22.
2. Make disciples of the students and help them become world

Christians by providing meaningful opportunities for ministry in the local and wider communities as well as around the world.

3. Check the school's mission or purpose statement to be sure that it includes equipping to live a servant lifestyle, modeling the commands of Christ (Matthew 28:19–20, Acts 1:8). Imagine the impact on students of a school that is committed to the following purpose statement: *Visionville Christian School seeks to challenge all students to a life of commitment to Jesus Christ, and to equip them not only to know the truth but to live it, taking Christ into the world, sharing His message, helping those in need, following His example.*
4. Provide quality teachers and staff who embody the "living curriculum." They need to live out before their students the principles they want their students to internalize. They should share with students their activities as world Christians outside the school context. James warns us, "Not many of you should presume to be teachers, my brothers, because you know that we who teach will be judged more strictly" (James 3:1, NIV). If students are to become world Christians, willing to reach out to those around them, sharing the gospel message, and ministering to people's needs, they must first see that spirit in those who are their primary models—their parents and teachers.
5. Build school unity that is both practical and spiritual. Students need to see biblical principles at work in the school. They need to become a part of a unified, caring community and to experience what true biblical living is all about. For example, if families or individuals within the school are in need, the school community should seek to be supportive and meet those needs.

The Christian school has a mandate to help train children and young people in a way that gives them every opportunity possible to become what God created them to be.

The warning is clear. "Things that cause people to sin are bound to come, but woe to that person through whom they come. It would be better for him to be thrown into the sea with a millstone tied around his neck than for him to cause one of these little ones to sin. So watch yourselves" (Luke 17:1–3, NIV).

The call is clear. "Therefore go and make disciples of all nations ... teaching them to obey everything I have commanded you" (Matthew 28:19–20, NIV); "and you will be my witnesses in Jerusalem, and in all Judea and Samaria, and to the ends of the earth" (Acts 1:8, NIV).

The challenge is clear. "I tell you, open your eyes and look at the fields! They are ripe for harvest" (John 4:35, NIV).

Conclusion

What an awesome privilege and responsibility belong to the Christian school! Can you think of what could be done for Christ in the world if just half the students in Christian schools caught the vision and began to witness and minister to the society around them? It's an awesome task, but the Christian school is in the position of presenting ministry in such a way that the Holy Spirit can reach into the hearts and lives of young Christians and call them to a life of service. It is the Christian school's spiritual mandate and challenge!

About the Author

James W. Braley has served many years as an educator in Christian schools. He was a teacher at Pasadena Christian School for twelve years, and superintendent for six years. In addition, Braley was Director of Educational Services at ACSI for ten years, managing editor of *Christian School Curriculum* for two years, principal of Maranatha High School for seven years, and missionary-at-large to Christian schools for twelve years.

Strengthen Your Foundations

1. Review your school's mission or purpose statement. If it does not clearly state your school's mission in regard to creating world Christians, rewrite the statement.

2. Investigate possible opportunities in your local community for service that would be appropriate to the different age levels in your school. When appropriate, seek approval to experiment with some of the opportunities.

3. Develop a program for involving students of all ages in ministry and service.

4. Develop a method for emphasizing the importance of the "living curriculum" in your school.

5. Using the suggestions in the book *A Mind for Missions,* develop a systematic curriculum for major subject areas that incorporates concern for different countries of the world.

6. Organize your class or school for effective prayer.

References

Borthwick, Paul. 1987. *A mind for missions: Ten ways to build your world vision.* Colorado Springs, CO: NavPress.

Johnstone, Patrick, and Jason Mandryk. 1993. *Operation world: When we pray God works.* Reprint 2001. Grand Rapids, MI: Zondervan.

References

Agnew, John E. 1985. The grading policies and practices of high school teachers (March /April). Paper presented at the annual meeting of the American Educational Research Association, Chicago, IL.

Akers, John. 2000. *This we believe: The good news of Jesus Christ for the world.* Grand Rapids, MI: Zondervan.

All Kinds of Minds. www.allkindsofminds.org.

Anderson, James D. 1988. *The education of blacks in the South, 1860–1935.* Chapel Hill: University of North Carolina Press.

Anderson, Rebecca S. 1998. Why talk about different ways to grade? The shift from traditional assessment to alternative assessment. *New Directions for Teaching and Learning* 74: 5–16.

Andrade, Heidi Goodrich. 2002. Understanding rubrics. Retrieved July 2, 2002, from http://learnweb.harvard.edu/alps/thinking/docs/rubricar.htm; retrieved July 17, 2003, from http://www.middleweb.com/rubricsHG.html.

Astley, Jeff, and Leslie J. Francis, eds. 1992. *Christian perspectives on faith development: A reader.* Grand Rapids, MI: Eerdmans.

Ausabel, David. 1963. *The psychology of meaningful verbal learning.* New York: Grune & Stratton.

——. 1977. The facilitation of meaningful learning in the classroom. *Educational Psychologist* 12, 162–78.

Austin, Susan, and Richard McCann. 1992. Here's another arbitrary grade for your collection: A statewide study of grading policies (April). Paper presented at the annual meeting of the American Educational Research Association, San Francisco, CA.

The Baptist faith and message: A statement adopted by the Southern Baptist Convention. 1998, revised. Nashville: LifeWay Christian Resources.

Barbe, Walter Burke, and Raymond H. Swassing. 1979. *Teaching through modality strengths: Concepts and practices.* Columbus, OH: Zaner-Bloser, Inc.

Bauman, Zygmunt. 1997. *Postmodernity and its discontents.* New York: New York University Press.

Beechick, Ruth. 1982. *A biblical psychology of learning: How your mind works.* Denver, CO: Accent Publications, Inc.

Berkhof, Louis. 1939. *Manual of Christian doctrine.* Grand Rapids, MI: Eerdmans.

Bewes, R., P. Blackman, and R. Hicks. 1999. *The essential Bible truth treasury and journal.* Bath, Avon, England: Gospel Gifts.

Bigge, Morris L., and S. Samuel Shermis. 1998. *Learning theories for teachers.* 6th ed. New York: Addison Wesley Longman.

Blamires, Harry. 1963. *The Christian mind.* Ann Arbor, MI: Servant Publications.

Blanchard, John F. 1970. Toward a Christian approach to grading. *Christian Teacher* (November/December).

Bloom, Benjamin S., and David R. Krathwohl. 1956. *Taxonomy of educational objectives:* Book I: *Cognitive domain.* New York: Longmans.

Boice, James Montgomery. 1986. *Foundations of the Christian faith.* Downers Grove, IL: InterVarsity Press.

Borich, Gary D. 1999. *Observation skills for effective teaching.* 3d ed. Upper Saddle River, NJ: Prentice-Hall.

Borthwick, Paul. 1987. *A mind for missions: Ten ways to build your world vision.* Colorado Springs, CO: NavPress.

Bounds, E. M. 1966. *Heaven:* A *place, a city, a home.* Grand Rapids, MI: Baker Book House.

Boyce, Amanda. 2002. Lights, camera, ACTION! A unit on communication in the media. Unpublished curriculum unit. Trinity Western University.

Braswell, J. S., A. D. Lutkus, W. S. Grigg, S. L. Santapau, B. Tay-Lim, and M. Johnson. 2001. *The nation's report card: Mathematics 2000,* NCES. Office of Educational Research and Improvement. National Center for Education Statistics. Washington, DC: U.S. Department of Education.

Brightman, H. J. 2002. Student learning and the Myers-Briggs type indicator. Retrieved August 3, 2002, from Georgia State University, Master Teacher Program: www.gsu.edu/~dschjb/wwwmbti.html.

Brookhart, Susan M. 1994. Teachers' grading: Practice and theory. *Applied Measurement in Education* 7, no. 4: 279–301.

Brown, Diana. n.d. Homework ... help or horror experience? FEA/United. Retrieved June 2, 2002, from http://www.yesiteach.org/homework.htm.

Brown, L. D. 1980. *Truths that make a difference.* Nashville, TN: Convention Press.

Bruner, Jerome. 1960. *The process of education.* Cambridge, MA: Harvard University Press.

——. 1966. *Toward a theory of instruction.* New York: W.W. Norton.

Bubna, Donald. 1988. *Encouraging people.* Wheaton, IL: Tyndale House.

Bursuck, William D., and Dennis D. Munk. 1997. Can grades be helpful and fair? *Educational Leadership* 55, no. 4: 44–47.

Caine, Renate, and Geoffrey Caine. 1990. Understanding a brain-based approach to learning and teaching. *Educational Leadership* (October): 66–70.

——. 1991. *Making connections: Teaching and the human brain.* Alexandria, VA: Association for Supervision and Curriculum Development.

——. 1997. *Education on the edge of possibility.* Alexandria, VA: Association for Supervision and Curriculum Development.

Campolo, Tony. 2000. *Let me tell you a story: Life lessons from unexpected places and unlikely people.* Nashville: Word Publishing.

Carper, James C. 2001. The changing landscape of U.S. education. *Kappa Delta Pi Record* (spring): 106–10.

Carper, James C., and Jack Layman. 1995. Independent Christian day schools: Past, present, and prognosis. *Journal of Research on Christian Education* 4, no. 1: 7–19.

——. 2002. Independent Christian day schools: The maturing of a movement. *Catholic Education: A Journal of Inquiry and Practice* 5, no. 4: 502–14.

Center for Applications of Psychological Types. 2000. http://www.capt.org.

Chadwick, Ronald P. 1982. *Teaching and learning: An integrated approach to Christian education.* Old Tappan, NJ: Fleming H. Revell.

——. 1990. *Christian school curriculum: An integrated approach.* Winona Lake, IN: BMH Books.

Chafer, Lewis Sperry, and John F. Walvoord, eds. 1974. *Major Bible themes.* Grand Rapids, MI: Zondervan.

Christian Learning Center, associated with the Christian Reformed Church and Schools, 2520 Eastern Avenue Southeast, Grand Rapids, MI 49507.

Cizek, Gregory J. 1998. The assessment revolution's unfinished business. *Kappa Delta Pi Record* 34: 144–49.

Cizek, Gregory J., et al. 1995. Further investigation of teachers' assessment (April). Paper presented at the annual meeting of the American Educational Research Association, San Francisco, CA.

Clark, Gordon H. 1981. *A Christian view of men and things.* 2d ed. Grand Rapids, MI: Baker Book House.

Clark, Kenneth B. 1965. *Dark ghetto.* New York: Harper & Row.

Cochran, Leslie H. 1989. *Administrative commitment to teaching: Practical, research-based strategies to strengthen college teaching effectiveness.* Cape Girardeau, MO: STEP UP, Incorporated.

Coles, Robert. 1998. *The moral intelligence of children.* New York: Putnam.

Colson, Charles. 1987. *Loving God.* Grand Rapids, MI: Zondervan.

Colson, Charles, and Nancy Pearcey. 1999. *How now shall we live?* Wheaton, IL: Tyndale House.

Comenius, John Amos. 1967. *John Amos Comenius on education.* New York: Teachers College Press.

Counts, George. 1952. *Education and American civilization.* New York: Teachers College Press.

Criswell, W. A. 1966. *The Holy Spirit in today's world.* Grand Rapids, MI: Zondervan.

Cross, Lawrence. 1995. Testing Memo 6: *What kinds of grades should be averaged?* and Testing Memo 11: *Absolute versus relative grading standards: What does a percentage mean?* Blacksburg: Office of Measurement and Research Services, Virginia Polytechnic Institute and State University.

Culbertson, Linda Doutt, and Mary Renck Jalongo. 1999. But what's wrong with letter grades? Responding to parents' questions about alternative assessment. *Childhood Education* 75, no. 3: 130–35.

Curren, Randall R. 1995. Coercion and the ethics of grading and testing. *Educational Theory* 45, no. 4: 425–41.

Damon, William. 1988. *The moral child: Nurturing children's natural moral growth.* New York: Free Press.

Danielson, E. E. 1982. *Missionary kid (MK).* Manila: Faith Academy.

D'Archangelo, M. 1998. The brains behind the brains. *Educational Leadership* (November): 20–25.

Deakin-Crick, Ruth, Patricia Broadfoot, and Guy Claxton. 2002. Developing an effective lifelong learning inventory: The effective learning profile (ELLI). Center for Assessment Studies, University of Bristol. Unpublished manuscript.

Dewey, John. 1944. *Democracy and education.* New York: Macmillan.

——. 1964. *A common faith.* New Haven, CN: Yale University Press.

Dick, Walter, Lou Carey, and James O. Carey. 1996. *The systematic design of instruction.* 4th ed. New York: HarperCollins.

Dobson, James. 2001. *Bringing up boys.* Wheaton, IL: Tyndale House.

Dollar, T., J. Falwell, A. V. Henderson, and J. Hyles, eds. 1977. *Building blocks of the faith: Foundational Bible doctrines.* Nashville: Fundamentalist Church Publications.

Donahue, P. L., R. J. Finnegan, A. D. Lutkus, N. L. Allen, and J. R. Campbell. 2001. *The nation's report card: Fourth-grade reading 2000,* NCES 2001–499. Office of Educational Research and Improvement. National Center for Education Statistics. Washington, DC: U.S. Department of Education.

Douglass, Frederick. 1845. *Narrative of the life of Frederick Douglass.* Mineola, NY: Dover Publications.

——. 1894. The blessings of liberty and education. An address delivered in Manassas, Virginia (3 September). In *The Frederick Douglass papers* 623. Edited by J. Blassingame and J. McKivigan, 1992.

Dowd, Tom, and Jeff Tierney. 1992. *Teaching social skills to youth.* Boys Town, NE: Boys Town Press.

Dunn, Janet. 1985. Inspiring others. *Discipleship Journal* 5, no. 4 (July).

Durant, Will. 1926. *The story of philosophy: The lives and opinions of the greater philosophers.* New York: Simon & Schuster.

Edlin, Richard J. 1999. *The cause of Christian education.* Colorado Springs, CO: Association of Christian Schools International.

Education Week on the Web. 1998. Quality counts '98: The urban challenge. Retrieved April 10, 2002, from http:/www.edweek.org/sreports/qc98/intros/in-n.htm.

Eggen, Paul, and Don Kauchak. 2001. *Educational psychology: Windows on classrooms.* 5th ed. Upper Saddle River, NJ: Prentice-Hall.

Elkind, David. 1984. *All grown up and no place to go: Teenagers in crisis.* Reading, MA: Addison-Wesley.

Elmer, Duane. 2002. A pilgrimage to servanthood (January). Keynote address delivered at the International Christian Educator's Conference, Quito, Ecuador.

Engel, S. M. 1994. *With good reason: An introduction to informal fallacies.* 5th ed. New York: St. Martin's Press.

Evans, William. 1974. *The great doctrines of the Bible.* Chicago: Moody Press.

Failing grades for late assignments: Teaching responsibility or giving permission to fail? Retrieved July 2, 2002, from http://www.middleweb.com/INCASEfailingrades.html.

Fenstermacher, Gary D., and Jonas F. Soltis. 1998. *Approaches to teaching.* New York: Columbia University, Teachers College Press.

Fowler, James. 1992. Character, conscience, and the education of the public. In *The challenge of pluralism: Education, politics, and values.* Edited by F. Power and D. Lapsley. Notre Dame, IN: University of Notre Dame Press.

Frisbie, David A., and Kristie K. Waltman. 1992. Developing a personal grading plan. *Educational Measurement: Issues and Practice* (fall).

Gangel, Kenneth O., and Warren S. Benson. 1983. *Christian education: Its history and philosophy.* Chicago: Moody Press, Wipf & Stock, 2001.

Gangel, Kenneth O., and Howard G. Hendricks, eds. 1993. *The Christian educator's handbook on teaching*. Grand Rapids, MI: Baker Books.

Gardner, Howard. 1984. *Frames of mind: The theory of multiple intelligences.* New York: Basic Books.

Gibbs, Ollie, and Jerry Haddock. 1995. *Classroom discipline: A management guide for Christian school teachers.* Colorado Springs, CO: Association of Christian Schools International.

Glenn, Charles Leslie Jr. 1988. Ch. 3, The common school as a religious institution, and Ch. 4, The opposition to common school religion, in *The myth of the common school.* Amherst: University of Massachusetts Press.

Greene, Albert. 1998. *Reclaiming the future of Christian education.* Colorado Springs, CO: Association of Christian Schools International.

Greene, Jay P. 2000. *The effect of school choice: An evaluation of the Charlotte Children's Scholarship Fund Program.* Civic Report No. 12 (August).

Guskey, Thomas R. 1994. Making the grade: What benefits students? *Educational Leadership* 52, no. 2: 14–20.

Hales, D. 2000. Teaching boys, teaching girls. *Parents* (September): 202–8.

Hart, Leslie. 1975. *How a brain works.* New York: Basic Books.

Heatherley, E. X. 2000. *Our heavenly home.* Austin, TX: Balcony Publishing.

——. 1997. *The parables of Christ.* Austin, TX: Balcony Publishing.

Hendricks, Howard G. 1987. *Teaching to change lives: Develop a passion for communicating God's Word to adults or children—in the church, in the home, in Bible study groups, or in schools.* Portland, OR: Multnomah Press.

Hobbs, Herschel H. 1960. *Fundamentals of our faith.* Nashville: Broadman Press.

Hoffecker, W. Andrew, 1986. *Building a Christian world view,* vol. 1. Phillipsburg, NJ: Presbyterian and Reformed Publishing Company.

Hofstede, Geert. 1997. *Culture and organizations: Software of the mind.* New York: McGraw-Hill.

Howell, Russell W., and W. James Bradley, eds. 2001. *Mathematics in a postmodern age: A Christian perspective.* Grand Rapids, MI: Eerdmans.

Howell, William G., Patrick J. Wolf, and Paul E. Peterson. 2000. Test-score effects of school vouchers in Dayton, Ohio, New York City, and Washington, DC: Evidence from randomized field trials (August). Retrieved July 23, 2002, from http://data.fas.harvard.edu/pepg/.

Hurley, P. J. 1977. *A concise introduction to logic.* 6th ed. Belmont, CA: Wadsworth Publishing Co.

Hyerle, David. 1996. *Visual tools for constructing knowledge.* Alexandria, VA: Association for Supervision and Curriculum Development.

——. 2000. *A field guide to using visual tools.* Alexandria, VA: Association for Supervision and Curriculum Development.

Jacobsen, David A., Paul Eggen, and Donald Kauchak. 1999. *Methods for teaching: Promoting student learning.* 5th ed. Upper Saddle River, NJ: Prentice-Hall.

JAF Ministries (Joni Eareckson Tada). PO Box 9333, Agoura Hills, CA 91376.

Jarolimek, John, and Clifford D. Foster Sr. 1993. *Teaching and learning in the elementary school.* 5th ed. New York: Macmillan.

Johnson, David, and Roger Johnson. 1994. *Learning together and alone: Cooperation, competition, and individualization.* 4th ed. Needham Heights, MA: Allyn & Bacon.

Johnson, James A., Victor L. Dupuis, Diann Musial, Gene E. Hall, Donna M. Gollnick, Janet W. Lerner, eds. 2003. *Essentials of American education.* Boston: Allyn & Bacon.

Johnstone, Patrick, and Jason Mandryk. 1993. *Operation world: When we pray God works.* Reprint 2001. Grand Rapids, MI: Zondervan.

Joyce, Bruce, James Wolf, and Emily Calhoun. 1993. *The self-renewing school.* Alexandria, VA: Association for Supervision and Curriculum Development.

Joyce, Bruce, and Marsha Weil. 2000. *Models of teaching.* 6th ed. Needham Heights, MA: Allyn & Bacon.

Kagan, Spencer. 1994. *Cooperative learning.* San Juan Capistrano, CA: Resources for Teachers.

Kaminsky, James S. 1993. *A new history of educational philosophy.* Westport, CN: Greenwood Press.

Keenan, Derek. 1998. *Curriculum development for Christian schools.* Colorado Springs, CO: Association of Christian Schools International.

Keener, Craig. 1993. *IVP Bible background commentary—New Testament.* Downers Grove, IL: InterVarsity Press.

Keirsey, David W. 1998. *Please understand me II: Temperament, character, intelligence.* Del Mar, CA: Prometheus Nemesis Book Company.

Keirsey, David W., and Marilyn Bates. 1984. *Please understand me.* Del Mar, CA: Prometheus Nemesis Book Company.

Kellough, Richard D., and Patricia L. Roberts. 1998. *A resource guide for elementary school teaching: Planning for competence.* 4th ed. Upper Saddle River, NJ: Prentice-Hall.

Kennedy, D. James. 1980. *Why I believe.* Nashville: Word Publishing.

Kessler, Rachael. 2000. *The soul of education.* Alexandria, VA: Association for Supervision and Curriculum Development.

Kirk, S. A., J. J. Gallagher, and N. J. Anastasiow. 2000. *Educating exceptional children.* Boston: Houghton Mifflin.

Kohn, Alfie. 1994. Grading: The issue is not how but why. *Educational Leadership* 52: 38–41.

——. 1996. *Beyond discipline: From compliance to community.* Alexandria, VA: Association of Supervision and Curriculum Development.

Kozol, Jonathan. 2000. *Ordinary resurrections: Children in the years of hope.* New York: Perennial.

Kroeger, Otto, and Janet M. Thuesen. 1988. *Type talk: The 16 personality types that determine how we live, love, and work.* New York: Dell Publishing.

Kuhlman, Edward. 1986. *The master teacher.* Old Tappan, New Jersey: Fleming H. Revell.

LD Online: www.ldonline.org.

LeBar, Lois. 1958. *Education that is Christian.* Old Tappan, NJ: Fleming H. Revell.

Lemann, Nicholas. 1986. The origins of the underclass. *Atlantic Monthly* (June). http://www.theatlantic.com/politics/poverty/origin2.htm (accessed August 7, 2003).

Levine, Mel. 2002. *A mind at a time.* New York: Simon & Schuster.

Lewis, C. S. 1952. *Mere Christianity.* New York: Macmillan.

Lewis, Gordon R. 1976. *Testing Christianity's truth claims.* Chicago: Moody Press.

Lickona, Thomas, and Catherine Lewis. 1997. *Eleven principles of effective character education* (video). Port Chester, NY: National Professional Resources, Inc.

Little, Paul. 2000, revised and updated. *Know why you believe.* Downers Grove, IL: InterVarsity Press.

Lorayne, Harry, and Jerry Lucas. 1974. *The memory book.* Ballantine Books, reissued 1996.

Lowrie, Roy W. Jr. 1978. *To those who teach in Christian schools.* Colorado Springs, CO: Association of Christian Schools International.

——. 1980. *Inside the Christian school.* Colorado Springs, CO: Association of Christian Schools International.

MacDonald, Robert E. 1991. *A handbook of basic skills and strategies for beginning teachers: Facing the challenge of teaching in today's schools.* White Plains, NY: Longman.

MacIver, Douglas, and David A. Reuman. 1994. Giving their best: Grading and recognition practices that motivate students to work hard. *American Educator: The Professional Journal of the American Federation of Teachers* 17, no. 4: 24–31.

Maine, Karen, n.d. Let's worry more about assessing students and less about grading them. Retrieved July 2, 2002, from http://www.middleweb.com/INCASEgrades.html.

Manning, Duane. 1971. *Toward a humanistic curriculum.* New York: Harper & Row.

Marsden, George. 1994. *The soul of the American university: From Protestant establishment to established unbelief.* New York: Oxford University Press.

Marzano, Robert J. 1992. *A different kind of classroom: Teaching with dimensions of learning.* Alexandria, VA: Association for Supervision and Curriculum Development.

——. 2000. What are grades for? In *Transforming classroom grading.* Retrieved July 17, 2003, from http://ascd.org/publications/books/2000marzano/chapter2.html.

Marzano, Robert J., and Debra J. Pickering. 1997. *Dimensions of learning teacher's manual.* 2d ed. Alexandria, VA: Association for Supervision and Curriculum Development.

Marzano, Robert J., Debra J. Pickering, and Jay McTighe. 1993. *Assessing student outcomes: Performance assessment using the dimensions of learning model.* Alexandria, VA: Association for Supervision and Curriculum Development.

Marzano, Robert J., Ronald S. Brandt, Carolyn Sue Hughes, Beau Fly Jones, Barbara Z. Presseisen, Stuart C. Rankin, and Charles Suhor. 1988. *Dimensions of thinking: A framework for curriculum and instruction.* Alexandria, VA: Association for Supervision and Curriculum Development.

McClellan, V. A. 1983. Dewey, John. In *Twentieth-century culture: A biographical companion.* Edited by Alan Bullock and R. B. Woodings. New York: Harper & Row.

McDowell, Josh. 1999. *The new evidence that demands a verdict.* Nashville: Thomas Nelson.

——. 2002. *The disconnected generation.* Dallas, TX: Josh McDowell Ministries.

McGrath, Alister E. 1991. *I believe: Exploring the Apostles' Creed.* Downers Grove, IL: InterVarsity Press.

Mead, James V. 1992. *Teachers' evaluations of student work.* East Lansing, MI: National Center for Research on Teacher Learning.

Minirth, Frank B. 2002. A brief digest on everything you ever wanted to know about the chemistry of emotions: Thirteen medication types that can change brain chemicals and emotions. Retrieved August 2, 2002, from www.minirthclinic.com/digests.html.

Moreland, J. P. 1997. *Love your God with all your mind: The role of reason in the life of the soul.* Colorado Springs, CO: NavPress.

Morris, Henry, and Henry Morris III. 1974. *Many infallible proofs.* Green Forest, AR: Master Books.

Moynihan, Daniel Patrick. 1987. *Family and nation.* San Diego: Harcourt Brace Jovanovich.

National Institute for Learning Disabilities, 107 Seekel Street, Norfolk, VA 23505.

Nicholson-Nelson, Kristen. 1998. *Developing students' multiple intelligences.* New York: Scholastic Professional Books.

O'Conner, Ken. 1995. Guidelines for grading that support learning and student success. *NASSP Bulletin* 79, no. 571: 91–101.

Ornstein, Allan C., and Francis P. Hunkins. 1993. *Curriculum foundations, principles and issues.* Boston, MA: Allyn & Bacon.

Orr, C. E. 1959. The education of missionaries' children. *Occasional Bulletin of the Missionary Research Library* 10, no. 9: 1–11.

Overseas Schools Profiles. 2001. Colorado Springs, CO: Association of Christian Schools International.

Ozmon, Howard A., and Samuel M. Craver. 2003. *Philosophical foundations of education.* 7th ed. Columbus, OH: Merrill Prentice Hall.

Palladino, Lucy Jo. 1999. *Dreamers, discoverers, and dynamos: How to help the child who is bright, bored, and having problems in school.* New York: Ballantine Books.

Pazmino, Robert W. 1988. *Foundational issues in Christian education: An introduction in evangelical perspective.* Grand Rapids, MI: Baker Book House.

Pentecost, J. Dwight. 1965. *Things which become sound doctrine.* Grand Rapids, MI: Zondervan.

Perkins, David N., Heidi Goodrich, Shari Tishman, and Jill M. Owen. 1994. *Thinking connection: Learning to think and thinking to learn.* Reading, PA: Addison-Wesley.

Peterson, Michael L. 2001. *With all your mind: A Christian philosophy of education.* Notre Dame, IN: University of Notre Dame Press.

Pippert, Rebecca M. 1989. *Hope has its reasons: Surprised by faith in a broken world.* New York: HarperCollins.

Plato. n.d. *The republic.* Translated into English by Benjamin Jowett. New York: Modern Library.

Pressley, M., Levin, J. R., and Delaney, H. D. 1982. The mnemonic keyword method. *Review of Educational Research* 52, no. 1, 61–91.

Ravitch, Diane. 1983. *The troubled crusade: American education 1945–1980.* New York: Basic Books.

Ray, Susan. n.d. A teacher researches a middle school's grading practices. Retrieved July 2, 2002, from http://www.middleweb.com/INCASEgrdresrch.html.

Reedy, Randy. 1995. Formative and summative assessment: A possible alternative to the grading-reporting dilemma. *NAASP Bulletin* 79, no. 573: 47–51.

Renicks, Philip M. 1986. *Perceptions of administrators in a worldwide study of orientation and induction practices of member schools in the Association of Christian Schools International in overseas locations.* Tuscaloosa: University of Alabama.

Richards, Larry. 1970. *Creative Bible teaching.* Chicago: Moody Press.

Robinson, Glen E., and James M. Craver. 1989. *Assessing and grading student achievement.* ERS Report. Arlington, VA: Educational Research Service.

Rush, Myron D. 1983. *Richer relationships.* Wheaton, IL: Scripture Press Publications.

Ryrie, Charles C. 1972. *A survey of Bible doctrine.* Chicago: Moody Press.

Schaeffer, Francis A. 1976. *How should we then live? The rise and decline of Western thought and culture.* Wheaton, IL: Crossway Books, 1983.

Schneider, Tom. 2000. Everybody's a winner. Retrieved July 2, 2002, from http://www.connectingwithkids.com.

SchwabLearning.org: www.schwablearning.org.

Shuell, Thomas J. 1996. Teaching and learning in classroom context. From D. Berliner & R. Calfee, eds. *Handbook of educational psychology.* New York: Simon & Schuster, 726–64.

Silber, John. 1989. *Straight shooting: What's wrong with America and how to fix it.* New York: HarperPerennial.

Sisson, Richard. 1983. *Answering Christianity's most puzzling questions,* vol. 2. Chicago: Moody Press.

Sizer, Theodore R. 1984. *Horace's compromise: The dilemma of the American high school.* Boston, MA.: Houghton-Mifflin.

——. 1992. *Horace's school: Redesigning the American high school.* Boston, MA: Houghton-Mifflin.

Skinner, B. F. 1948. *Walden two.* London: The Macmillan Company.

Slavin, Robert E. 1995. *Cooperative learning: Theory, research, and practice.* 2nd ed. Needham Heights, MA: Allyn & Bacon.

Sobel, Dava. 2000. *Galileo's daughter: A historical memoir of science, faith, and love.* New York: Penguin Books.

Spears, Dana Scott, and Ron L. Braund. 1996. *Strong-willed child or dreamer?* Nashville: Thomas Nelson.

Sternberg, Robert J., and Spear-Swerling, Louise C. 1996. *Teaching for thinking: Psychology in the classroom.* Washington, DC: American Psychological Association.

Stoddart, T., M. Connell, R. Stofflett, and D. Peck. 1993. Reconstructing elementary teacher candidates' understanding of mathematics and science content. *Teaching and Teacher Education* 9, 229–41.

Stott, John R. W. 1992. *The contemporary Christian: Applying God's Word to today's world.* Downers Grove, IL: InterVarsity Press.

Stringfellow, Alan B. 1981. *Through the Bible in one year,* vol. 3. Tulsa, OK: Hensley Publishing.

Stronks, Gloria, and Nancy Knol. 1999. *Reaching and teaching young adolescents.* Colorado Springs, CO: Association of Christian Schools International.

Sutton, Joe P., ed. 1993. *Special education: A biblical approach.* Greenville, SC: Hidden Treasures Ministries.

Sweet, Leonard. 1999. *Aqua church: Essential leadership arts for piloting your church in today's fluid culture.* Loveland, CO: Group Publishing Incorporated.

Sylwester, Robert. 2000. *A biological brain in a cultural classroom: Applying biological research to classroom management.* Alexandria, VA: Association for Supervision and Curriculum Development.

Terwilliger, James S. 1989. Classroom standard setting and grading practices. *Educational Measurement: Issues and Practice* 8, no. 2: 15–19.

Thiessen, Henry. 1979, revised. *Lectures in systematic theology.* Grand Rapids, MI: Eerdmans.

Torrey, R. A. 1998. *What the Bible teaches.* Peabody, MA: Hendrickson Publishers.

Tripp, Ted. 1995. *Shepherding a child's heart.* Wapwallopen, PA: Shepherd Press.

Turnbull, Ralph G., ed. 1967. *Baker's dictionary of practical theology.* Grand Rapids, MI: Baker Book House.

Uecker, Milton V. 2002. *Biblical foundation for curriculum: Study guide.* Columbia, SC: Columbia International University.

U.S. Department of Education. National Center for Education Statistics. 2002. *The condition of education.* NCES 2002–025, Washington, DC: U.S. Government Printing Office.

Van Brummelen, Harro. 1994. *Steppingstones to curriculum: A biblical path.* Seattle, WA: Alta Vista College Press.

——. 1998. *Walking with God in the classroom.* Seattle: Alta Vista College Press.

——. 2002. *Steppingstones to curriculum: A biblical path.* 2d ed. Colorado Springs, CO: Purposeful Design Publications.

Van Dyk, John. 2000. *The craft of Christian teaching.* Sioux City, IA: Dordt Press.

Waldron, Peter W., Tani R. Collie, and Calvin M. Davies. 1999. *Telling stories about school: An invitation.* Upper Saddle River, NJ: Prentice-Hall.

Walsh, Brian. 2000. Transformation: Dynamic worldview or repressive ideology? *Journal of Education and Christian Belief* 4, no. 2: 101–14.

Warren, Jonathan R. 1975. *The continuing controversy over grades.* TM Report 51. Princeton, NJ: ERIC Clearinghouse on Tests, Measurement, and Evaluation.

Wasley, Patricia A. 1991. Stirring the chalkdust: Changing practices in essential schools. *Teachers College Record* 93: 29–58.

Wayside Language Center, 12721 Northeast 101st Place, Kirkland, WA 98033.

Weis, Nita. 1995. *Raising achievers: A parent's plan for motivating children to excel.* Nashville: Broadman & Holman.

Wendel, Fredrick C., and Kenneth E. Anderson. 1994. Grading and marking systems: What are the practices, standards? *NASSP Bulletin* 78, no. 558: 79–84.

Whitehead, John. 1985. *Parents' rights.* Wheaton, IL: Crossway Books.

Wiggins, Grant, and J. McTighe. 1998. *Understanding by design.* Alexandria, VA: Association for Supervision and Curriculum Development.

Wilkinson, Bruce H. 1991. *Teaching with style: What your students wish you knew about teaching but were afraid to tell you.* Atlanta: Walk Thru the Bible Ministries, Incorporated.

——. 1992. *Almost every answer for practically any teacher!* Portland, OR: Multnomah.

Willard, Dallas. 1999. Jesus the logician. *Christian Scholar's Review* 28, no. 4: 605–14.

——. 2000. How reason can survive the modern university: The moral foundations of rationality. Paper presented at the American Maritain Association, Notre Dame University.

——. 2002. *Renovation of the heart: Putting on the character of Christ.* Colorado Springs, CO: NavPress.

Williams, Clifford. 2002. *The life of the mind: A Christian perspective.* Grand Rapids, MI: Baker Academic.

Williams, Joseph E. 1993. Principles of discipline. *American School Board Journal* (February).

Willmington, Harold. 1981. *Willmington's guide to the Bible.* Wheaton, IL: Tyndale House.

Wolters, Alfred M. 1985. *Creation regained.* Grand Rapids, MI: Eerdmans.

Wolterstorff, Nicholas. 2002. *Educating for life.* Grand Rapids, MI: Baker Academic.

Woodson, Carter G. 1999. *The education of the Negro*. Brooklyn, NY: A&B Book Publishers.

Yancey, Philip. 1997. *What's so amazing about grace?* Grand Rapids, MI: Zondervan.

Zemelman, Steven H., Harvey Daniels, and Arthur Hyde. 1993. *Best practice: New standards for teaching and learning in America's schools.* Portsmouth, NH: Heinemann.

Index